Guttersnipe

A tabloid hack's memoir of Fleet Stre

Dick Durham

Cover photo: Bob Aylott

Legal note:
I've seen the inside of enough courtrooms to last a lifetime and
have therefore changed the odd name here and there. Otherwise
what you are about to read is the truth and nothing but the truth.

Introduction

Has democracy been nobbled?

Lord Justice Leveson's investigation into the culture, practices and ethics of its watchdog, the press, heard from many who felt it has. The relationship newspapers have with the public, police and politicians, is rotten, they said.

Mi'lord Leveson's job was to help the government decide if the newshounds should be muzzled and if so what impact press regulation would have on its 'integrity, freedom and independence.'

His inquiry was spawned in the cauldron of the phone-hacking scandal which brought Rupert Murdoch's News International empire to its knees, including the closure of the News of the World in July 2011.

But Dick Durham's book reveals that newsgathering has been in the hands of irresponsible bandits for decades and probably needs to be.

For more than 20 years Durham pursued 'red –top' excellence in Fleet Street. He arrived there from the provincial newspaper route where the moral murkiness begins because what sells papers is, as has been famously stated, always what the public are interested in, but not always what is in their best interest. In Fleet Street he discovered that, under pressure from editors, the cultural relationship newspapers have with the public is one of ingratiation, insensitivity and indecency. The practices newspapers employ with the police and politicians is one of bribery, bullshit, and bullying. As for ethics, come back Plato all is forgiven.

The red-top 'scalps' he reveals, include the closure of a mental hospital, in what appeared to be a public duty but which in fact led to scores of patients having nowhere else to go; the outing of a TV celebrity for heroin addiction: he died of an overdose a week later; and supplying champagne to a famous alcoholic sports star to get him posing for a photographer.

He has wined and dined senior police officers and Customs men; bought a yacht for his editor while on a job; and 'turned over' a small time TV celebrity as part of a personal vendetta on behalf of his superiors.

He tells how a photographer considered having his mortgage paid off by a million pound newspaper Bingo winner; how the grieving father of a murdered fifteen year old was told by a reporter he'd have been paid more if she'd been killed before the newspaper's deadline; and asked the family of an IRA victim, too young for legal sex, whether she was pregnant when she died, to 'spoil' a rival newspaper's story.

He has bought a wreath to lay at the entrance to King's Cross Station to 'symbolise' the tragedy of a fire which killed 30; had to placate a Muslim football supporter whose photograph was doctored to show him as a cross-dresser after he jokingly said he would dress as a woman to use his girlfriend's ticket for a seat at the World Cup; and climbed into the back of an ambulance to get a picture of an emergency patient, incorrectly identified as a radiation victim.

These stories are just some examples of the ruthless culture, the dodgy practices, and the ethics-less world of the newspaper reporter, which Guttersnipe reveals. This is what happens every day in Britain's newsgathering world. This is without one mobile phone being hacked, or police officer supplied with cash...all of it perfectly legal, simply the quintessential mechanics of newsgathering which, for better or worse, defines a free, not to say free-for-all, press.

As you turn the pages of Guttersnipe you, Lord Justice Leveson, and actor Hugh Grant will discover what really makes a true tabloid hack tick: how he finds the stories which fill those pages every day.

The next time you open your door to a guttersnipe intent on acquiring your innermost secrets, your family photograph album and your soul... you will be better armed.

Pulitzer prizes, public interest and probity apart, this is the real world of Fleet Street hackery where spin, artifice and disingenuousness are the tools of the trade.

Prologue

Twenty-five years after the United Nations enshrined the principle of a free press in its Declaration of Human Rights, I walked into Fleet Street for a job. I only dimly realised then that a free press was an important factor in my liberty. Unfettered by state intervention, national newspapers, especially the tabloids, are constrained only by the market. To sell them in their hundreds of thousands so much 'entertainment' is packed into them that matters of state take a back seat. This is because in the world of the globalised market a free press is the fourth estate only as long as it sells newspapers, or earns money from internet advertising. If it can't make money it dies and with it go the much vaunted 'checks and balances' of democracy.

It took me a while to understand that hacks are just as ephemeral as the newspapers they serve. But eventually I came to know what every reporter knows, namely that 'you're only as good as your last story' and while yesterday's newspapers are at least used to keep fish suppers warm, when the reporter gets his chips they don't even come wrapped.

My secondary modern education had tried and failed to teach me to play a recorder, chisel a dovetail joint or carry a decimal point. Even my single 'O' Level in Geography smacked of failure as it suggested I had been trying.

I had been hopeless at anything in the real world, until I discovered that through watching or listening to others I was able to make a living vicariously.

I was a paid voyeur. A very well paid voyeur: my annual salary was a five figure sum. I earned as much as a doctor, a headmaster even a novice lawyer. But they, unlike me, did not enjoy private health insurance, a company car, seven weeks holiday a year, a four-day week and a huge expense allowance.

HOLD THE FRONT PAGE:

'I'm bloody glad I didn't do anything useful, I could have been a plumber's mate, someone who's never been anywhere in his life. Instead I've lived the life of Riley. I've been all over the world, spent huge sums of money, had nice dinners, stayed in the best hotels, done everything that millionaires would do and somebody else has paid for it.'

James Sutherland, former Deputy Editor of the Daily Star.

Chapters

1. Doorstepping Fleet Street
2. Hard news
3. Becoming an 'operator'
4. The Editor's new clothes
5. The Animal Kingdom
6. Fancy dress
7. Crime
8. Foreigns
9. Features
10 Brand awareness
11 War
12 Showbusiness
13 Royals

1. DOORSTEPPING FLEET STREET

The first thing I noticed about Fleet Street was that here be dragons and they'd apparently won. It was early one spring morning in 1973 while walking up Fleet Street searching for the offices of D.C. Thomson where I was to be interviewed for the job of editorial assistant on something called The Sunday Post. On the corner of Fetter Lane, where their office was based, I looked up at the City Arms to check the street sign. It was emblazoned with the cross of St George and I noticed that the devil-slaying patron saint of England was missing. All that remained was his indigestible sword, shield and helmet between two rampant dragons licking their scaley jaws with forked tongues. He'd been sucked in and spat out and I was, unwittingly, about to follow suit.

If the street sign symbolised a journey into the morally unknown, I, as a 23-year-old drifter was unaware of it, having, until then, been employed ony in jobs which exercised my brawn. I was good at humping things about. I humped bricks, dirt and planks for a builder, branches, trunks and foliage for a tree feller and - underwater this time - pipes, sand bags and steel rods for a diving company.

As a jobbing labourer I'd saved enough money to pay for a back-packing trip through the Middle East, India, the Far East and Australia on the last knockings of what was called the Hippy Trail. It was a sort of Grand Tour for the rabble.

But my Fleet Street masters had a much bigger adventure planned. The world was their oyster and they would send me to see much of it as long as I could return with evidence it was a dodgy mollusc. For this they paid me more than I could dispose of gracefully, gave me access to unlimited expenses, and insisted I join them in the bars of Fleet Street for as much time as they saw fit. Ever mindful of our welfare, The National Union of Journalists had balanced such demands upon body and soul with a negotiated four-day week to compensate.

My ignorance of the life Fleet Street promised had led me to its environs for an interview still dressed as though I was trying to find myself in Rajastan. I clomped up Fleet Street in wooden-soled Breton clogs, over which flapped bottle-green, flared, denims, a cheese cloth shirt, and a brown leather flying jacket. I was half-hoping my appearance would abort the job of 'editorial assistant' with The Scottish Sunday Post which my father half-hoped I would secure. He had agreed to lend me the air-fare back to Sydney, Australia, where my globe-trotting had come to a halt, but was insistent I try for a 'proper job' first. If I didn't get the job I would get the loan.

Fetter Lane, was a street name I recognised from the back of The Beano which was pretty much the last periodical I had read. The tall, narrow building's upper storey windows were tapped by the lofty plane trees opposite, overshadowing the office of David Norrie, the beetle-browed London editor of The Sunday Post who set me a questionnaire which, I was told, had determined the suitability of applicants for the Chicago police department. I can recall just one of the questions, all of which had multiple answers: 'If you found a baby in the street would you (a) take it to a shop (b) leave it there (c) take it to a police station (d) take it home with you. Chicago was clearly no place to be a baby, but a pushover if you wanted a job in the police department. Next I had to write an essay on the person who had made the 'biggest impression' upon me followed by a brief interview with managing editor, Robin Needham. He was a well-tailored man whose perfectly round body suggested an ease and symmetry of movement which, had he been a ball, he doubtless would have enjoyed. But as he was not, he faced instead the effort of manoeuvering a sphere on legs which caused him to glitter with beads of sweat. His round, florid face seemed to throb and suggested many years of heavy investment in lunch at El Vinos, the exclusive journalists' wine bar just a short waddle across Fleet Street. His eyes fought to focus between the swellings of flesh folded neatly above and beneath his eyelids and when he blinked they temporarily lost the battle. He looked like a 19th Century cartoon from Punch magazine: the British Empire morphed into Mr Round carving up the world with a knife and fork before eating it. For all the distention caused by appetite his voice was disarmingly kindly and commanded respect. He had an accent you don't hear anymore, one which summoned an atavistic deference from a pool of inferiority you didn't realise you lived in. He was what middle class people call 'old school' when what they really mean is privileged.

'Do you think you would enjoy going out and interviewing people?' he asked. To a fellow applying for a job as a journalist it appeared an artless question. Together with the Chicago questionnaire I began to wonder if potential journalists went through a selection procedure which ensured only the disingenuous were recruited.

Although I was too old for the 'copy-boy-to-Harold-Evans-route' I was still young enough to imagine the world had been constructed for my sole pleasure and that this was an initiative test for the next stage.

My father kept his money and I started at D.C.Thomson's 12 Fetter Lane office on £25 a week. I wanted now to be a reporter. That I had started with a company which had enriched itself by producing comics did not then seem prophetic. The customers of The Sunday Post - the readers - sent in the raw material for The Dandy, Beano, and Beezer, according to a wheezy, old man, who lived on cigarettes and whisky and was 'front of house' before the days of brand awareness. Danny Israel's job was to tie up out-of-date comics and newspapers and send them back to the company HQ in Dundee. He told me through his slipping false teeth that these publications were made partly from the readers' mulched down letters. It was pure Scottish parsimony and would be congratulated in today's recycling-obsessed world.

My first job was as 'The Garage Man', as the paper's motoring column was entitled. The fact I'd never owned a car nor knew anything of what went on under the bonnet, didn't stop me collecting driving anecdotes from family and friends.

Soon I was onto to grander things. The Sunday Post editorial – the newspaper's opinion, also known as the leader - was a column of short statements called 'As We See it', which all staff were encouraged to find material for. A visit I made to Moorfields Eye Hospital gave me my first example of spin. Commuting to work on the platform of the number 9 bus a gust had blown dust in my face and a speck of grit had become lodged in my cornea. At Moorfields Hospital my head had been locked into a brace, anaesthetic had been squirted into my eye and the grit picked out with a needle. I had been impressed with the exceptional treatment that I had received from the number of different ethnic groups working there.

I mentioned this to Norrie and was encouraged to write an As We See It. It became my first lead editorial:

' Last week, a Glasgow tourist (me) in London went to Moorfield's Eye Hospital to have grit removed from his eye.

At the reception, he was advised where to go by an African.

In the waiting room, he was ushered in by a Pakistani.

In the clinic, he was inspected by a West Indian.

A British doctor plucked out the grit. A Spanish girl gave him his prescription. A Jamaican nurse said he need not come back.

A real eye-opener!'

That was what The Sunday Post published. However what I had written contained the penultimate sentence which read: ' They were all working together in perfect harmony – a real eye-opener in fact!'

My 'As We See It' ,thanks to a subtle omission, had been turned completely on its head.

Instead of 'Isn't it great that all these different racial groups are working so efficiently together to save folks eyesight' the reader got 'Coo, look at all these foreigners holding down a job in London.'

It was as D. C. Thomson saw it and my first experience of news management.

The Sunday Post's 'investigative' section was headlined 'Customers' Complaints', abbreviated to Cuscom in order to save transmission money on the internal 'wire' service between London and Glasgow, it dealt with readers who had been ripped off by all types of shady traders and I would be despatched to Companies' House in Old Street, Shoreditch to root out the addresses for the directors of the rogue companies concerned. Unfortunately I had never been shown the procedure and thus the first story published as a result of my enquiries included the address of the company which had SET UP the rogue company in question. Being the first named on the records it was incorrectly included and condemned as the villain in The Sunday Post. A libel which, a perspiring Needham told me during the office Christmas party, had cost the paper £11,000. Still they had impugned the reputation of Moorfields Eye Hospital and got away Scot-free, I thought.

Other 'investigations' for Cuscom produced my first crop of headlines, which included: 'Trouble With The Double-Glazing', 'Why Such A Dear Pinta?', ' Are Light Bulbs Lasting As Long As They Used To ?' and 'Blast Those Jacket Buttons'. The Sunday Post dug deep into the fearful psyche of the Scottish Presbytarian shopper.

My first summer at The Sunday Post was gloriously sunny and one morning I walked to the office from my rented bed-sit in Warwick Avenue off Kensington High Street, through all the parks – Hyde, Green and St James – in sandals. That was until David Norrie's brows stiffened when he espied my dusty feet beneath my white cotton Safari suit: 'I canna send yae to see the Queen with yae taes poking oot,' he said in his strange squeaky, and permanently exclamatory Dundonian accent.

If I arrived in Fleet Street early I would walk down towards Ludgate Circus absorbing the great newspaper office facades and smile absurdly at the rotund commissionaires as though ingratiating myself with them would help me over the threshold. Breakfast was a slab of home-made bread pudding and a mug of tea in Mick's Café, romantically open 24 hours a day, and where invariably a newspaper vendor in a white coat with Daily Express printed on the back would be sleeping off a hangover.

I would sometimes wander round St Brides Church, reading the memorial plaques of great journalists. I was by now hooked on the glamour of Fleet Street and I didn't want to dress like a hippy anymore, instead I wanted to look like a reporter. I had a charcoal suit with a waistcoat made at Dombey & Son in Fleet Street. I discarded my Breton clogs for a pair of black, double-brogue shoes. I corralled my neck with a Paisley pattern tie and with confident self-delusion started to power mingle along the world's most famous street.

The suit is the reporter's chrysalis. I was an uneducated labourer with one O-Level developing into a guardian of democracy. My plausibility was gestating within the pupa of collar and tie.

Another of The Sunday Post's columns was by the 'HON man'. HON stood for 'Holidays On Nothing'. It was the legacy of a long since forgotten cub reporter who had hiked round the Highlands of Scotland. He survived on the sniff of boiled haggis and Irn Bru, a hideous ethnic cola the colour of a diabetic's urine. This delighted the Thomson management who had not been faced with any vast expenses. They assumed it would delight the readers, too, who, they believed, related warmly to such parsimony.

Holidays On Nothing had sparked a permanent column, written in the first person, the HON man's journalese accompanied by a cartoon image of a reporter in trench coat and trilby hat.

Norrie decided a newsworthy task for HON man would be to obtain an interview with Frank Sinatra who was appearing at the London Palladium. A phone call to Celebrity Bulletin, a service that newspapers subscribed to for showbusiness information, revealed the crooner was staying at the Savoy Hotel.

'You may need a wee advance,' Norrie said, 'I'm giving you an IOU for five poonds.' After spending most of it in the American Bar on gin and tonic and gleaning nothing on the whereabouts of my quarry, I wandered instead through the hotel, taking the lift up to various floors. I stopped a chambermaid and, posing as a guest who was seeking Sinatra's autograph for his mother, was told the singer had hired an entire floor. At the end of a long corridor on the third floor of empty rooms a desk had been placed. Behind it sat a burly minder who was happy to take my request for an autograph to Sinatra's suite. As he stood up his name was emblazoned on his track suit. I quickly scribbled it down. It was a 'fact'. A name that could be used in a story. I heard a muffled voice sounding a negative and the autograph did not materialise but now I had established Sinatra was in residence. All I had to do was find out which entrance he would leave from. The chauffeurs who service the hotel, can always be found drinking in the pub next door, The Coal Hole. Still posing as a guest I spent the last of my IOU buying them halves of bitter, and from them discovered that Sinatra always slipped out of the kitchen entrance when leaving the Savoy. I waited in the dark for an hour listening to rack loads of cutlery being washed up, until a large Jaguar arrived. It parked at the kerbside and waited with its lights on and engine running.

Shortly after this a light came on in the kitchen doorway and as I stepped forward for a clear view, Sinatra came through a revolving door and almost bumped into me.

'Frank?' I said, and with that one word, the world's most famous entertainer was immediately surrounded by minders who elbowed me into the gutter and bundled him into the back of the Jaguar. The car sped off into the night, tyres squealing.   I was left at the kerbside next to one elderly woman fan who had proved equal to my own sleuthing. I explained why I had been lurking in the dark.

' You know what you done wrong?' she said ' you should have called him Mr Sinatra.' With that she, too, disappeared into the night.

Having ruined my chance of a full and fearless interview with Old Blue Eyes, I strolled up to the Strand where not a single fan was to be seen. Frank could have used the main entrance – no one would have been the wiser. Perhaps he was only too aware of that.

'Have You Heard?',the paper's diary, was another section that budding reporters had to fill. Cub reporters were encouraged to lift and re-write celebrity gossip from the national dailies. If we could get a fresh quote from an agent fine, if not, a date-sensitive re-write was perfectly acceptable.

As a result, yes, most people had already heard as the gossip we published was, in newspaper terms, historical fact. Occasionally we would initiate our own. A colleague who had been promoted to The Sunday Post from the Dundee Courier, was reporter John Hayes. He was assigned the job of knocking on the front door of ex-King Constantine of Greece's home and ask him what it was like living in exile in Hampstead. Hayes, acerbically but accurately, assessed the paper's naivety when he commented: 'They expect him to come to the door wearing a crown.'

The Sunday Post boasted a 'saturation' circulation and was mentioned in the Guinness Book of Records for this distinction. Apparently just about everybody in Scotland either bought the newspaper, or read it second-hand. Certainly many copies were sent on from Scottish homes to friends and family living overseas. The widely held belief in the Dundee HQ, of the comic and newspaper empire, was that people had grown up with 'Oor Wullie; and 'The Broons': cartoon Scottish archetypes in a sort of newspaper soap opera, which the paper felt, its readers could not live without. The unchanging folksy nature of the paper reassured it's conservative readership. Russia and its Soviets were the enemy; America was a fascinating land of technology, and unhinged superlative. The rest of the world was a place toured by 'Glasgwegian tourists', or where resourceful Scotsmen temporarily worked. Scotland, as the centre of the universe, was the only sane and safe place to be.

England was Scotland's playground when Scots played the English at Wembley every other year. For one of these clashes I was sent to cover the news story – the expected trouble - as opposed to the match itself, which was left to the sports' journalists. As the only man in a suit, I arrived in a land of tartan-covered corpse-like drunks either lying or sitting on the concrete steps around the stadium. These were the ones who could not get inside. I felt distinctly uneasy as I walked among them. Add to this the fact that all London Transport Underground trains and buses had been cancelled in a large zone around the ground, I felt isolated, too.

The chill spring air kept the smell of urine puddles to a tolerable level and when the stadium 'burst' – I was outside the Coliseum-like walls as briefed. The tartan army marched forth. There were two distinct types: tall, fiercely handsome, flame-haired warriors and short, ugly, threatening, types sporting lurid spots presumably a legacy of the fish suppers and 'soor ploom' diet I was forever being encouraged to write about. Never having been to Scotland , now, like Dunsinane Wood it came en masse to me. There was no trouble really, though the man running the hot-dog stand who had his own mustard squirted over him might have taken a different view. I tried to walk along in my collar and tie surrounded by the chanting tartan horde as though it was the most natural thing in the world. Denial had not then been invented but I that's what I was in.

A mile or two from the ground I managed to find a bus and with some relief set off back to central London. My sanctuary was short-lived however, when, at the next stop, a hundred or so fans got on and commandeered the vehicle. As the sole English passenger I again practiced my mental escapism by staring reflectively out of the window as though fascinated with NW London. The conductor was trapped upstairs by the sheer number of fans and was powerless to stop the mob taking control. The driver clearly thought the best way to help his colleague was to keep going. So the bus was belled past every stop by the fans who stuck two fingers up at astonished queues as the runaway, double decker roared past. One of the shorter kind of spotty, abscessed, toad-skinned Scots who had been standing on the platform and until now had miraculously not noticed me, now did. Perhaps my study of passing suburban London had been overlong to be convincing.

'Whose that coont a shittin' hissell?,' chanted the toad, his retinas fissured with so many veins they appeared to have rolled 360 degrees in his skull . I affected an absent-minded look, trying to make eye contact with no-one.

'Whose that coont a shittin' hissell?,' he repeated with more volume. First one then many started chanting. As in-bus entertainment it happened to be uncannily well observed. But before the whole mob joined in we reached Notting Hill Gate where I leapt off and made my escape.

2. HARD NEWS

After I had worked for just a year on The Sunday Post, D.C. Thomson moved its office around the corner and into Fleet Street itself. I now had a wallet full of business cards marked with the most prestigious address any reporter could hope for. But I knew it was a delusion. 'We're on Fleet Street but not in it,' Hayes, who now works for the Financial Times, accurately observed. Even the office pub, The Clachan, wasn't one used by the thirsty journalists of our neighbouring national brothers. So near…

I started firing off what must have seemed very peculiar letters to the editors of the national dailies. I would walk around Fleet Street with a Have You Heard, As We See It, HON-Man mentality, composing application letters based on my observations of the newspapers' environs. I was under the illusion that being a writer was what newspaper editors were looking for. The Daily Mirror got a description of Holborn Circus, the Evening Standard one of Shoe Lane. In other missives I endeavoured to seem interesting by chronicling my chequered career since leaving school.

The news editor of the News of the World wrote back: 'I thought I was getting your life story but it seemed different,' and gave me an interview. Another of the letters secured an interview with Charles Wintour, legendary editor of the Evening Standard. But neither mentioned my brilliant prose and instead asked me about something called 'hard news': and had I done any? Whatever hard news was, it clearly did not include the journalese I'd turned out for The Sunday Post. Even so I started to get a few casual shifts and the Standard sent me off to find 'overnight' pieces: any old bumpff around London which would fill the early edition before the real news was gathered in by the day's reporting team. From this I began to realise that hard news was basically bad news. Human beings are only interested in good news if it's personal. As newspaper readers they are comforted by the misfortunes of others – not because they are heartless beasts – but because as everyone in life has a cross to bear it's an easier burden if you are able to read that others are sharing the 12 stations. Newspapers are in the hugely successful business of reporting that shit happens everywhere.

I was delighted to see my copy in print and even had a by-line : 'Mick Durham' –not very subtle, but changed enough so I could deny any knowledge to Norrie.

You could literally view the hard news at the Evening Standard's old office at 47 Shoe Lane whizzing overhead as it passed through an umbilical tube which connected the newsdesk with the compositor's room. The typescripts of news were sealed in translucent capsules and by means of air suction sped across the ceiling between the ventilation ducts. The noisy process, designed to preserve the news' rapidly evaporating novelty, added a sense of urgency to the scene, as did the chattering typewriters, serial cigarette smoking, shouted curses, and desks covered in plastic cups full of cold coffee.

The Evening News, off Tudor Street, had a different method of swiftly dispatching copy from the newsdesk to those who physically put the paper together: it trundled along on a little conveyor belt, rather like a toy train, which ran between a narrow metal channel and connected the reporters' desks with the newsdesk and the newsdesk with the sub-editors and so on. On a 'quiet news day' on the Evening News one winter's morning, the newsdesk decided that London was in for the snow that was affecting some parts of the Midlands. Reporters were ordered to call the AA, RAC, London Transport, the ambulance service, British Rail (as it then was), the British Medical Association, Help the Aged and other agencies to 'stand up' a threat of snow. As the sun rose that morning the first edition screamed "Blizzards Blast Thousands' only lower down did the reader discover, via the selective and tortuous inquisition of a multitude of agencies, that London was under 'threat' of snow. And for the closing editions, commuters were told 'Blizzard Pulls Back for Return Home' as they were about to find out for themselves.

On a Daily Mail nightshift I discovered the magic of reverse telephone directories, purloined from a postal worker with a backhander of hard cash from somebody at the General Post Office. In these the streets of UK cities were listed alphabetically with the names, addresses and telephone numbers following on so when an assault, fire or robbery occurred somewhere, calls could be made to everyone in the road for eye-witness accounts. My night shifts on the Daily Mirror were at the old Holborn Circus building which looked like a harmonica on end. On my first Mirror shift I introduced myself to a burly chap in a Prince of Wales check suit who was sitting with highly polished loafers propped up on a large, combined news and picture desk. A shock of raven curls, like a black cauliflower, sat atop his large head. 'Hello, my name's Dick Durham. I was told to check in with the newsdesk.'

The cauliflower tilted downwards as its owner squinted along the barrel of a large gun. He appeared to be using the highly polished loafers at the end of his crossed legs as a sight. He squeezed the trigger and Thwat. A steel dart hit a bullseye target pinned up on the tin wall of a side office.

Then he turned to me.

'Oh hello dear,' growled the bass Cockney voice of Tom Merrin, the night news editor. 'Have a shot at this: pound a go'. I had about £6 jangling in my pocket and soon lost £2 before being detailed to the canteen for bacon sandwiches and tea all round. Having run my chore I sat at the bench furthest from the newsdesk and hid behind the Daily Telegraph hoping I would not get anything to do in case my hard news was too soft for Merrin's taste.

The desks were covered in black Formica and ran away in rows like glossy railway sleepers down through the voluminous and important-looking news room to the key and lamp system news shrine. All the typewriters were chained down. This was not because the reporters wanted to take their work home with them, but, as the conflicting demands of closing time and deadlines clashed, it was to ensure nothing bigger than a ball point pen or litter basket could be used as a missile.

Suddenly the phone rang on my desk. 'Hello ? Daily Mirror,' I chirped.

'I know it's the Daily Mirror, love, this is an internal phone. You're so far away I've had to call you,' came the rich East End voice of Merrin.

'Oh sorry.'

''Ave a word with this woman will you? She thinks she's found another planet.'

I was put through to an excitable Daily Mirror reader from Dagenham, who had seen a light shaped like a cigar which was flashing on and off and had hovered close to the ground then lifted into the air, moved sideways, then descended and hovered close to the ground again. I can recall it all so clearly because I took copious notes.

Merrin watched the pages flick over in my wire-bound note-book, then he bellowed right down the length of the newsroom: 'Mr Durham ? What's she going on about?'

Covering the receiver with my palm I stood up and stammered out a verbatim account of the reader's experience.

'Tell her to fuck off!' roared Merrin. I lifted my cupped hand and began to tell her diplomatically that we would call her later and could I have a contact number? Could I have an address ? Perhaps a work number ?. But on and on she went, how the light had changed shape to a sphere, how it had shot away and then come back. How it was there NOW, hovering. How I should come down and see it myself.

'I SAID, tell her to fuck off,' came Merrin's roar I was sure it had echoed in the receiver. But she was not going to let go of a sympathetic ear AND one on HER paper the Daily Mirror. Caught between loquacity and profanity I cut her off. I didn't know what else to do but I never sat at the back again.

'Mr Durham, have a look at this will you?' said Merrin, handing me a sheet of Press Association copy. It was about Manchester United fans arriving in London en masse for some away game. 'Go and have a look Mr Durham, see what the animals are up to,' said Merrin, who then turned to his colleagues on the picture desk enquiring; 'Who's hungry?'.

There was no reply.

'Well I am, can't we send a monkey down to Tubby Isaacs?' Chuckling inwardly at the name I had supposed was being used to summon a messenger I was startled to see a photographer stand up and receive an order from Merrin for a large portion of jellied eels.

21

It seemed the natural thing to do was head straight for Piccadilly Circus. It was a good choice: the 'Red Army's' perception of metropolitan London was about as sophisticated as mine: Eros and his roundabout was alive with them.

I witnessed a lot of shouting, a few windows pushed in, the odd policeman bated and I filed accordingly. Naively I believed that the copy 'takers' actually wrote the story and that all I had to do was dictate my notes. Not once did the 'telephone reporters', as they were known, stop me and ask why I wasn't using paragraphs or grammar of any kind. When I got back to the Daily Mirror, Merrin called me over. This time he spoke softly.

'Mr Durham, what's all this old crap? United supporters? What united? West Ham ? Leeds ? You've never filed by phone before have you?' I had not and admitted so. I explained that on The Sunday Post we got back to the office and wrote it up.

'Fuck me! Even when the Sunday Mirror comes down here on Saturdays to play at being a newspaper, they file by phone,' Merrin, a hard news man who saw feature-packed Sunday papers as no better than magazines, said reflectively.

I crept back to my furthest bench flushed with shame but very grateful that Merrin had aired his observations sotto voce. I was fortunate both Merrin and his deputy, Terry O'Hanlon, treated novices kindly.

I resolved to go back to my Sunday Post world and try and get news hardened. I did not expect to get any more shifts on the Daily Mirror.

Back at my prosaic D.C. Thomson post I was given another of the Post's franchises : 'The Honest Truth' as if the truth in The Sunday Post had to be qualified. This was the major interview of the week and took the form of a question and answer session. The questions were collated from editorial staff including those in Glasgow, Dundee and London.

It wasn't exactly a grilling. I was briefed via a telex from the big chief in Dundee, Harold Pirie, to ask the following question of TGWU leader Jack Jones: 'What has been your sheet anchor in public life?' whatever a sheet anchor was; of TV tycoon Lew Grade 'Are you a millionaire?'; of Labour veteran Manny Shinwell, who had been the 'most impressive' person he'd ever met? Once I even got through to former Prime Minister Harold Macmillan on the phone, but confronted with some asinine question he answered simply: 'I am very old, you know.' There was nothing in that which could be taken out of context.

He was too polite to put the phone down and I was too polite to be pushy then, so I thanked him and *I* put the phone down!

When Norrie sent me along as HON man to a press conference at the Park Lane Hilton to welcome former heavyweight boxing champion Muhammad Ali to London I sat next to all the top national reporters. Ali arrived wearing black trousers, a black cowboy shirt and black hobnail boots. Though tall, he was not as broad shouldered as he looked on TV. The master of ceremonies said: 'I don't think I need to introduce our guest.'

'Why you talkin' then?,' quipped Ali.

'Thank you for coming,' answered the host.

'You're paying me, but they still say the nigger talk too much,' Ali continued, transfixing the crowd of newspapermen.

A microphone on a mobile lead was passed around the room as the raised hands of reporters requested it. I self-consciously raised my arm and watched nervously as it headed heron-like towards me. I asked Ali if he ever caught the bully who stole his bicycle at school, a fact I had gleaned from the library of the Press Association, the national news agency to which all national and regional newspapers subscribe. The question did stop the pugilistic poet in mid-flow and I for once I felt among peers as the real Fleet Street scribes also paused to watch his reaction.

'No, and I'm glad I never did,' he said as he pummelled one palm with a fist.

My moment of peer equality evaporated as a reporter from the Daily Mail told me: 'You don't ask exclusive questions at press conferences. Anyone who's silly enough to ask questions with everyone else here will forfeit them.'

I then compounded my loss of status by asking for the heavyweight's autograph !

'Sit down,' screamed the melee of photographers as I lunged forward with proffered notebook, 'some of us are trying to work here.'

To my astonishment I discovered I'd been given three more night shifts at the Daily Mirror, perhaps Merrin was hoping I 'd exercise my losing streak at gun-darts again. Whatever the reason I never filed by phone again without first writing out my copy.

A few lines of Press Association tape were handed to me on my next assignment at the Daily Mirror. They recorded the stark fact that a young woman had fallen to her death from the 18th storey of a high rise in East London. The desk were interested because there was no suggestion Rosemary Bailey had taken her own life. I would later learn that suicidees are not a source of good copy for newspapers because such stories wander into the realm of mental illness and therefore invalidate the paper's normal vice of exploiting culpability. If you are mad the only way to get into the papers is to be related to the Queen or other royals. Both Katherine Bowes Lyon, a relative of the late Queen Mother and Idonea Fane, a cousin of the Queen, made the nationals when it was discovered they had been shut away in a mental asylum where the NHS picked up the tab until it was closed down. Fane's death also made the papers because she was given a pauper's funeral after she died in 2001.

After a check call to Scotland Yard's Press Bureau I got the outline of the story. It seemed the girl had argued with her live-in boyfriend – they were both of West Indian extraction – about his white lover. The row had culminated in his peremptory eviction of the 19-year-old girl from their council flat in James Sinclair Point in Plaistow. While the boyfriend was at work, Rosemary had let herself back into the home and then set up a barricade using his voluminous Hi-Fi PA system. There had also been a row between Rosemary and the new girlfriend who, in turn, was rapidly evicted from the flat. Having created a self-imposed siege, it was thought Rosemary's anger had cooled and she had begun to have second thoughts – possibly something to do with the inevitable return of the boyfriend who enjoyed body-building. She decided to get out herself, but desirous, still, of keeping her rival from the domicile she left the barricades in place and climbed out of the window by lowering herself from the balcony to the one immediately below. Her tool for the descent was a length of curtain wire. She was a well-built girl and the home-made abseil 'rope' was not strong enough.

The Mirror photographer assigned to the job was Bunny Atkins who showed me down to the car park. Depositing his camera bag in the boot of his smart Rover automobile he said: 'Where is it?'

'Plaistow.'

We set off.

'What's the story?'

I told him.

'Colour?'

'Sorry?'

'Colour. What colour is she?'

'I believe she's West Indian.'

'I know a nice little pub down the road. We'll stop off for a beer if you like.'

'I'd rather push on,' I said.

'Look, she's black,' he said,'they'll never use it.'

I persisted and we drove to Plaistow in silence.

We arrived at the tower block and automobiles in various states of dis-assembly lined the precinct of the homes in the sky. Atkins was clearly loath to park his own immaculate saloon in the vicinity and continued to lobby for a visit to the nearest pub from where we could make 'check calls' to the office and while away the shift. 'There's no way they'll use it,' he said again.

We entered the urine-reeking, tin-can lift and jerked up towards the 18th floor. I had not got the exact address and therefore knocked on a couple of doors. No one answered.

'Let's fuck off to the pub,' said Atkins, 'this is a waste of time. The desk aren't interested in coons.' I knocked on another door and a tiny, petrified old lady opened it just a crack. Her head barely came above the door chain. On receipt of the name she thumbed towards the next door flat and put her forefinger to her lips.

Her neighbour was a short, stocky, well muscled man, Melvin Sinclair, the estranged boyfriend of the unfortunate Rosemary. He ushered us in to the lounge where about a dozen black males were sat smoking. Among them was an attractive blonde. I had said we were from the Daily Mirror but I do not think this fact had registered and it became clear they thought we were police officers. We got the full details of the story plus a 'collect' photograph -an existing print handed over from a photo album - of the dead girl and also permission from the recently bereaved muscleman to pose for a photograph with his new girlfriend. I turned to Atkins. 'My gear's in the car,' he said lamely. Not only did he have no faith in the story ever seeing the light of day, he did not believe we would actually GET a story or picture. Worse, he feared he would be mugged for his equipment and had left it locked in the boot of his car.

We had lost the moment, as now the dead girl's relatives, carrying baseball bats, turned up to demonstrate their displeasure with the sequence of events. We then realised why so many fellows in the rival 'camp' were enjoying Sinclair's hospitality. It was most definitely time to leave.

Back at the Mirror Atkins was congratulated for 'securing' the collect!

But at least he put in a good word for me and the story was used as a page lead – albeit re-written by staff reporter Garth Gibbs, who got the by-line. Atkins' intemperate language about the protagonists in this particular story sounds shocking, especially as race was not a hindrance to secure coverage in the Mirror. Atkins, however was no racist, he was already middle-aged, had the big car, the house in Spain and simply wanted a quiet life doing his shift, taking his money and knocking off early. He did not relish a tough doorstep with a keen young casual out to prove himself and put up a barrier to hinder what he perceived as being a hard night's work. His 'macho' language was merely a camouflage for his idleness. But I was hooked, this was 'hard news' and the process of acquiring it was infectious. The 'night shift' seemed the appropriate time to gather stories on the darker side of life and I'd got the taste.

Meanwhile back at my day job, human interest replaced hard news once more as HON Man, alias myself, went from strength to strength. He spent a day with the Wombles who were 'competing' against disc jockeys and a pop group called the Bay City Rollers at Brands Hatch in Kent. He wore an electro-cardiogram for a day to test his heart out and he interviewed a 'boffin' who could turn leaves and grass into protein fit for human consumption.

I interviewed a 42-year-old security guard, Joe Incles, from Corby, who sat in a urine-stained armchair and sounded like an amateur ventriloquist while telling me of his insatiable appetite through jaws wired to stop him exercising it. Failed teetotaller and Coronation Street actor Peter Adamson told me about the pills which turned him red if he drank, which he used deliberately as a devilish party trick. Dwarf Nottingham factory workers, Iris and Mavis Allen, revealed to humanity their life at knee height as the 'Shortest Twins in Britain.'

But I now knew these assignments were all 'soft news', they were features and not what the big beasts of Fleet Street were after. The Sunday Post's grittier gathering of hard news was carried out from the Glasgow office. Any move towards trying to get involved in news-gathering from the London office was actively discouraged by Norrie who existed in order to arrange the supply of his trifle-like articles to the Dundonian HQ. News was tricky, news invited litigation, news meant proper training which in turn meant expenditure. Far better to have a staff of safe youngsters playing at being reporters and turning out acres of copy on the cheap.

So my old colleague Hayes and I stopped wandering Fleet Street in the lunch hour 'star-gazing' – picking out great correspondents from their picture by-lines and following them into El Vinos and other hostelries in Fleet Street trying to get our shoulders rubbed – and left D.C.Thomson. By taking a drop in pay we secured jobs on a London borough bi-weekly, the Ealing Gazette, whose editor was impressed with our D.C. Thomson experience and was prepared to let us catch up on news-gathering skills.

I was given a copy of the newspaper group's guide to their titles. The 'Westminster Press House Style' book stated in its forward: 'This book is an attempt to give guidance on the way our newspapers ought to be written………. Perhaps the most surprising feature of the subject is the frequency with which even highly educated writers offend in matters of style. For example, it is not uncommon to see Negro spelt with a lower case n although this is highly offensive.'

The guide also advised that writing in 'the active' was 'better' than in the 'passive': '"man bites dog" is better than "dog is bitten by man" .' The book also stated: 'Avoid the shorthand possessive, e.g. Egypt's President Nasser,' thereby condemning every national newspaper in the land.

My first lesson in court reporting - at Ealing Magistrates – was that the grandly titled fourth estate was a fine check and balance within the unwritten constitution of the land as long as the judiciary's fare would sell the Ealing Gazette. Thus any number of felons would escape having justice being seen to be done to them unless they were famous, involved in sex crimes or were serial killers.

I was expected to drop in and out of various courts looking for a 'news worthy' story.

One of the earliest of these concerned two carloads of youths racing each other down the Uxbridge Road. At traffic lights the occupants of the 'losing' car battered their rival with hammers and screwdrivers smashing windows and denting panels. I got carried away with my despatch and described it as a 'Starsky and Hutch' style race after the popular TV cop series. Nobody in court had used such a description which became part of the headline although surprisingly none of those prosecuted later complained of defamation.

I developed a taste for the macabre. Being young and therefore distant enough from my own mortality, I was interested in death and relished my regular visits to West London Coroner's Court, where the inquests of Ealing citizens' were heard.

That there is no dignity in death soon became apparent as I sat in the gloomy courtroom listening to police officers detailing clinically their 'facts' . One demise that sticks in my mind was that of a hotel proprietor who, while walking beside his swimming pool, had a seizure and fell in. The officer who arrived at the scene thought the man's cat had drowned with him, until the unfortunate victim was hauled from the water. At first he could not be positively identified as all those who knew him remembered a man with a full head of hair.

The other thing I soon realised about court houses is that they are the unavoidable address for the quarry you are trying to nail. People can be 'doorstepped' for days without uttering a word, but once the court is involved their elusiveness is over. On a local paper the only juicy copy available that is realistically publishable is garnered from the privileged arena of the local courts.

On the Ealing Gazette we were interested in a suspected double-suicide attempt. This suicide was 'news worthy' as the pair were not mentally ill - in the recognised sense of the phrase – just in love. The pact had gone wrong and the male had survived. The lovers were living in Southall in the heart of the Sikh community, the UK's largest sub-continental community. The girl, Tara Meisuria, was one half of an unhappy arranged marriage and her husband was due to join her from Bombay. Her lover, Rajinda Sahib, a twenty-year-old trainee chef, survived and of course an inquest was opened. At the inquest we got the chance of photographing the surviving male. This infuriated both his family and the bereaved family of the dead girl, an 18-year-old chemist's assistant. Our car was chased back to the office on Ealing Broadway. I ran inside with the film but later the photographer's car was covered in paint stripper.

Southall was to figure large in my cub life. The district has some of the oldest council houses in the country and when the option for tenants to buy their council homes was first mooted I was sent down there to get reaction from residents. The first front door I knocked on was that of a good-sized, three-bed, semi facing a canal which was lined with well-established plane trees. It seemed a good place to live. The elderly gent who opened the door invited me in.

'Olive,' he called out to his wife, 'got a young man here from the newspaper wants to know if we want to buy our house! What I want to tell you, young man, is that we've bought it several times over with the rent we've paid.'

It turned out that the 76-year-old resident had moved in straight from the trenches of Flanders Fields.

'It was terrible,' said the toothless old gent.

'What the war?'

'No, the house. All the window frames were creosoted – we had to leave the windows open for six months to get rid of the smell. It was like living in a creosote pig-sty.'

I said I thought it was a lovely area in which to live what with the canal and trees.

The old fellow looked at me and beckoned me outside to his back garden.

Here he had made a pond so his gnomes could fish and a cement stork could wet its bill. He jerked a thumb over the fence I looked at a bald lawn scattered with engine parts and washing up bowls full of sump oil.

'Asians' said the man. He thumbed the other way. I looked at another garden, this one overgrown and supporting tall thistles which had snared several plastic bags blown in from the street.

'Asians' repeated my host. At the bottom of his garden was an allotment. His patch was manicured with erect runner bean sticks and a well painted shed. The others were much the same as the gardens I had seen earlier: running wild, untended: a habitat which supported deflated footballs, car tyres and supermarket trolleys.

'I'm being wogged out!' croaked the old tenant with a cheeky grin.

Desperately trying to salvage something I could actually use I said: 'But they were called the Homes fit for Heroes weren't they?'

'Homes fit for Heroes? You 'ad to be a fucking hero to live in one,' came the candid reply which terminated an unpublishable interview.

But nevertheless Ealing was a great 'patch' for stories. We had celebrities living in it, 'good' crimes - I covered the fatal shooting of a Securicor guard and the stabbing to death of a newsagent in my first couple of weeks on the paper. Ealing was also a rich source of 'industrial' stories, ie strikes or job losses including the closure of AEC the bus and truck manufacturers. Ealing's complex cosmopolitan mix gave us exotica - as well as the Oriental flavour of the Sikh community there was a healthy Polish ex-pat contingent.

A retired British Rail worker Marion Skoczek was one of only twenty who survived the 150-strong militia he had lead through the drains of Warsaw in that city's uprising against the Nazis. We pictured him holding a medal display case longer than the rifle he carried as a 30-year-old captain. It included the Virtati Militari, the Polish VC.

The 'Queen of the suburbs' as Ealing had once dubbed itself even had a link to the notorious Kray twins, who came from another kind of suburb altogether: Bethnal Green. Canon Richard Hetherington had come to Ealing to retire, but had known the twins since they were boys when he was their local vicar at St James' Church in the Bethnal Green Road.

He told me how he was trying to get Reggie moved from Parkhurst on the Isle of Wight to a mainland prison to make it easier for the twins' mother, Violet, to visit, as Ronnie was on the mainland, too, in Broadmoor.

But the one big story in Ealing while I was there were the Southall riots. Or I should say while I was not there. What a time to be on holiday - after the Anti Nazi League clashed with the National Front in Southall and during the subsequent fighting, an Anti-Nazi League member, Blair Peach, a local school teacher, was killed after witnesses observed a police officer on horseback hitting Peach over the head with a long truncheon.

Subsequent enquiries found Blair had a) a thin skull b) was hit by a lead-filled cosh as opposed to a truncheon.

Anyway I was staying with my parents in Cornwall when it happened: in the wrong place at the right time. In my dreams I imagined great events would be laid out before me every day of the week, but that was true only for those on the national newspapers. The death of Blair Peach was a national story happening in Ealing and I had been on holiday!

I caught up, though. An attractive reporter on the neighbouring Acton Gazette, Aileen Doherty, who went on to become one of the Daily Mail's freelance feature editors and who shared a damp flat near the Hammersmith flyover with Lorraine Heggessey who went on to head up BBC 1, had good contacts with the Peaches. While sleeping off a good dinner paid for by me, I rifled through her handbag, found her contacts book and got Blair Peach's

widow's phone number. She would have given me the number
had I asked, but obtaining it by hookery suited the 'ratlike
cunning' I had read reporters required. Next morning a
photographer and I presented a plausible manner to Celia Peach
at her Hackney, East London home for an exclusive interview.
By now I felt ready to walk Fleet Street again, no longer gazing at
the stars on the national papers but as an equal. Or so I
Imagined. I was interviewed by Stuart Kuttner, cleared at the Old
Bailey in 2014 of any wrong-doing in the News of the World
phone-hacking scandal, but then managing editor of the London
Evening News, for a reporter's job. Kuttner, tall dark and
Levantine-looking leapt at me as I entered his office.
'Coup d'tat?' he yelled.
'Sorry?'
'Coup d'tat, I said, have you ever covered a coup d'tat?'
'Er, not in Ealing no,' I replied but if he had a sense of humour he
was saving it for later.
I thought this must be the Evening News' version of the Chicago
Police psychological profiling test and prepared myself for
further unpredictabilities.
Kuttner seemed a man much pre-occupied with what he wanted.
He certainly wanted somebody, it certainly wasn't me. But he
appeared to enjoy going through the motions anyway.
'What books do you read?'
I was still plodding through my recommended reading list, and
had entered a Kafka phase for though he was not on it, he had
become vogue and I was trying to develop an enigmatic
approach to impress newspaper secretaries in the Wine Press on
Fleet Street.
'Well I've been reading some Kafka,' I said.
'What relevance has Kafka got to journalism?' Kuttner asked.
I tried to jokingly suggest that Kafka's protagonist in The Castle,
who spends the whole book trying to get into the place, was not
unlike trying to get into Fleet Street.
He suddenly became interested and scribbled down notes.
'So what have you covered in Ealing then?,' he asked looking up
from his desk.

'Well there's the Southall riot, which as you know resulted in the death of Blair Peach. I got an exclusive interview with the widow.'
'Who killed him?'
'Who killed who?'
'Who killed Blair Peach?'
'Well, I don't know it's been suggested a police truncheon......'
'Yes but which police truncheon, eh? Don't you think that as a reporter on the Ealing Gazette you should make it your business to find out eh? That's the story isn't it? That's the one for you eh?'
'Yes, quite !' I said as the interview ended and somewhat crestfallen I rumbled back to prosaic Ealing on the prosaic District Line.

Many years later when I heard what the reporters at the Evening News had telexed to the editorial of the Evening Standard, where Kuttner was moving to, it struck a chord: 'For what you are about to receive may the Lord make us truly thankful'.

I then started trying to sell my Ealing stories to Fleet Street, and quickly discovered there were no takers for the local community race relations lobby attacking the Metropolitan Police for 'losing control' over the Southall riots. Nor could I raise anything louder than a yawn over a public service workers' proposed strike for a basic wage. I was puzzled – was this not hard news? Instead they wanted the story of a retired coal miner whose lumbago had forced him to dig up the geraniums in his front garden and replace them with plastic flowers. They also bought the yarn about the family whose gnomes had been kidnapped and ransomed. Strangely it seemed that the nationals liked their hard news soft, after all.

Back at Holborn Circus I sat on my Daily Mirror night shift one evening listening to a senior reporter on the bench in front. It was Garth Gibbs, the reporter who'd re-written my first story, talking to his wife.

'Yes I've been to the doctor,' he said drawing on a cigarette, 'What did HE say? He said that if I start exercising, if I stop drinking so much, if I quit smoking, if I have a diet which takes in more vegetables and fruit I'll be OK.

'What did *I* say? I said I know that, that's why I've come to you, can't you give me a fucking pill?'

Another time I glanced over the shoulder of Stuart Greig, as he typed out his weekly expenses. The amount in total was nearly twice that of my weekly wage! Greig, who kept a bottle of Scotch in his grey steel desk drawer diluted his tea with it to help him concentrate on the 'reason for expenditure' column.

Having by now learnt that the proper brick road to yellow journalism was paved with the cobbles of hard news I knew I would have to move on from Ealing, and its twice weekly delivery of news, to an evening newspaper. I got a job on the now defunct Evening Post-Echo which covered Luton, Watford, St Albans and Hemel Hempstead. The received wisdom was that working for an evening newspaper – a paper which comes out every weekday – is a a more demanding role. With their daily deadlines, the fledgling reporter's speed and accuracy is put to the test and so evening newspapers are therefore the next logical step to the national dailies. The trouble is receiving wisdom is for parrots and it's owls that are wise.

I was regularly disappointed when I had copy ready to file by lunchtime from some magistrates court only to be told by news editor Paul Brown, who became Environment Correspondent for The Guardian,: 'It's too late for the edition. We'll have it as an overnight!' Hard news, if no-one else was chasing it, was given a longer sell-by date.

The Evening Post-Echo had been a proper paper in it's day. It had won prestigious awards and was a journal through which many reporters went to Fleet Street, but, an early victim of modern production methods, it had, by the time I joined the staff, become more interested in design than content.

It's greatest asset, from a news perspective, was the fact that the M1 ran right through it's circulation area, and therefore was a regular conduit of hard news stories, from fatal pile-ups, to record traffic jams and motorway madness.

While on a Saturday shift, alone, I drove out to a Road Traffic Accident (RTA) near St. Albans. I got to within a mile of the motorway before having to dump the pool car and walk because the whole carriageway on both sides had been cordoned off. It struck me how beautiful the meadows and copses of Hertfordshire were, once the blacktop highway running through them was void of traffic noise. The peace, as I walked across the fields towards the great road, was strange. The empty and silent motorway, surreal.

I got there just as the firemen had finished hosing down the carriageway surface. One of the officers said the crash which involved a fibreglass three-wheeled car somersaulting after the nose wheel fell off, was the worst he had ever seen in 20-odd years service, but by then I knew you always needed a quote like that and normally had to secure it with a suitable leading question as I did that sunny spring day. The broken vehicles had already been cleared away. The blood and gore hosed free of the tarmac. My notebook filled I began to stroll back along the eerily empty highway and then noticed something incongruous hanging slimily from the roadside hedge. I stepped closer. It was a swinging strand of brain tissue. Then I noticed a small piece of fissured, convex-shaped bone like a broken piece of Easter egg sitting on the tarmac. Though I had not seen one before I knew instinctively I was looking at a piece of skull.

During my next Fleet Street shift this time for the Daily Star I started recounting my brush with death to others in the pub. This started a sort of horror contest and Syd Brennan, an old Fleet Street hand, became particularly animated.

'I've covered eight air crashes,' he said, 'there was one, a flight from Manchester landed on top of the Pyrenees. There was a man sitting like The Thinker on a rock but you went round the other side and there was no bottom half. I've covered train crashes, too, there was Hither Green. Remember Hither Green? And Lewisham, remember the Lewisham train crash ?'
Nobody did.

'They were mainly in one carriage. It crushed up like a packet of cigarettes. Legs were cut off inside, dismembered arms dropped out of the window, terrible.' So terrible Brennan warmed further to his subject.

'I covered a train crash in Manchester one winter – it was so cold the ice froze the carriages together. I was walking through the frozen snow along the embankment when my foot kicked a round thing. It was a head.'

Fascinated, I waited in silence as Brennan broke off to scribble something in his notebook. He had filed a story earlier, he explained, and had just remembered omitting a vital detail. Moving to the payphone in the bar he called the copytakers: 'Hello, love, yes it's Syd Brennan B- R- E- N- N- A-N, as staff, love. Could you mark it Add YETI, Y- E- T- I?....' Hard news ?

After he added the vital information he returned to his subject. 'It does no good to dwell on these things, Dick, because you'd never be able to do the job, matey. When I was in Aden, I don't mind telling you, I was frightened. When the Scot's Guards marched into the town you've never seen anything like it. But then you don't need to go abroad to witness horror. In Northern Ireland I saw a boy shot dead from a ricochet bullet.......'

Brennan, a pale–faced, tall figure with black hair, who always dressed in black, was dubbed 'the undertaker' by news editor, Phil Mellor, who sent him to cover comedian Arthur Askey's funeral. Askey had died after having a leg amputated and Brennan was warned not to 'put in a bid for the single slipper' and 'Don't ask if there are two coffins.'

My lack of formal training was laid bare at the Evening-Post Echo. While trying to harden up a rather boring prang between two cars I went into graphic detail spelling out the manoeuvres of each car, the dents, the shattered windscreen, the fear and who hit who. This understandably incurred the wrath of one Graham Butterworth on the newsdesk who gave me a humiliating and noisy dressing down because I had not used the statutory and legally safe term 'collision' which keeps such news stories neutral. It had been the one word I had deliberately tried to avoid using as it seemed so dull!

But at least I was acquiring a killer instinct. From an innocuous press release distributed by a local Scout group I got a page lead with the headline: 'Youngsters frightened by Scout "baptisms".' The Scout leader I had chatted to over the phone clearly didn't realise his claim, that boys had always been nervous of having their bottoms buffed with boot polish, was going to be published.

In the next Scout 'press release' was an apology from the Scout leader:

'Some of you may have read a dubious and would-be sensational report in one of the local papers last month, purporting to be a report of our District Gathering at Phasels Wood. That report was the result of a telephone call to me at my place of work and a persistant series of questions at a time when I was thinking more about my business problems than of the implications of the questions. That is no excuse for me, only an explanation of how it came about. I apologise most sincerely to all members of this District for any harm that may have come to our reputation as a result of my carelessness. It will not happen again.' I had drawn my first blood.

I had by now increased my regular shifts in Fleet Street from the Daily Mirror to include The Sun, the Daily Mail, the Evening News, The People, the Sunday Mirror and the Daily Star. As a result I left the Evening-Post Echo and went 'full time casual' as the slot is called.

The circulation of the Daily Star was increased by at least one the day I got my first national by-line as until then my mother had not been a reader. But I did not bathe for long in the glory. Calling up The Sun for my regular allotment of shifts I was told by the newsdesk secretary: 'You had a by-line in the Star this week didn't you?'

'Yes,' I proudly confirmed.

'Oh well we don't have any more shifts for you'

'Why not?'

The cleric asked me if I should like a word with the news editor, Ken Donlan. I said instead I would come in and see him.

Donlan looked like a small, bald turkey. But his fleshy, hanging face was pointed up by a pair of uncompromising Scottish eyes that were like lazers of interrogation. He didn't ask questions, he didn't need to. Most people in his presence gave unsolicited answers, blabbing away and digging an ever deeper hole while the hugely respected and much feared Donlan sat on in effortless judgement.

I had waltzed in expecting to use my breezy, doorstep charm on the old reptile.

'So you don't like sharing your shifters out?' I started. He stared at me. 'Er, presumably because you're worried any stories I hear about at the Sun might find themselves in the Star?' He nodded, still staring. 'But then I would never do that. It would make no sense would it? I mean the Star would then think I was doing the same to them if I give them a Sun story wouldn't they?'

'If you decide you want to work for the Sun then you'd better concentrate on the Sun!' he said, terminating the interview.

It wasn't much of a guarantee for regular work and I couldn't afford to chuck in all the other shifts on the rival nationals. In any case I liked getting by-lines and on the Daily Star they were prepared to dole them out even to casuals.

One of the Daily Star newsdesk staff, Sylvia Jones, had watched a circus, Roberts Brothers, erect a tent up above her home in the grounds of Alexandra Palace. She had wondered whether a story could be had from the show and I was despatched to make some enquiries. I went along in casual clothes seeking a job as labourer or tent-peg polisher or anything – I was, I told the muscular gipsy-blooded ring-master – a former merchant seaman and out of work.

This fable I concocted as, under cross-examination, I could answer questions plausibly as my grandfather had been a sea-captain and my father a lifelong yachtsman, who had taught me how to sail. The suspicious ring-master took me on as 'elephant boy' and I was given a pair of red overalls to wear.

My job it was to roll out giant podiums on which the elephants performed whatever grotesque athletics they were called upon to do. Moving these monstrous pedestals was no small feat. They were so heavy they could only be shifted by rolling them on their edge. If you lost the balance they would flatten you. The elephant gymnasium had to be set up in double-quick time, too, so as not to spoil the choreography of the show. As soon as the podiums were in place I had to run back to the ring entrance and flatten myself against the tarpaulin walls as the giant mammals came padding out.

In between acts I witnessed a clown roughing up a kangeroo. He was goading it – slapping it around the face, to get it into fighting mood, before chasing it into the ring for a 'boxing match'. I got chatting to one of the main elephant handlers who told me how the beasts were chained up by the ankle for hours on end and how one once grabbed him around the leg with its trunk and threw him over its back in frustration.

A young lad who worked with the plumed ponies told me how they were whipped mercilessly in rehearsals to encourage equine choreography in the ring. Blessed with a half decent memory I jotted it all down later when out of sight. I then got the lad to defect so he could be an identified witness. The office ordered Neil Wallis, who went on to become deputy editor of the News of the World, and who , in 2015, was cleared of any wrong-doing by an Old Bailey jury in the News of the World phone-hacking scandal, but who was, in 1980, a reporter in the Daily Star's Manchester office, to 'turn over' another circus in the north to give us national 'outrage'.

Wallis, a short, half-shaven – before it became fashionable – figure, was known as Wolfman. Some said it was because of his gravelly voice. But I recall his eyes, they had a strange kind of backlit quality to them, more like the wolf's domesticated successor the husky, which gave him an unnerving dispassionate intensity. He certainly gained the reputation for being an utterly ruthless predator, not just for worrying his prey, but also for harrying competitors in the pack: many said the empire he eventually built, teetered on a mound of skulls.

The non-commital, toothless wonders at the RSPCA were too nervous to comment on our combined zoo expose but we ran a spread anyway after putting our findings to the respective circus bosses.

Unfortunately Roberts Brothers said they had nothing to hide and Invited the Daily Star back to it's circus at 'any time of your choosing'. Features Editor Bob Coole felt it right I should return and so I did to face the barely-controlled wrath of my former 'colleagues.' But the story 'sood up' and we published.

Working with animals was not such a bad thing after all: it had secured me a place on the staff of a national newspaper. On the 1st June 1980 I became a Fleet Street reporter at last.

3. BECOMING AN 'OPERATOR'

By night The Daily Express building sat like some immense, black, glass spaceship on Fleet Street, its winking lights helping newsprint lorries dock like shuttles on one side where a hoist lifted off their giant rolls of paper. On the other side, cut and printed piles of tomorrow's newspapers rolled off a chute into a flotilla of distribution vans.

By day the spaceship's Art-Deco doors hissed open to swallow an army of reporters, sub-editors,photographers,designers, and printers.

The black Lubianka, as it was called, named after the notorious Soviet prison, was also the home of the Daily Star, which nestled nervously among its grander sisters: The Daily Express, Sunday Express and Evening Standard. I was immensely excited to be able to walk in off that great street and through the doors of Lord Beaverbrook's imperial pile. I even got my father to come up and, like children, we went in, activated the automatic doors, and stepped out onto the street again. The former glories of the British Empire were symbolised in the front hall by an intricate relief of aluminium foil exotica from tigers and Maharajas to the great steamships and cogged wheels of industry.

But despite its grandiloquence I was quickly to become more interested in the uniformed commissionaires who sat beneath the montage like panjandrums disposing the petty cash drawn as an advance by hacks on receipt of a blue docket signed by the news desk. The fund was supposed to be for reporters racing to the scene of some major news story and who had no time to draw money from their bank: there were no 'holes in the wall' then.

However the cash usually did not travel much further than the watering holes of Fleet Street where it was rapidly dispensed in quenching thirsts including those of the news desk signatories. Not long after joining the staff a little poster stuck up in the front hall was brought to my attention: my first experience of the memorandum, forerunner of the email. Both are a remonstration in literary as opposed to oral form, and all the more chilling for the fact they cannot be shrugged off as an aside: they physically exist. This one was from the London editor, Brian Hitchen:

'TO ALL STAFF
In clear view alongside the commissionaire's desk in the Front Hall is a List of Shame.
It is taped up for all to see. On it are 23 names – 13 of them belonging to members of the Daily Star staff. I am not concerned with the other 10 people on the list – they do not belong to this newspaper.
I do however, find it humiliating to see that the bulk of the names on this stop list are our people and I am determined that it will not happen again.
I want all those arrears clearing off immediately and anyone who transgresses to this extent in the future will be put on a PERMANENT, but much more discreet stop list in this office.
I don't find it amusing to hear clerks sniggering over the fiscal foolishness of highly paid journalists.'

A curving stone stairway led up to the third floor where behind all the grandeur at the end of the corridor was squashed the tin partitions of the Daily Star editorial. We were next to the canteen – the office invariably smelled of stale chips and baked beans. Like the monster hidden away in the attic we sat ontop of the great one, the Daily Express, which was on the floor below. The Express reporters treated us with lofty disdain.
Lord Matthews, dubbed 'Lord Whelks' by Private Eye Magazine, because of his working class origins, was the Trafalgar House building tycoon and proprietor of Express Newspapers. He had, with a no-nonsense Bill of Quantities style, discovered a whole bank of printing machines in Manchester which were lying idle and so in just 12 weeks he founded The Daily Star in order to have them doing something. The newspaper was launched on 2 November 1978, the first new national daily for 75 years, although this was a paper born of pragmatism rather than vision: the concern of a businessman to get full use of his infrastructure.

'I see the new Daily Star as something that will reduce our overheads and use spare production capacity in Manchester,' Lord Matthews candidly announced, and then unsentimentally warned, '.....if I find we are adding overheads instead of cutting them that will be the end of the paper.' The Daily Star was to be promoted as the cheapest of the down-market dailies: one penny below The Sun and two below the Mirror. Daily Express editor, Derek Jameson, the Daily Star's editor-in-chief, was also re-christened by Private Eye, as Sid Yobbo, because of his Cockney glottal stops. He said the paper was to be 'caring' and not 'just about tit and bum'. Kelvin MacKenzie,editor of The Sun, wasn't convinced and shifted the paper's topless girl, Jilly Johnson, from Page Three and spread her instead across the middle pages on the day the Daily Star arrived.

'A Star is Born' the publicity posters revealed to the citizens wandering the length of Great Ancoats Street in Manchester where the new paper was initially printed on those spare machines. The posters were defaced by 'Gay Liberation activists and women's rights movements', according to Jameson, so that they read 'The Star is porn'. He was reassured by a taxi driver: 'You should worry – it will double the circulation.'

According to The Times: 'in those important Manchester newspaper establishments: the Land o' Cakes, the Crown and Kettle and Yates's Wine Lodge, even the dismissive Express journalists joined in the chorus of a song composed for the new paper's launch and sung to the tune of 'Deep in the Heart of Texas': A Star shines bright deep in the heart of Ancoats.' Star staffers, meanwhile, wore badges which read: 'I am a Star gazer'. But behind the chutzpah was deep resentment from the Daily Express hacks, jealous of the fuss being made over their new sister. They formed a posse and took all the chairs away from the Star's editorial so that during the first shift on the new paper,the staff had to work standing up.

The Daily Star's editor, Peter Grimsditch, who, The Times noted respectfully was 'an Oriel College graduate' but then added, for balance, 'and a former deputy editor of Reveille,' said of The Sun's middle page spread of female flesh: 'They are panicking.' The 'Starbird', as she was named, got her own poster, never mind picture, on page seven, the idea being that purchasers might actually read the news carried over the first six pages. Much work had also gone into producing an easily accessible TV guide.

If The Sun could counter tit and bum with more tits and more bums it could do little to beat the Daily Star's late breaking coverage of sports events, as it was then publishing only in the cramped confines of Bouverie Street, just off Fleet Street. As The Times put it :'the vast readership of sports-loving Northerners cannot always be satisfied by the London-printed Sun.'

The first edition of the Daily Star was well timed, because the night it went to press was the night of the European Cup Final – a cup final involving only northern clubs. The paper carried the sports news of all the European Cup ties with Northern Clubs. The front page 'teased' the readers to look inside with the promise of former football star Jimmy Greaves talking about 'My life on the booze' and 'The Nude and the Priest picture special'. There was also a competition to 'double your wages' an offer which another kind of star, The Morning Star, mouthpiece of the UK Communist Party, criticised.There was, the paper complained, '......not a word of support voiced for the Ford strikers who are merely seeking to add a few percentage points to theirs.'

The Morning Star was morally outraged at the Daily Star's assertion that the paper would be 'politically independent', because they claimed Lord Matthews had said, just a day before, 'the paper would be backing anyone who supported capitalism'. They also reported the adulteration of 'A Star is Born' posters by 'feminists angered by the sexism of the new tabloid.'

The Morning Star did not have the same qualms about another 'capitalist-supported' vice: gambling. In the same news column attacking the Daily Star, headlined 'Their Star is porn' they announced that the Morning Star's horse racing correspondent, Cayton, had tipped a 12-1 winner at Southwell race course the day before. 'If you picked up a copy of the Daily Star in error you really missed out,' the paper gloated. The name of the horse ? Double Star.

The Morning Star had accurately recognised that people might confuse their organ with the new tabloid. For years after the Star's launch, reporters were continually asked, when introducing themselves as being a representative of the Daily Star: 'That's not that communist paper is it?'

The Labour Prime Minister, Jim Callaghan, said: 'I am very happy to send good wishes on the birth of the new Daily Star.' Opposition leader Margaret Thatcher said the launch of the paper was a 'triumph for Press freedom'.

Personally I shall always be grateful that Lord Matthews'pragmatism secured me a job, even if he did say he wouldn't have the Daily Star in his house because of its pictures of topless girls. Jameson described the Daily Star as a 'downmarket tabloid newspaper – a working class tabloid paper. It is a cross-breed between the Mirror and Sun.' The Daily Mutant, perhaps.

The working class they were after were the Cs the Ds and the Es. These are categories of consumers defined by marketing anthropologists and based on earnings coming into the household. A C1 is a lower middle class person, a C2 a skilled working class person, a D person is just working class and those with an E number are working at the lowest level of subsistence. The marketing men believe that, unlike the As, upper middle class, or the Bs, middle class, all of the C, D and E households have more than one breadwinner. Dad, mum and all the kids are likely to be holding down not very good jobs to survive, but nevertheless are producing a pooled income which the High Street wants spent on consumer wares. If a newspaper can show the business world it is appealing to the Cs, the Ds and the Es, advertising revenue will flow into that newspaper. Incidentally, most Star hacks, when trying to secure an interview with As or Bs, introduced themselves as being from 'Express Newspapers' for fear of getting the brush off if they announced they were from the down-market C, D and E-targeted, Daily Star.

The news desk was made up of the news editor, Brian Steel a tall, dark Scot with a Velasquez-style beard which appeared an unwitting atavistic choice: a throwback to the blood of a shipwrecked Armada sailor, as he became a serious offshore yachtsman in retirement.

His deputy was Kingsley Squire who would chivvy reporters along by throwing an arm round their shoulders and giving them a friendly shake. He was an avuncular figure of ample girth, grey-bearded, with a thatch of greying hair worn at the same length he had grown it in the Mop-Top sixties. He still wore the cowboy boots, too. They called him 'The Flying Armpit'. He had come from the Daily Express and was hugely enthusiastic about the Daily Star, although he occasionally could not resist a self-deprecatory dig: I heard him answer the telephone more than once and say: 'Hello, Daily Star, the newspaper that scours the parts of the gutter the other papers refuse to stoop to, how may I help you?'

Sylvia Jones, at number three, was unfairly likened by some to 'a female SS officer' – mainly because she wore her hair back in a severe bun, had glasses and appeared an austere figure. She had also been through the windscreen of a car but good Slav-style cheekbones gave her face a finely-boned profile nevertheless.

Loudest noise in the newsroom was Don Mackay. He was a classic case of nature and nuture. What qualities he was born with to help him become a newspaperman: tabloid style writer, provocative asker of questions and bully to the silent witness, were more than compromised by the effort he made himself to become a quintessential Fleet Street man: huge imbiber of alcohol, punch-throwing debater and company car crasher. Mackay, it was fair to say, would do anything to get the story. He could be utterly charming if required, he could persuade in a plausible way, he could even burst into tears if he thought it would secure the family photo album. Mackay was much more than a legend in his own lunchtime he'd created a mythology before his bacon and eggs were cleared away. On behalf of his newspaper he was a liar, con-man, cheat, bad debtor, sycophant. You couldn't help but admire him. He was, to use the vernacular, 'a good operator', and behaved appallingly to prove it. He was touchy about his age as the contrary way he had decided to live had demanded much of body and soul. Prematurely bald, and with false teeth – as likely from untreated gingivitis as affray –

his fingers glistened gold with nicotine. His brawny physique had distended over his trouser belt from a lifetime of 'liquid lunch'. He would have a 'heart starter' at 10.30am usually a pint of 'lagger' in The Old Bell.

The width of a Marlboro tip above 5ft 8in, Mackay let it be known he was from Highland stock. He certainly tossed his company cars around as thought he spent the weekend lobbing elm trunks as javelins. Mackay would borrow twenty quid and give you a petrol receipt as repayment. He once spent a lunchtime explaining what he was going to do with industrial reporter, Tom McGhie's head once he had removed it from his shoulders until it was explained to Mackay that Tom had boxed for his year at public school. Mackay, who on the way to lunch had read Tom his fortune, on the way back from lunch said: 'I'll let it go this time, but if you ever do that again ......'

He managed to row with everybody and was affectionately known as the 'scrapyard alsation'. But while crashing his third company car on his way home to Kettering after a heavy day's defence of democracy, he managed to pick up another sobriquet. There was an advert at the time for the new Ford Sierra it's catch phrase being 'man and machine in perfect harmony' This became Mackay's nickname with the added rider – 'they're both fucking wrecks'. He eventually tired of the daily struggle to get back home to Kettering after a heavy shift, and decided to sleep in the office. For a time he lived under the newsdesk, his jacket on a coat hanger clipped over the Wendy-house style partitions of the newsroom. When the cleaners came round in the morning to empty the ashtrays and litter bins, they would give Mackay a shake and he'd shower off and shave in the Daily Express loos, a floor below, and then join the printers for an early breakfast in the canteen, which appropriately enough, was staffed by local homeless folk.

Mackay's interview technique often involved bellowing down the telephone: 'With the greatest respect' at interviewees who deserved to be 'turned over'. Whether this ever elicited any printable quotes was neither here nor there, it all added to the Mackay myth.

With Mackay on the staff a bench mark for behaviour was set. The rest of us felt that as long as we did not stray beyond the parameters set by Mackay we would be safe from having to earn a living in the real world. Though whether any human being could physically or mentally go beyond such limits was debatable.

Another of the Star's great characters was James Nicholson, Also known as 'Jimmy Nick', the 'Caped Crusader' or the 'Prince of Darkness'. He was an old Fleet Street hand who had worked as a crime reporter on most of the nationals and had been transferred to the Daily Star from the Daily Express. His title as 'chief crime reporter, Daily Star' he revelled in. Nicholson at most times wore a black single-breasted suit, and occasionally a black cape, one of which, to his undying shame, was stolen in a Fleet Street pub. He had created this image for himself years before when it counted for something. Now he still used it, though more in self-parody than with any operational effect. His mystique was thanks to a legendary contacts book. He could not write to save his life but this did not matter because he could always bring in the story and someone else would write it up. Nicholson never bought a drink but remained one of the most popular legends of the Street, quite simply because he was so funny. The first time I met him he was on the phone in the Star office. He had his feet up on the desk and the receiver extended to his ear. 'Hello, is that King's Cross?' he asked, 'This is James Nicholson, chief crime reporter Daily Star, get me a train ready I'm going North!.' He liked to travel by train as it gave him the opportunity to walk along the carriages asking to see people's tickets. In his strange, black single-breasted suit he could pass himself off as a ticket inspector and Nicholson, always on first name terms with the incumbent Metropolitan Police Commissioner, liked to make sure he was not surrounded by law-breakers.

Nicholson used a strange kind of flippant lingo that sounded like a cross between a Raymond Chandler character and Kojak the TV cop.

'Hi baby what's going down?' he might ask. If mocking another reporter he would describe him as a 'Hitman for Mother care' If he called you 'Top gun' it made you nervous – was he taking the piss?

I prefered 'Hi, smallface' which seemed fairly innocuous, to 'big noise' which, again as a compliment, bordered on the ambiguous. Anyone below editor he referred to as 'deputy dog'. If a news editor got on his case he was 'the biggest bozo of them all' if on the other hand Nicholson was praised by the news editor he would refer to him as a 'top gun.'

When Arabistan separatists took over the London Iranian Embassy in the summer of 1980 Daily Star reporters, in common with all the nationals, took shifts 24 hours a day at the Metropolitan Police barrier in Knightsbridge.

The days rolled by and Nicholson became bored. 'It's a bad 'B' movie baby, I'm splitting I've seen this film before' he repeated like a mantra to all and sundry. When the stun grenades exploded announcing the arrival of the SAS down ropes and through the windows of the Embassy, we all ran like hell: away from the story! Nobody knew what the loud bangs were of course, and it seemed prudent to get out of harm's way.

As Nicholson ran past Roger Tavener of the Press Association, Tavener asked him: 'Have you seen this movie before James?' Nicholson was egotistical, nothing rare in the Boulevard of Broken Dreams, to use Kingsley Squire's phrase – a cynical rebuttal of the phrase, Street of Adventure, coined by a Daily Mail hack, Sir Philip Gibbs in 1959, but his love of self-promotion had a hidden agenda. His days as top crime man had been long and illustrious but could not go on forever so when his chance came for role-play on a 'less serious' paper he leapt at the lifebelt the Daily Star threw him, even allowing himself to be filmed in a black flowing cape walking across the roof of the Black Lubianka for TV ads which were used to launch the paper. A black and white photograph of this escapade hung in the editor's office and when it was Brian Hitchen's turn at the helm he would turn the picture to the wall if Nicholson had not 'delivered'.

He claimed to have covered 'every siege since Troy', and to have stood on more doorsteps than any milk bottle.

At one stake-out another former Daily Star reporter, Chris Boffey, who later moved upmarket to The Observer, heard James

stagger back to his room one night full of gratuitous Guinness.
He heard him bounce along the cheap hotel corridor walls, stab
at his door with his key before two loud thumps in different
corners of the room: the sound of Nicholson removing his
characteristic, zip-sided ankle-boots, then finally as his head hit
the pillow an exhausted sigh: 'Ah, the Prince is tired' whistled
through the chipwood wall.

Specialists did not have to work nights or weekends, so
Nicholson, angry at being called in to work one Sunday after a
huge armed robbery, announced as he came into the newsroom:
'This is a cartoon paper except the characters aren't animated,'
he said looking round at those of us ordinary hacks doing our
Sunday duty, but without the gravitas to handle such a big crime
story, 'they're all Plutos, big noses and no knickers,' he added
cryptically.

Self-belief is a virtue in Fleet Street, especially belief in one's own
publicity. I told Nicholson one day I had heard another classic
story about him and his ripostes: 'What did I say?,' he suddenly
asked keenly,'What did I say?'.

Nicholson actively promoted his meaness in the bars of Fleet
Street by making parsimony part of his zany 'character'
meanwhile saving a small fortune in bottled Guinness. He would
reinforce such tight-fisted-ness by telling stories against himself.
One classic was when the body of a small time gangster was
found rolled up in a carpet and dumped on the streets of south
London.

Scotland Yard had phoned Nicholson in the early hours – not to
tip him about the story but to ask him if he knew anything about
a note found in the dead man's pocket which read: 'Daily Mail
£100, Daily Mirror £85 The Sun £50, James Nicholson, Daily Star
£5.' The villain had been making the rounds trying to sell his
story and Nicholson had dismissed him as a 'front hall nutter'.
This is the name given to all those members of the newspaper
reading public who call in on newspaper offices with impossibly
complex, but sometimes half plausible, stories of their council
house rent going up because of some local government
conspiracy; of NHS incompetence in dealing with their chronic

illness; of encounters with aliens. Being sent down to talk to the 'front hall nutter' was a punishment meted out by the newsdesk. Anyway Nicholson's nutter was, having sold his 'story' for a fiver, later caught in bed with another hood's girl and swiftly despatched. After the laughter died down, I said naively 'Bloody good story, though James?'

'Made a page lead in "Carpet News"' came his droll reply.

The Daily Star staff were a mixture of freshly appointed young hopefuls and proven old-hands from the long established Daily Express. The 100 journalists who made the move from the Daily Express were re-seeking their youth, they said.

They wanted fun again, they said. They should have known better: the threat of redundancy had been hanging over the Manchester office staff for years. They were just part of that extra capacity Matthews was fretting about.

During my first weeks on the staff, The Observer ran a story about a facility for mentally ill children, Smiths Hospital, in Henley-on-Thames which was locking children away in 'time out' rooms. I called the main protagonist of the story to discover The Observer had missed half the yarn. The woman, a nurse at the establishment, had a letter from Tory health minister, Dr Gerard Vaughan, who was promising to take action. We ran a much harder piece, confronted the minister and pressured him to make further commitments, which resulted in the hospital being closed down. It seemed a triumph until I subsequently learned there was now nowhere nearby for these desperately ill children to go to and worse that they might end up far from where their families lived in far more draconian establishments. As a result of the story, I received a letter from a distraught mother who had a mentally ill child at another hospital where a lock up was used. She wrote in graphic detail about the 'Victorian' methods used to deal with her daughter, a girl of 16. Posing as relatives photographer Tony Sapiano and I paid the place a visit, along with the mother, and took the tragic child for a walk in the grounds, away from the staff.

The mother had managed to get the restraining tool, a mask, from the nurse on the excuse that it might be required. Sapiano and I wanted a picture of the girl trussed up in the mask – a hideous leather and steel muzzle which was used, the nurses said, to stop the child tearing at the flesh on her arms with her teeth. The mother had bestowed upon the daughter the things she craved – cigarettes and fizzy drink.

Then she pulled out the mask.

I will never forget the child's reaction: 'Sorry, sorry, sorry, sorry' she wailed as the mask was buckled on, 'sorry, sorry, sorry' she continued as Tony used his motor-drive to get the mask pictured as quickly as possible so it could be removed. The girl was now very unsettled, and adopted a devilish kind of unctuousness towards us in the hope she would not incur our 'displeasure' again.

We drove away leaving the child with her cigarettes and sugar water.

The news editor decided that the pictures were too disturbing to use, they were also worried about the legal consequences of Sapiano having taken them on private property and considered that the mask, hideous though it was, might be the only method of restraining the child. It was an area too grey for the tabloid palette upon which only black and white exist. What horrors lay behind the girl's pleas for clemency have haunted me since.

For editors, morality is a pulpit from which to have a go, a stance from which to facilitate judgement. Controversy is what newspapers are all about – find a fire, fan the flames; then name the arsonist. Readers love it. In the days when newspapers sold in the hundreds of thousands it is undoubtedly what the readers wanted. So while a newspaper in full moral flow may be like a pederast priest, blame the choir.

Newspapers are privately owned organs with shareholders. They must make money. If moral outrage colours editorials and sells newspapers it is nothing other than sensible commercial policy.

The first example of this I came across was when Buster Edwards, one of the Great Train Robbers, and the gang member widely believed to be the arm behind the cosh used on train driver Jack Mills, had his south London flat burgled.

'Poetic justice old boy", cried Kingsley Squire, as he read the Press Association wire copy, "are you free Dick?"

"Yes."

"Top hole," said the Flying Armpit hugging me in anticipation of a good Sunday for Monday, Sundays are slow news days.

The only other newspaper eager to join the schadenfreude fest that day was the Daily Mail. Its reporter Gareth Woodgates and I stood outside Edwards' tower block home. As it turned out Edwards was either away or would not come out. His daughter emerged briefly to tell me and Woodgates to "piss off", her words were not reported verbatim in the following day's Mail instead they exclaimed she had used a 'pithy South London phrase' to tell reporters to go away.

'Loony left-wing councils' were another guilty party among the favourite targets for the tabloids. They are safe to villify as they don't sue, and all politicians are fair game. One of my early stories in this vein was about Lambeth Council in South London who banned Tufty the Squirrel, a road safety character for being 'racist and sexist' and also his pal Willie Weasel for talking 'too posh.' The pair, the council said, should be crossing the road in multi-ethnic Brixton not on rural highways.

The headline was simple 'Nuts'.

And the readers response was massive. Here is one typical letter I had from a teacher in Surrey:

'I live in Mitcham, England, not Mitcham, India, China, Japan or anywhere else. I am tired of being made to feel guilty of what I am. I can't see the councils in other countries making anything typically English to suit a minority.I am proud of my Proper English and take great pains to teach Proper English.......it's time all these do-gooders realised immigrants are here by choice therefore they should speak English.'

And an eight-year-old girl from Stockport wrote:

' I do not think Tufty and his friend Willie Weasel talk too posh, I think he talks very nice and I like his colour I think he is very nice and I do not think he is sexist and racist I think he is OK for the boys and girls so please keep him.'

I began to sense the truth of the claim made about newspapers: that they had power without the responsibility. Certainly it never ceased to amaze me how much faith ordinary folk had in their daily paper. Such faith struck me as pathetic and symptomatic of a deep loneliness out there, a deep need to belong. For some folk, their newspaper was their friend, their counsellor, their daily link to the world outside their consciousness. It was scary to think there were people actually relying on the Daily Star, but they did so simply because for many of them it was the one consistent thing in a life of disappointments, a life of let downs. 'Your caring Daily Star' turned up, without fail, through the door every day.

Take this letter which came in from a 57-year-old woman from Walsall:

'Dear Sir or Madam,
On reading your paper about having a balloon inserted in stomach. I would like something done like this as I have tried and tried no end of diets and they have not worked. And I have got to lose weight to have new knee caps in. I have got to lose four and a half stones before I can have it done. I had a hysterectomy and that is why all this weight has gone on, as I have never been overweight before. I would love it done.'

The Daily Star has been described as the 'thinking man's bin liner' and I also once heard somebody say of it that, without it, there would be two million people reading nothing. Certainly some readers appear to have fallen through the educational system and, barely literate, are left to fend for themselves in a complex world. And yet they remain touchingly selfless. When on one story the Daily Star made an appeal to find a kidney donor for an ailing child, a reader rang in and offered her liver. It had to be explained that this particular organ did not have a twin. Another time we ran a series on 'Violent Britain.' A reader wrote in offering her condolences to the victims who had been battered, starting her letter: 'Dear Violet, I hope you don't mind me using your Christian name........'

There are some bounds beyond which a newspaper will not stray and during the hot summer days that actor Peter Sellers spent dying in Middlesex Hospital: 'Desperate Battle to Save Sellers', I was offered, by two hospital maintenance workers, the chance of a photo of the comic lying in intensive care. They said they could get access to Sellers if I were to provide them with an auto-focus camera – for cash.

The newsdesk ruled it out as being in bad taste and I instead joined the scores of other hacks eating, drinking and carousing in the busy West End streets which surrounded the hospital. This was known as a 'choice door step' because you could watch the main entrance from the pub and dart out for a quick quote from any friends and relatives who turned up.

The art of 'door-stepping' is one which the hack learns quickly if he is to be successful. The knack is similar to that used by credit card salesmen on a cold call. Those first few minutes of contact are vital You must be well-dressed in a suit and tie, you must keep talking, chatting constantly using good diction, unwavering delivery and a level, sotto voce, pitch. If they start talking you are half-way there. Listen, ever-ready to sympathise with them even on points against yourself. If possible get talking about anything other than the story itself. Just get over that threshold. Some believe good tactics are to leave your overcoat in the car – you are then psychologically in need of shelter. Others believe it is important to close the gate behind you, suggesting you are already part of the establishment and should also be behind a closed door. In my experience talking and more talking and keep on talking is the best way.

What certainly does not work is the mythical foot-in-the-door, hardman approach. I know, I once tried it.

Mackay had always nurtured the image of a foot-in-the-door, hardman. "S'cuse me, Her Majesty's press' he would bawl jokingly In the pub as he pushed to the bar. A routine in front of his colleagues for fun, but a tactic he liked people to believe he adopted for the job. In fact, Mackay, a good reporter, was much more likely to have notched up what success he had by the wheedling, pleading and persuasion we all used.

One Sunday I had been sent to Leighton Buzzard, Herts to follow up a News of the World story about a serial rapist known, because of the lair he built in his victim's bedrooms, as 'The Fox'. The modus operandi of The Fox was to target upmarket, out-of-town, housing estates which backed onto woods. Accordingly the police decided to set a trap in a house which fitted the target profile with the addition of an attractive housewife. Two uniform police officers were quietly smuggled in to the house to set up home with the well-heeled couple. So far so good, until the News of the World splashed an exclusive alleging that the husband had come home from work to find his wife, Doreen Knightley, in the arms of one of the cops.

I got to the house before the rest of Fleet Street but not before the local news agency. The husband with the door just open was understandably defensive, but hurt pride also nagged at him to offer mitigation for his wife's actions. But it was going to be a long job getting it out of him and certainly one that required the notebook to be left in the pocket and an ability for total recall. Employing polite interest in the estate – what a pleasant area it was, so peaceful, so well landscaped, so well placed for local amenities - I got a sentence or two from the hubby before he finally closed the door. I went back probably half a dozen times throughout the day and got a snippet more each time. At one stage I tried the neighbours, a hack always talks to neighbours when the one resident he is targeting won't talk openly. I rapped on a door and while waiting for an answer became aware of some movement – the Mr. had crept round the side of the house to come up behind me, and the Mrs. had done the same thing on the other side, clearly 'The Fox' was spreading caution if not fear. Finally I filed my story, well pleased with the amount of information I'd managed to glean and turned in for the night at my hotel room. At about 9.30 I got a 'call back': a query from the newsdesk. It was Ian Monk, rather unkindly dubbed 'Cyclops' by Mackay for having one eye focused off centre, a physical defect which has not put off 'top people' such as Cherie Blair's lifestyle guru Carole Caplin who allowed Monk to handle her public persona in his new role as PR man to celebrity. He was complaining that I had failed to get a quote from Mrs. Knightley herself – her husband had assured me she had talked to no newspaper. But The Sun – the first paper seen by the newsdesks, had a one line quote from her.

Now somewhat riled at having had the wool pulled over my eyes – or so I thought – I immediately drove back to the house. By now Mr. Knightley had tired of my calls and had set the lawn sprinkler in such a way that I got a shower of water before I could get to the front door. I decided to try the nasty approach. As Mr. Knightley opened the door I said: "Look here I've been very reasonable with you accepting what you told me about your wife, now the Sun have got this quote", before I could finish he screamed "Fuck off, fuck off, get off my fucking land" at the top of his voice and slammed the door.

Next day it transpired that a local news agency had been on the ground before I arrived and secured the one quote from Mrs. Knightley. They had filed it to every national newspaper accept the Daily Star because the paper owed them money. A hack can rarely expect to be a welcome guest on the doorstep of the newsworthy but my only attempt at 'foot in the door' had failed miserably.

On another occasion photographer Tony Sapiano and I doorstepped the father of an eight-year-old girl killed when a gale blew over a brick wall. The child's mother was hospitalised with broken limbs. The pair had been on their way to a Christmas mass. When I pushed the doorbell a pre-recorded carol started to play: 'Oh come all ye faithful', the door opened, 'joyful and triumphant'. The poor wretch stood there too stunned to switch it off.

"I'm very sorry to trouble you at this time.'

'Oh come ye, oh come ye to Be-eth-le-hem…'

He invited us in and talked away nine to the dozen while in a state of shock then finally flipped when we asked him for a photograph of the dead child.

Of course there are times when the question you need to ask is so outrageous that no amount of grinning, no amount of careful framing can sugar the pill. I have never descended to turning up with bouquets of flowers – believing that there is not a person in the land incapable of seeing through such grotesque fawning.

One of my lowest points on the doorstep involved the family of Danielle Carter, a little girl killed by the IRA bombing of the Baltic Exchange in the City of London in 1992 , which killed two others and injured 90 more.

This family had been 'bought up' by The Sun, that is to say their 'story', such as it was, had been paid for and would appear only in an opposition paper. I was despatched to Danielle's home anyway as the then news editor claimed he had been given a tip that the girl – only 15 – was pregnant. This had come from Hugh Whittow a chunky, professionally charming Welshman from the unlikely town – to produce worldly wisdom - of Haverfordwest. Whittow was ribbed by news editor Phil Mellor who accused him of being vain. 'We used to say that if Whittow lived to be 65 he would have wasted six years looking in the mirror saying: "Who's a pretty boy then?"'. And features editor, Mike Parker, actually christened Whittow as 'They're all wet for me isn't it?' Now that Whittow was on the desk he was able to preserve his charms for sending reporters on missions impossible he himself once faced.

'Just give it a try Dick,' he sing-songed down the phone at me. 'You never know they might spill the beans if you hit them with that.'

So to Basildon I went and surprisingly found Danielle's home unguarded by Sun minders. Danielle's parents had separated and the girl had lived with her mother Kay Meekings, who was too distressed to come to the door. Instead a close family friend answered my call. He, too, was clearly emotionally drained and red-eyed and holding a crumpled can of lager.

I fumbled for words and asked if Danielle had had any boyfriends and if so would they be attending the funeral. The tear-stained fellow stared at me uncomprehendingly.

'Had she dreamed of starting a family?' I wondered, effecting innocence.

The fellow continued to gape.

'Only it's just that we heard she may have been pregnant,' I finally spat out.

What would you do on the morning of the funeral of your friend's 15-year-old daughter just a week after she had been blown apart by an IRA bomb, if a tabloid newspaperman turned up and asked if she had been having illegal sex?

That's what my interviewee did too. Fortunately it was a council house in good repair and the door stayed on it's hinges.

Trouble was I still had a story to stand up. I tried an aunt. She didn't think it likely and so I made my way to St Martin's Church in Basildon where the funeral service was to be held. The clergyman, Canon Lionel Webber, was an understanding man, he showed me the Order of Service – meaningfully it included some pop songs which were among Danielle's favourites. Then I quietly put it to him that her death may have hidden a double tragedy. He said he knew the police pathologist and would make discreet enquiries. By the time he returned with his answer all the national press and TV were lined up outside the church.

He came up to me as I jostled in the line of hacks and photographers and whispered in my ear: 'There was no sign of a foetus.' The mark of becoming a successful 'operator' is when you have gone beyond the capability to self loath.

But whether the story stands on its own two feet with the flying buttresses supplied by the hack or not, it still costs money. I had failed to stand up what was probably a mischevious 'spoiler'. Whittow was not happy that the Sun had the story and we didn't as his memo to me for that job underlines:

'I can only put these expenses down to severe sunstroke. We are looking at half a bottle of wine less than £200. Your expenses for East Anglia are almost as much as it costs to cover the rest of England.'

As I mentioned earlier, Sundays are quiet news days and the most worrisome for newsdesk staff trying to fill the day's schedule. It was on a Sunday that I covered my only coup d' etat, the category of story I'd missed while working for the Ealing Gazette. The newsdesk were excited because this particular uprising involved spear throwing. It was in Espiritu Santu and the line was not good.

'Hello? Can you hear me? Is that the British Consulate? Hello ? Yes it's the Daily Star here. THE DAILY STAR in London. Good. I understand there's been some trouble on your island...TROUBLE.'

Fellow hack Joe Clancy had got in before me and was engaged on the juiciest follow up from the Sunday papers – 'The Human Jig-Saw:

Police hunt for chopped up torso parts.' Clancy's inquiries centred on South London.I was lumbered with the South Pacific. 'Is there any trouble? You know, WAR? Is there a CIVIL WAR going on? Hello?'

'OK leave that,' said the duty news editor, 'have a look at this instead – a horse that's got hooves so small it has to wear Wellington boots.'

The line to Perivale, West London was much clearer, I didn't have to shout and Sunday would produce for Monday after all. Talk about newspapers 'making it up' is exaggerated. That they have done so it is true. But such cases are rare and usually to do with self-indulgent one-upmanship, of one tabloid trying to better another in an esoteric Fleet Street game of cheat and counter-cheat. Day-to-day news gathering of the more prosaic things never need 'making up'. Some journalists are lazy and will invent quotes to back up a story, which are actually quicker to get for real, by either phoning people or simply stopping folks in the street for a quick reaction. That way you get to use a real name too. If the man in the street is a dullard, simply swamp him with your own personality until his bland outlook on things becomes opinionated, colourful, and preferably bigoted, then get this fascinating fellow's name and address. Authentic sentiment – even by proxy - always puts the lie to sham dialogue.

Sub-editors, the journalists who read, check and make the copy fit into the news pages are also guilty of hardening up the story with make-believe. At arm's length from the realities of gathering the story itself, sitting in front of a piece of text rather than the person it represents, it is tempting to tweak it into a better preconception. This is especially so if the reporter who wrote the article can't be raised because he's busy 'contacting' in the pub.

There was a period when adjusting quotes caused concern at the Daily Star and the following memorandum was sent to all sub-editors from John Penman, Sports Editor of the time:

'This is a memo that should not have been required to be written. Unfortunately events of the last couple of weeks necessitate it. Quotes must NOT be invented. There is no excuse for changing quotes or for making them up. This is a capital offence.'

The problem of inaccuracies still plagued the Daily Star four years later when news editor Graham Jones sent the following memo to all reporters:

'The Editor is concerned about the number of solicitors' letters we are receiving. Although many of these are merely belly-aching some are clearly with foundation. Could you make sure you check everything that could conceivably lead to legal problems. It is not enough simply to rely on cuttings because a lot of these are incorrect. When they are repeated the inaccuracies become fact – until we get a writ. So less reliance on cuttings and more questions asked of the subject.'

Newsdesks are under pressure from editors and don't want to know how reporters get quotes or stories they just want them got.
When Prince Edward dropped out of becoming a Royal Marine Commando at Lympstone in Devon, there was a news blanket thrown over the whole camp and anyone to do with it. No one arriving or leaving from Lympstone would say ANYTHING to us gathered hacks outside.
When I phoned the desk to tell them this , David Mertens who was then news editor said: 'For God's sake, Dick it's only a fucking newspaper story. Find someone, anyone, anything who will say something!' The inference was clear: make it up.
Though popular, Mertens, with his public-school education, Country Life-subscribing wife and well-bred sense of fair play, was the last gentleman standing among the sordid Star rogues. He was like Lord Snooty without the pals. It was Mertens with his plummy voice, ever-ready smile and a continuous cackle which he used whether registering amusement or condemnation, I spoke to from Gatwick Airport when Elton John,

returning to the UK for his 40th birthday party, said only these words: "Get these fucking animals out of the way" to his minders when confronted with H.M. Press. I know because I was right behind him when he said it. The showbiz scribes then sat down in a terminal bar and started writing their articles. Quotes such as: 'I'm not too old to rock' and 'Life begins at 40' flowed out of their pens.

I offered Mertens a report with what the singer actually said and the one with the quotes attributed to him by my showbiz colleagues. The latter was used. John did not complain because what he 'said' was innocuous.

What is truly false in a newspaper is its sense of outrage. It must be outraged at everything, day in and day out, whether the matter is scandalous or not. It wants those C's, D's and E's engaged in a 'good talker': an issue which will be discussed in the pub or wine bar. It is hard work having an opinion about everything, if not downright unnatural. The only way a newspaper's columnists or editorial can be so opinionated on a daily basis is to see things in black and white. I indeed if it were not for the newspaper's prejudice as a guide it would be an intolerable burden for the hacks whose job it is to write 'issue' essays, but fortunately for them, today's burka-wearing Muslims are yesterday's multi-partnered, Giro-collecting mothers and history's homosexuals.

On quiet news days the Daily Star reporters not actually engaged in 'news –gathering' gathered instead across the street in the Old Bell Inn, constructed in 1670 by Sir Christopher Wren to house the workers who were re-building St Bride's Church next door. The original had been destroyed in the Great Fire of London. The Old Bell now accommodated those of us constructing a very different and secular beast: a tabloid newspaper, a task once described as the construction of a Gothic castle on the head of a pin. It was common to be told: 'Take an early break' by the newsdesk and I began to drink at lunchtimes – something I had previously reserved for eventide. Quite frequently it would start with lager in the Old Bell Inn, then shift to gin and tonics in the Snooker Club, The Tipperary, The Printer's Pie – known as the Peanut Parlour because of its free monkey nuts - where a double whisky was known as a 'trumpet', a triple a 'euphonium' and anything more a 'full orchestra', or The Punch. Drinking became part of the culture. Everyone did it. This was where the great - and genuine camaraderie for which Fleet Street became legendary – arose. The upstarts from the Daily Star would move in a body to drink with the Daily Mail hacks in their upstairs bar at The Harrow, which was virtually a private club. Any member of the public who wandered innocently in would have a job getting served: he would be taking up valuable square meterage, a thirsty hack would drink and buy rounds for other thirsty hacks at a rate far greater than any half-pint tourist.

The Daily Mail was and is the purveyor of the most professionally-honed pre-conceptions in the UK, consequently its staff were and are the most vicious gossips of all and if one tired of them there were our Daily Express colleagues in The Poppinjay. The Sun gang used the Cheshire Cheese and up Fetter Lane, the Daily Mirror boys could be found in the White Hart, always referred to as the 'Stab' which was short for the 'Stab in the back', and the location for the assassination of many a Mirror man's character.

One of the Daily Star's feature writers, Brian Wesley, had come across to the paper from The Sun and still enjoyed meeting his former workmates in the Cheshire Cheese, indeed so often was he in there that he had his 'own' bar stool. When one hot summer's day he found the pub packed with American tourists and was unable even to get to the bar he returned to the office and persuaded a telex machine operator to type out a 'news snap' that American Express had gone into administration. Armed with the early 'news story' ripped from the telex machine he ran into the Cheese and, waving the piece of paper, shouted out the news to a pal across the bar which immediately emptied. The banter in these great Fleet Street pubs was competitive and some of the hardest and most stoic imbibers were to be found in the King & Keys: 'office' of the Daily and Sunday Telegraph.

In The Old Bell, our pub, the landlord – a big, shrewd Irishman – knew the names ofus all and he would be briefed as to our supposed whereabouts for when the newsdesk called the bar telephone – pre-pager and mobile phone days.

During my break from a night shift on one occasion, I fell in with a sharply suited Cockney fellow who was well oiled and dispensing pints to those gathered round him. He was a great raconteur and we were all having a jolly good time when I bought my way out and said I must get back to the night desk. My new friend was disappointed and insisted I stayed on for another drink. I explained to him that I had to get back in time to see the first edition of The Sun, a copy of which we used to get at around 8.30 pm. This gave us time to 'match' any exclusive story they had in time for our last edition.

'I'll stop the fucking Sun,' he said and with no more ado walked round to Bouverie Street and did indeed hold up the paper's run for an hour. He was a News International machine minder 'working' nights, but had in fact been up the West End with his wife for a meal and had not yet changed back into his overalls. When I rang the desk to explain why I had not come back I was hailed a hero and encouraged to stay on and continue the industrial sabotage.

I have often gaily trooped off to drive my office car across England at the orders of the newsdesk after a six hour drinking session – a session also held at their behest. I was not alone. And to ensure this was perfectly normal I paid £90.00 to a specialist to be told I was not an alcoholic,something I knew already, but my wife wanted a second opinion. The specialist's advice was to carry on drinking EVERY day rather than drinking a shedful on the weekend.

Sensible chap and I took his advice. I drank a shedfull on a daily basis. Other, shrewder reporters bragged about their great thirsts 'Christ I was pissed last night,' or 'I feel lunch coming on,' but in fact drank strategically with those who would assist their ambitions, pacing themselves by the glass as they measured their career path. I didn't. I also drank with the wrong people: the drinkers. Like the newspaper I was helping to create I lived for the day, but I monitored my grasp of sobriety by calling up my home number and leaving a message on the answer phone. Next day I would replay it and check for slurring.

I soon developed a super-liver and taking a good drink became second nature and with that second nature came my first serious scrape.

It happened to be my 30th birthday when I found myself on a Townsend Thoresen ferry, the Viking Valiant, enroute from Southampton to Cherbourg. The ferry was packed to the gunnels with 700 frustrated Brits who, with their cars, were trying to commence a holiday on the continent but had been turned back by French fishermen who had blockaded Cherbourg in a typical Gallic dispute and had forced the ferry to return to the U.K. The ferry company, sensing major publicity, invited the whole of Fleet Street to sail back to France, with the frustrated holidaymakers, to 'run the blockade'. Their PR chap a friendly, and unusually wise fellow by the name of Bob Bevan, told us that the ferry would ram the chain the French had allegedly stretched across the mouth of the ferry berth. So, on the way across the English Channel, we were filing scene-setter pieces about Nelson's ancestors "Britannia Rules OK', was the Daily Star headline. It was a long crossing and for the hacks everything was free: a fact quickly grasped by the 'punters', some of whom had already threatened to throw French passengers overboard. I was approached by a father from the home counties who was worried he might not get a refund should his holiday be cancelled. He had a thin voice and the nature of a whingeing rate-payer and jobsworth. He would always be one of life's complainers. A loser by nature he spread his discontent generously among passengers and crew alike. To find he had the nation's press aboard was a heaven sent opportunity to this inveterate man of complaining letters, and reader of guarantee small print. He was potentially perfect tabloid material, too, with his exaggerated sense of moral outrage and so I led the fellow to the purser's office where he was reassured his fare would be returned to him should he not be able to drag his fully warranty'd caravan into Normandy. Then it was back to lunch. By evening time the ferry had approached the blockade but failed to break through. At dinner, after a day spent celebrating my new job, my first 'foreign', it now seemed time to celebrate my birthday.

Another shedful of Muscadet was sunk and I announced to the gathered dining room where passengers, who were paying for their supper, ate alongside hacks groaning with complimentary fare: "You are all pawns on a PR voyage". I had brewed up some perverse idea that the ferry company owed me a good yarn having failed to act like corporate Lord Nelsons. However, perhaps due to my delivery, my attempt at creating cross-Channel mutiny was ignored, even by the unfailingly civilised Bob Bevan who would have been fully justified in having me keel-hauled.

So there was nothing left to do but let the passengers go to bed while we hacks kept a 'watching brief'. Trouble is few journalists go on standby with a good book and a mug of cocoa. For us the bar never closes. By the time we were ready to take a break from the 'watching brief' I had thrown a punch at Evening Standard photographer Mike Moore for reasons I can no longer recall. I missed, fell over and landed on the well-built Keith Dovkants, reporter of the same organ.

Keith flattened me on the floor of his cabin where the ensuing melee caused the neighbouring occupant to complain about the noise. As my eyes rolled into the back of my head I thought I vaguely recognised the whining tone of the passenger concerned. There was something inquisitorial about his appeal.

Next morning as the itinerant ferry rolled about off the Cherbourg Peninsular I was approached again by the irritant passenger. He looked well-fed and rested. I felt hot with booze, tired and with a lurking half-memory of the night's escapade. I wanted to meet familiar faces, smile, say hello and quickly move on. Suddenly a thin voice whined at my side: "Have you got a card?" I handed one over to get rid of the man. I assumed he wanted to thank me for my assistance on the previous day and I asked him to let me know the consequence of his late arrival on holiday for a possible 'follow up'

Big mistake.

"Thanks, because your behaviour last night was dreadful and I wish to make a complaint" he said.

Ungrateful tosser.

"Here let me give you the Freephone number then it won't at least cost you anymore valuable holiday spending money," I offered perversely in hangover-induced, self-destruct mode. Some weeks later while on a job, the photographer I was with checked in with his picture desk and was told: "Tell Dick to return to the office immediately!"

I did, puzzled to be confronted by London editor Paul Hopkins, who handed me a letter. Hopkins was a sound man, he took tabloid papers very seriously.

He was genuinely angry. I was seriously ashamed. The letter was a literal version of the audible whine I'd already heard. It was cc'd to Townsend Thoresen, the ferry company which became P&O.

Hopkins said: 'What have you got to say?' I admitted that I had had 'a few'. Hopkins said: 'We are struggling. We are trying to get the Daily Star known and respected. That's not easy. Your behaviour is going a long way to jeopardise our efforts.'

'Sorry.'

'You'd better draft an apology.'

I immediately rang Bevan and crawled to him. I didn't need to. He knew nothing about it, though he certainly knew about me and the 'pawns' statement. He rang me back.

'He was a pain in the arse,' he said. It turned out my passenger had complained throughout the voyage to Townsend Thoresen about all and sundry. I deserved no quarter from TT, but they, thanks to the zealotry of their serially-complaining customer and the magnanimity and professionalism of Bob Bevan, remained benevolent and gave no support to their customer.

Hugely relieved that TT were not anti-me I was even more relieved when Hopkins came through to the newsroom and gave me a shoulder massage, he too had called them and was bounced to Bevan.

That still left me the apology letter, and I wrote four. 'You still haven't said sorry,' Hopkins said, 'We've either got to say sorry or tell him to fuck off!'

In weasel mode I struggled to compose a non-culpable 'apology'. Thus ended my first experience of post prandial peril.

Words and pictures get horse-traded in Fleet Street for although every journalist jealously guards his contacts and strives for exclusivity, he also knows that he cannot cover every angle on a story which may have several addresses to check out. This means big breaking stories are 'carved up'. One paper will agree to chase the parents, while another harries the police, another will keep pace with events at the scene of the incident, while another will bang on doors in the area. An agency may be put to use trawling through phone books to find relatives.

After the close of play – about mid afternoon - all the reporters meet up and pool their results. Then there is the temptation to take from everyone else but only hand out part of your own findings – especially if you have come across a self-contained exclusive and yet can cover your obligation by handing over innocuous quotes or meaningless details. Hacks are nothing if not ambitious and all have been in this position and abused the arrangement. Sometimes papers with bigger staff and serious commitment to editorial will flood the story with countless reporters to alleviate the necessity for horse-trading, but this can prove counter productive as one reporter working alone will bust his guts to cover every angle – two will each rely on the other to get them off the newsdesk hook. Sometimes The Sun or The Mail will send half a dozen reporters to a scene, then the remaining newspapers will band together to beat them.

With such Co-op style newsgathering, at the back of every reporter's mind as he decides to cherry-pick his handover quotes and guard his exclusive, is that one day he will be in the shit and need help from the opposition. That said, so too, will the pack who feel like punishing the cheat. But hacks are social animals, and frankly unconcerned about yesterday's stories. They are susceptible to the phoney charm of their colleagues even though they know it to be false, they like being flattered and having drinks bought for them.

Above all else is the genuine feeling of 'us and them'. Us being the hacks, them being the various newsdesks.

I can remember getting my first hand-out quote from the late Danny McGrory, who became a senior journalist on The Times, but who was then on the Daily Express.

In 1982 a transvestite villain, David Martin, had escaped police custody and been on the run for weeks. It had become a huge story because the Metropolitan police had shot and almost killed an innocent man they had mistaken for Martin.

Martin had been recognised in a restaurant in Hampstead and police had been tipped off. The Express had also been tipped off and were up in Hampstead an hour before The Star arrived. Martin had run through an underground train tunnel to unsuccessfully evade arrest.

McGrory – without being prompted – could see the look of panic on my face once I realised I would be left with only the Press Bureau version of events. He gave me enough quotes – including what Martin had said upon his arrest – to get me out of the mire. You never forget a move like that, which is why there were more than 500 people at McGrory's funeral.

A hack will do anything not to hear the phrase "Is this off the record?" He will soap, cajole and gently prod an interviewee along, chatting away about anything except the subject he wants to hear about. The idea is to win the interviewee's confidence, hope that something salient will slip out and if it does not, have gathered enough chatter to authenticate an interview before cutting his losses and whacking the subject with the controversy he wants addressed, the big question he wants answered, right at the end. Likewise he will never say to an interviewee 'Don't worry this is off the record' unless there is simply no other way of getting him to talk. If he is then fortunate enough to gamer a response he will later go into denial about the guarantee and say to himself: 'Yes, but it was not THIS part which I said was off the record!' It is shocking how mercenary one can become in print when confronted by an empty page or computer screen, hours after making such a guarantee and with a news-thirsty editor to placate.

Everyone who takes a reporter into his confidence gets burnt in the end. For a reporter it is painful having information if you can't share it. Even domestic gossip about the rise and fall of fortunes within Fleet Street itself is eagerly gathered. Although I noticed that those who were always first with the news on personalities in the industry itself were frequently the last to get anything worth publishing from the world at large.

Likewise I have given mouth-to-mouth on more than one occasion. I have even filed a complete story to an opposition newspaper when their own reporter has been either too drunk to do the same or in one case, in police custody, and unable to contact his newsdesk. The latter incident took place one Autumn when the whole pack was doorstepping Koo Stark, the soft porn actress who had once been a girlfriend of Prince Andrew, and as a consequence had become 'famous', in her own right. The pack descended on her new boyfriend's home off the Kensington High Street in London and though his door had been knocked repeatedly and variously by all the titles represented in the street outside, he was saying nothing. Lunch beckoned and we repaired to a restaurant on Kensington High Street while making regular contact calls to the boyfriend. Unfortunately the man from the Daily Mail went down in the post prandial Hall of Fame and had a blazing row with the rather snotty maitre' d over getting the bill apportioned appropriately between us.

The restauranter acted more like a provincial tea shop proprietor than the owner of a metropolitan eaterie and called the police. Our colleague was arrested and carted off to Kensington nick. I tried to get him out of the lock up by saying I should take him into my care until he sobered up, but the Old Bill were not impressed with my privatised offer of custody. The hack's photographer, an energetic freelance eager to prove himself and get on the staff, was worried: what could he say to the Mail newsdesk? To make matters worse the Stark boyfriend had agreed to say a few words. Not much but enough to write a story around, especially the Daily Mail's particular brand of moral essay. There was nothing for it but to hack out a story in Mailese and file it under the detained hack's name which I did. Normally a check call is made with the newdesk after filing to clear up any misunderstandings. We decided the best approach would be to ignore the newsdesk until they conferred with the picture desk as to the hack's whereabouts. Then the snapper would say he was busy ferreting out some fact or other, hoping he would be released before the desk demanded to speak with him in person.

Alas all newsdesk staff have been 'on the road' themselves and as rodent detectors are past masters. Fortunately for the reporter concerned, the desk man that day was Ian Walker, who I had broken much bread with myself over the years during 'lunch' . He was so excited at being the first to be in a position to break the gossip, he completely forgot about the news story instead telling his reporter:

'You've been Durham'd.'

From the rarified atmosphere of the 'royals' where a tiny scrap of information can become front page news, the hack can find himself at the other end of the social spectrum where the equivalent of an air raid needs to happen before the lower orders make news.

After Leeds Football Club had played away at Derby and the supporters had semi-rioted, smashing up the stadium, Chelsea F.C. were due to play at the Midlands ground the following week and the desk, fully expecting a 'replay' of bother, sent me along. I still had vivid memories of covering the Scots at Wembley and now, once more, I was to cover a football match – off the pitch.

The Saturday football special from St. Pancras was packed with Chelsea fans playing cards, and two journalists – myself and photographer Doug Doig. We were not suited this time, but in jeans and windcheaters, with Douggie's cameras well hidden: there would be no more nerve-racking bus rides for me. That said a hack attempting innocence at the scene he is to observe always feels his intent is showing.

At Derby we were herded between lines of police, all the way to the ground. I tried, to no avail, to get through the police line protesting I was a citizen with reasons other than football to visit the city.

In potentially dangerous situations I have always played it up front. While there was no point in attracting attention on the train journey to the ground, once there and on the terraces I wanted to get close. Not only that but Doig would have to be taking pictures anyway. So I introduced myself to a large group of fans and told them we were doing a feature piece on football and the people who supported the game. It is very unlikely they swallowed my story, but it guaranteed two things – firstly knowing they had the Daily Star actually witnessing their actions they were bound to behave abominably, secondly even though they actually revelled in the fact we were there, their macho code dictated that they pretended otherwise. We could now avoid the wrath they would have brought down on our heads had we been discovered as hacks posing as fans in their midst. It also meant that for a time, before they got fired up, I could talk to them taking notes, getting names, addresses, ages, occupations as well as their philosophy on life and violence. Always a tricky strategy, I have found that, nevertheless, it is a sure fire way of getting sound copy whatever else happens, not to mention a lessening of the chance of getting a good kicking.

I spoke to men in their 30s and 40s, men who ran antiques businesses in London's West End, men who worked as telecommunications engineers and in one case a City money broker. From our Chelsea cage segregating us from the Derby fans' cage, Doig and I watched in astonishment as two female Chelsea supporters who had become separated from their tribe and marooned among the Derby fans, were led back to their own side, along the edge of the pitch, by two police officers. Suddenly what sounded like a million spitting hoses started up as the girls were rained on by the phlegm of all Derby.

Having crossed into the Chelsea sector, the girls opened up their camel-coloured car coats and held them out like wings to show thousands of cheering fellow fans their dripping 'campaign medals'.

That was before the match even started. When it did the players were targetted with thrown coins, bottles and eventually plastic seats torn from their terrace fixings. It was good enough to 'make' and Doug and I had front row seats for 'Terror on the Terraces.' Such lowlife yarns are the daily fare of the tabloid hack, but on occasion he gets to doorstep the great and the good. On the morning of 9 December 1980 I wandered into the newsroom to witness the desk was in a state of great flux. 'Don't take your coat off – get to Paul McCartney's house' said the

'Flying Armpit' snatching at two telephones, 'It's down near Rye, there's a monkey on his way.'

I dimly remembered some half-baked story in one of the Sundays about an alleged McCartney love child but I didn't think the armpit could be at such an altitude over that. On the way out I stuck my head round the pale yellow partition where the copy boys sat and asked them what was happening.

'Call yourself a reporter? Lennon's been shot dead!'

Getting to Rye was difficult. East Sussex is not famous for its accessibility, doubtless one of the reasons McCartney and his family had chosen to live there. He had made an excellent choice as I discovered. I was still awaiting delivery of my new office car and getting to the doorstep required two changes of train and took me three hours before I arrived in a small village still a good many miles from McCartney's pile.

There were no taxis. I found a local garage where two ancient mechanics were peering beneath a Morris Minor which was up on a ramp.

I offered them hard cash to get me to McCartney's door. They first had a polite discussion about whose turn for lunch it was and the one not dining got the job. The Morris was gently and hydraulically lowered to the ground and away we went. My elderly driver was clearly at one with the pace of his rural district. I think he probably taught the Highway Code as well. We trundled along as he offered the normal observations about having a celebrity as a 'neighbour.' 'Keeps himself to himself. Never see anything of him.'

Suddenly, rounding yet another wooded bend, stood a cock pheasant all colourful plumage in the middle of the road. My sleepy driver immediately dropped a gear, put his foot on the accelerator and drove straight at the creature which began that curious, ungainly, prehistoric, running stride peculiar to pheasants, into the verge. The Morris followed and clipped the beast which then scampered, one wing hanging, into a ploughed field. My driver gave chase – fortunately not in the car – which he left, engine running at my disposal. Half way across the field my driver collared his quarry, lifted it bodily by the legs and proceeded to chop at it's neck furiously with karate blows.

Only when the bird was dead did my driver return to his half-sedated state. His reaction had been instilled from some rural, atavistic, survival impulse: years of country breeding. Now he seemed horrified at the fact he had killed the bird while trespassing – as it turned out on McCartney's land. Unabashed by the six inch turn-ups of mud he now sported on his dungarees, he turned to me.

'Here you'd better 'ad this,' he said thrusting the creature into my arms. He had done what a countryman has to do. He had acted instinctively. Now he wanted no further part of his action. The bird, of course, had been literally game on the road. The fact my driver had been obliged to apply the coup-de-grace on private property had unnerved him.

So when McCartney turned up at his arcadian doorstep, I stepped out with one of his pheasants, still warm, turning my briefcase into a bulging body-bag.

McCartney spoke briefly to me predictably about Lennon as a Messiah of peace but even on the day of his old colleague's murder McCartney was more interested in telling about the rip-off management The Beatles had suffered from. Nevertheless I was pleased we'd got an interview – everyone else had pulled out so we had it to ourselves.

McCartney, oddly, had made me promise I would give the 'story' to the Press Association before agreeing to talk. I said I knew where the PA man was staying and would see him later – without actually committing myself to the great man's oddly naïve request.

In those days – because the Star had been founded in Manchester - that good city was head office and we filed our copy there. I did so and checked in with a delightful old hand, Brian Sales who had been brought across from the Express where he had enjoyed a sinecure for many years as Motoring Correspondent.

Trying to sound as cool as possible I said: 'Hello Brian. I've just spoken exclusively to Paul McCartney you should have it soon.'

'Oh, is this the Beatles story?' he asked me.

'Er, yes'

'Oh Dick we've had so much stuff on that today I don't suppose there's any space left for it.'

People often ask reporters who have covered a major story 'What's the real story?' as though there is always some conspiracy the journalist is party to. They miss the point for ANYTHING a journalist gets to hear about which he can 'stand up', i.e. dress with facts and which is not libellous, goes in the paper. They rarely have more to tell.

Likewise with celebrities, yes you do meet them – occasionally. Unless you are a showbiz specialist, and even they are only hacks given the fulltime job of chasing stars rather than have their time interspersed with chasing fire engines or hassling police stations. Such meetings are, more often than not, fleeting. A five minute snatched interview with McCartney, while welcome on the day his musical partner is murdered, hardly constitutes an in-depth conversation. Yet that is all a tabloid man has to experience to be saddled as an 'expert'.

Thus I became the 'McCartney expert' and as such met him again over the next 18 years twice for a total of about 10 minutes. For a news editor however, that is a millennium – one fresh picture alone is a page lead or even a front page splash depending on the context.

Prince Andrew's girlfriend Koo Stark once said one word to me, after a two-day doorstep – 'No,' for 1.5 million newspapers to carry a 300 word story on how she was going to ignore the Duke of York that coming weekend.

To some extent dealing with celebrities is the easiest and quickest way of producing a newspaper story. They need no introduction for a start – no need for any 'standfirsts' here. The name is instantly recognisable and therefore a seller. Just one iota of difference in the circumstances is excuse enough to run a story.

Dealing with esoteric subjects is altogether a different ball game but much more satisfying when it works. Which it doesn't always. I spent weeks amassing 'evidence' against a doctor who was flogging blood plasma to private, wealthy clients – mostly Saudi oil sheiks.

One of the doctor's lab technicians promised to talk to me on the understanding I helped him to get a resident's visa for Australia, a country to which he hoped to emigrate. I contacted the press office of the Australian Embassy and met a friendly PR for drinks in the Strand. The technician, an Indian by birth, had already made the application but such matters could take months, even years. I explained what I was trying to uncover to the incredibly thirsty PR man and gave him the subject's name. Much to the technician's surprise and mine he got his visa within days and I got a lengthy interview. The trouble was that the wiley doctor was selling the whole of his service to his patient, the fact that the service included blood donated to the NHS bank was neither here nor there – one thing I had overlooked at the very start was that blood is given free to anyone who wants it. The doctor was acting unethically but not illegally. We killed the story – without the headline already dreamed up: 'Blood For Sale' as the desk lost interest.

4. THE EDITOR'S NEW CLOTHES

With his brutal domed head, jutting jaw and intelligent eyes the Daily Star's most respected Editor, Brian Hitchen, looked like Mussolini in peacetime. His burly chest stretched red braces under an expensive navy blue suit and a subtle, mocking smile always played along his wide mouth.
The Daily Star was his personal train set but he was going to do more with it than make it run on time. Power alone made him tick and being compared to the Fascist dictator suited the way he saw himself. But though he might have looked like Il Duce, there the comparison stopped. For Hitchen was further to the right. There were also no Latin histrionics about Brian Hitchen. He never ranted or raved, he didn't need to. He had that rare thing: natural presence, and natural authority. When he was in the news room you knew it, whether you could see or hear him or

not. Everyone in Ludgate House knew when Hitchen entered the building. By the mysterious telepathy of survival, legs would swing off desks, ties would be re-knotted, brows would be wrinkled over computer monitors. Everyone knew when he had left: hacks would head for the bar, office flirting would re-commence, holiday flights would be booked.

As editor, Hitchen was respected because he was an 'operator', a real newspaperman unlike so many others who were production men. Here was a man who could get people –from cabinet ministers to binmen - eating out of his hand. And he never missed an opportunity to manipulate. When he organised a birthday party for Lloyd Turner – then Editor himself – he called upon favours from the custodians of HMS Belfast - we had run glowing stories about the Royal Navy- to use the ship as a venue and the Salvation Army - we had covered their good works in a campaign - to provide a brass band.

His climb to the top started in the classic way – as a copy boy for the Kemsley Newspaper Group in Manchester. He carried bits of paper between the editorials of the Empire News, Graphic, Evening Chronicle, and the Sunday Times. One of his duties included washing the false teeth of the news editor of the Daily Despatch which fell out when he was drunk.

'Nobody notices a messenger boy – you walk in and out of places seeing and hearing and your knowledge is growing all the time,' he said.

At the age of 15 Hitchen started as a reporter on the Bury Times and one of his first jobs was collecting bottles of beer in a wooden Remington typewriter case for the news editor. He soon moved to the Manchester Evening News where he was sent to Cyprus with the Lancashire Fusiliers. Hitchen was shot through the left kneecap by an EOKA terrorist. But it did not deter him living in a tent on £3 a week.

All the national newspaper correspondents, meanwhile were far from the front line living in hotel luxury. As a saving on editorial spending it was a lesson Hitchen would recall when his turn came to allocate the budget. His proximity to the action produced vivid despatches which he filed from a cable office while soldiers armed with sten guns stood guard. They also provided an armed bodyguard while he went swimming at Kyrenia and so Hitchen's life-long respect for the Army was born. His stories were soon noticed not just in Manchester, but nationally. He was offered a job on the Daily Mirror and arrived in Fleet Street aged 20 – then the youngest staffer ever to make the Street. Hitchen's natural charm and ability to listen – with his ear wire-triggered for the seed of a story – made him a network of contacts and a cuttings book full of page one bylines. Of those early stories, a most sensational scoop, was headlined JOSHUA MACMILLAN WAS A JUNKIE. This was Prime Minister Harold Macmillan's grandson, Hitchen had got a tip from a drugs squad officer that Macmillan had died from an overdose.But the establishment closed ranks and everybody denied it – including the police press office. At the inquest nothing came out during the morning hearing to substantiate the Daily Mirror story. 'People were moving away from me, in the courtroom,' Hitchen said, 'I thought they were going to hang me out to dry. "Good bye you've had it". Then in the afternoon the family doctor told the court Macmillan was a heroin addict. I don't remember the rest of the evidence. They could take in P.A. as far as I was concerned.'

Hitchen first became aware of how stories could shift from the sublime to the ridiculous when he was covering the launch of a new invention, double-glazing - at Heathrow Airport, where it was used to cut out the noise of jet engine scream for waiting passengers. He was ordered to drop the press launch and instead cover the Indo-Pakistan War which had just broken out because he was nearest to the airport! The newsdesk told him to get the next flight going in the general direction which was to Kabul, in Afghanistan because 'Pakistan is only about half an inch away on the map'. He had £8 on him and was promised 'we'll get you some money once you're there.'

Hitchen's 'fieldcraft' - learnt the hard way in Cyprus – credited him with a 'good war' in Pakistan and the Daily Mirror told him they were going to post him to Paris.

'I don't speak any French,' he said.

'So what?,' said executive Roly Watkins.

A native tongue was not required for his first major assignment: interviewing a British climber of the north face of the Eiger in Switzerland. Always a smart dresser, Hitchen turned up at the base of the Eiger in his Church's shoes and Aquascutum raincoat 'looking like the man from the Pru'.

His newspaper had sent late on the story. So Hitchen headed straight for the funicular railway while the opposition waited in the restaurant of the hotel where a reception had been organised for the climbers. Hitchen got alongside the climber as he alighted from the mountain and escorted him all the way to his room. He then ran him a bath laid in some beer and interviewed him in the tub, joining his colleagues in the hotel restaurant after he had filed his exclusive.

Hitchen spent nine months in Paris before being sent to New York on a two-year posting. He was there over seven years – North Dakota and Hawaii being the only two states he did not visit in that time. While there his stories caught the eye of one Generoso Pope, proprietor of the National Enquirer, the down market grocery store weekly and hugely successful tabloid. But before his time with the Enquirer Hitchen accepted a job as news editor on the Daily Express and was brought back to Fleet Street. Here he masterminded one of Fleet Street's greatest stories of all time – the unearthing of Great Train Robber Ronnie Biggs in Brazil. But he was unhappy when ex-Economist editor Alastair Burnett left the Express as editor and went into television leaving instead Roy Wright at the helm. Hitchen felt Wright pulled too many good stories and 'played safe' and on the day they argued about the exclusion of a salacious story on Liberal leader Jeremy Thorpe which one of Hitchen's hacks had brought in, a call came through from Generoso Pope.

'How's your Wellington Boots, Brian?'

'What do you mean?'

'Well it's always raining over there. When are you going to come over here?' Hitchen prevaricated.

'They tell me you've got balls?'

'Well I did have in the shower this morning Mr Pope'

'I want you to be photo editor.'

A picture editor's slot in the US was a huge job.

'I don't know anything about photos'

'Well you know what a good picture is?'

''Yes'

'And you can control those fucking photographers?'

'Yes'

'Take it, take it'

'OK'

'You ain't asked about the salary?'

'What's the salary?'

'Fifty five thousand US'

That was then a £12,000 annual increase on Hitchen's Express pay. Hitchen prepared his wife Nelli for a return to the States and then there was a change of plan. Pope called up again, raised Hitchen's pay by 20,000 US dollars and told him to set up the London bureau of the National Enquirer.

Hitchen did so and was soon poached by entrepreneur Sir Jimmy Goldsmith to be news director of the short-lived Now magazine which was a 'journalistic success and a marketing failure' because the hubristic marketing team kept telling Goldsmith the circulation would be 250,000 and so advertising revenue was pitched at that. When the magazine only sold 100,000 -actually a phenomenal success for a news magazine in the UK- they had to keep giving money back to advertisers. So the magazine failed and Hitchen went back to the Enquirer, this time in the US, in time to fire most of the photographers before the paper moved lock,stock and barrel 'like a circus' on trains from Englewood, New Jersey to Lantana, Florida.

Generoso Pope Junior was the man who had the greatest impact on the way Hitchen ran the Daily Star. Founder of the world's most outrageous tabloid newspaper The National Enquirer, Pope was the son of a multimillionaire businessman who left a £3 million fortune in 1950 when he died, to Pope's brothers and sisters. Pope himself had to get a proper job and did so with the CIA, working in intelligence, dreaming up colourful propaganda stories to undermine communists.

It was great training for creating a sensational newspaper which he reportedly did with a loan from Mafia boss Frank Costello. By the time Pope had finished with the moribund New York

Enquirer it was read by more people across America than any other weekly. It was filled with horrific car crash stories, Hollywood glamour, UFO sightings and the paranormal, and medical breakthroughs. From his HQ in Lantana, Florida, Pope, a heavy smoker, sent reporters all over the world investigating cancer cures while he puffed on regardless. He also had somebody flying around the world – on a permanent mission – trying to find Shangri-La.

'The reporter would ring in from Bora Bora – or somewhere like it – and say "I've found it: the people are all smiling, the sun's always out, they want for nothing. Pope would listen and answer "Nah that ain't Shangri-La."' Bizarre though all this appeared to the hard-nosed man from the Daily Express he was impressed with Pope's standards of accuracy.

'If there was one thing I learned at the Enquirer it was never to settle for a second-hand anecdote or a cutting – all the journalists I'd worked with up until then would not have lasted five minutes on the Enquirer - all that stuff about making it up was not true – you made the story FIT, yes because you had to, but you never made it up.' Certainly Pope had recruited many journalists from the UK because Fleet Street was world famous for producing can-do, self-starters who could run rings round the US-produced reporters of 'record'. Any fool could write up the record, Pope wanted newsmen to MAKE the record. Working on the Enquirer was like being in the Foreign Legion: 'Everybody was running away from something. Same as me. I had a mid-life crisis. I was fed up with Britain, fed up generally.' When in 1977 Elvis Presley died, virtually all staff on The National Enquirer were despatched to Memphis, Tennessee to interview paramedics, policemen, doctors, pharmacists, neighbours, relatives and friends.

'Pope was driving me nuts. He thought on a story like that he'd got to have 18,000 people on it. I'd always figured blanket coverage was crap. Only one guy can really write it in the end and I don't believe in re-write editors. Pope kept saying "How many choppers you got up?"

I told him: "What do you want choppers for ? Choppers can't see into Gracelands." He didn't like that. You couldn't argue much with Pope. So he sent this huge team up there.'

Among the army of journalists was Jimmy Sutherland, a gangling lowland Scot. Though he was 'low on the totem pole' of Enquirer snappers he was, thanks to Hitchen, later to become assistant editor news and pictures for the Daily Star. Sutherland checked in with Hitchen and told him he could not get a camera into Presley's Gracelands home as security men were checking everyone queuing up to see the King lying in his coffin and there was a metal detector the 'mourners' had to go through. All he heard on the end of the phone was an unimpressed Photo Editor say: 'I want pictures of him dead. There's gotta be a weak link in this. Try the guards, try money, try SOMETHING.'

Sutherland, in fear of losing his job, eventually found a security man who was prepared to smuggle in a camera and try for a snap of the bloated pop star. He supplied him with a plastic Minox camera, Hitchen had found in the company safe. Sutherland taped over the controls so that the focus was set for between four to five feet. The guard had to spend the night shift inside Gracelands and re-appeared the next day a nervous wreck. Sutherland was ordered to send the guard, his uncle – who was chaperoning him – and the camera on flight back to Florida. Pope was a man of simple tastes: he wore $2 shirts and drove a 'working man's car' but when it came to scoops for his newspaper no expense was spared. Hitchen knew this and had no compunction about hiring a Lear jet from Palm Beach Airport and keeping it on standby in Memphis ready for the flight back to the Sunshine State. The Lantana police chief lived in Pope's wallet and was also one of Hitchen's contacts and he met the plane - airside - in a squad car and took the two, plus the valuable film back to the office. In the dark room Hitchen had ordered everybody out except the trusted manager. A security guard with a gun drawn stood in the doorway. The office was locked on the inside.

'I stood there under the red light while the film was developed. There were five pictures on it. The first one was of the guy himself all out of focus: this great swimming face – he'd got the camera the wrong way round.'

Hitchen's heart was pounding: 'That's it I'm fired,' he thought. 'The next one was of the chandelier above the coffin........the next two were pin sharp looking down onto the face of Elvis in the casket and the last one was of his face in profile peeping over the casket.' The guard and his uncle had been locked in a room with booze and TV.

Now the time had come to negotiate a price for the film, Hitchen's hostages, to the Enqurier's fortune, were released. 'Look, two pictures are no good but I'll give you eighteen thousand, two hundred and fifty dollars and I'll never tell anybody who did it,' Hitchen bluffed, simply pulling a figure out of thin air, but one which sounded as though it had been authentically calculated from Enquirer rates. It was a bargain and the deal was struck.

'It just about blew Pope's mind......suddenly he didn't need an army and all the helicopters flying about,' said Hitchen.

No newspaper or magazine in history had ever doubled its circulation on the strength of one story. The National Enquirer was about to do so. The front page and the spread were devoted to The King in his coffin and the Enquirer made American newspaper history by becoming the largest-ever selling issue at almost seven million copies. In Kentucky a supermarket was robbed – not for its cash, the till was left untouched – but for the pile of National Enquirers by the checkout.

The paper which officially sold for ten cents, was now changing hands at 100 dollars a time. The following week Hitchen suggested to Pope that they run the pictures again as a 'service' to readers who did not get a copy.

'Couldn't do that,' said Pope.

'Why not?'

'That'd be commercialism.'

Not long after the greatest scoop in the paper's history two journalists were caught in an FBI 'sting' operation trying to sell the negatives of Presley to a third party. They were taken, in irons, from the building, although Pope never pressed charges.

To his mind never working again for the National Enquirer was punishment enough for any journalist.

Pope could be more eccentric when it came to sacking staff: one greenhorn was fired on the spot for asking 'what the hell' the strange man dressed in slacks, sandals and short-sleeved shirt was doing standing on a desk adjusting the air-conditioning. What no-one had told the tyro was that only Pope was allowed to touch the thermostat. When a female journo's scent irritated the Pope nostrils and she refused to stop using the offending perfume, she, too was summarily fired.

The Presley scoop was the making of Sutherland and as he flicked his tie over his face, his party piece in the bars of Fleet Street, he would candidly claim: 'My most famous picture was a collect.' Hitchen took a couple of days off to wind down from the story and went on a pic-nic with another former Express colleague, Stuart Dickson. They drove into the Everglades and parked up near a swamp and unpacked a hamper and chilled wine.

'Suddenly there was this clinking sound and all these niggers appeared wearing orange uniforms and started to dig a ditch. Dickson said:"My God isn't this wonderful" I remember we gave the guards some wine,' said Hitchen.

Hitchen was never to forget the glory days in Florida and he tried to apply the Generoso Pope school of fear tactics ie get the picture or the story or get fired, when he got back to Fleet Street. The trouble was Britain is not a place where you can just hire and fire people at will. His capricious nature – he wanted to fire one photographer, Tim Cornall, because he had protruding teeth, and a reporter Chris Boffey for being 'gormless', after he told Hitchen that ''there was no story' in an assignment to build a case against a landlord who was making a Hitchen friend's life a misery. I was sent on the same mission, without knowing Boffey had refused, and stood the 'story' up. He also wanted to sack Bob Aylott, who he dubbed 'blind'. This was after an assignment at Mr Kipling's cake factory in Eastleigh, Hants at which Aylott took photos of the workforce who were baking cakes for Britain's brave boys fighting in the first Gulf War, which the paper were to fly out to the Middle East. Hitchen declared the women were 'too ugly' to appear in the Daily Star.

Hitchen also fumed at stories that were detrimental to his beloved South Africa. A South Africa which had Nelson Mandela banged up and apartheid as the policy of multi-ethnicity. A South Africa where he holidayed and where he became an admirer of the Zulus. Thus when feature writer Rob Gibson wrote a piece about how black men were hanged at the end of sisal rope but that white silk rope was used to execute white men, a piece which slipped through and was published in the Daily Star, he wanted to fire Gibson, too.

Although favoured by many Boers, Hitchen was biased against people with beards and would not employ anyone sporting one because: 'People don't trust them. You can't get into council houses at night with a beard in the rain looking like a wet holly bush. So I don't like beards. They're dirty. I think they are great at sea but they're no good in newspapers.'

He did not like suede shoes either, again because he believed people were suspicious of those who wore them. And anyone turning up for duty without a collar and tie – including photographers – were sent home to change. Drinking was fine, however.

'I wanted people who brought the bacon back. If they were harum
scarem, so what? I didn't want choir boys working for me.'

Instead of sacking people Hitchen let off steam with the memos he enjoyed writing almost as much as his bigoted column:

'To: All Reporters
If I see one more mention in copy of someone having "danced the night away", I will come out there with an axe.
The same goes for people "keeping themselves to themselves". People don't "keep themselves to themselves". There is always someone somewhere who knows all about them. Good reporters find the people who know. Even if it means "knocking the night away" on doors.
Also on the leave-it-out list are "sleepy picture postcard villages".

There are no "sleepy picture postcard villages" in England anymore.
Rustic habitations are now within diesel fume distance of motorways, and the inhabitants are either "dancing the night away" in rowdy pub discos, or "keeping themselves to themselves" hunched over bingo cards in the church hall.
Let's keep the stories coming but leave the cliches to The Sun.'

He would rail against professional standards:

'This morning's Daily Star was a prize winner – A BOOBY PRIZE WINNER!!
It was, without doubt, the worst 14p worth on any news stand.......
Our pictures were rotten. They were so static that a traffic-warden could have pinched them for parking. Page 13's picture of the angler's car being towed out of the Oggin would have been better suited in the Doncaster Advertiser – which is what we are rapidly beginning to look like. The Back Bench can't make bricks without straw. As it is they were hard pressed to find the clay, never mind the God-damned straw.'

He raged against the crumbling pre-computer infrastructure:

'I am well aware that many of our typewriters bear a resemblance to Arkwright's Spinning Jenny.
I also know how frustrating it is, with a hot intro in your head, to pick up a machine that has a jammed carriage, or type keys that have been twisted into a FairIsle knitting pattern.
..........With typewriter carcasses stacked against the walls like a brontosaurus's graveyard it is somewhat difficult for them (the typewriter mechanics) to sort out the quick from the dead.
The message therefore, is simple: when a machine breaks down report it to the mechanic immediately.'

All executives have the paranoid habit of ringing up their newsdesks pretending to be readers to see what reaction they will get. Woe betide any hack who does not treat each call with patience and respect, for one day the 'reader' will not be one who is easily brushed off:

'I am sure that one of the things that gets up all our noses is to be answered by a dummy on a switchboard, or a half-wit on a telephone extension.
Therefore, it was particularly galling to hear that some dumwit – I have not the faintest idea who it is, but if I had they would be seeking alternative employment – picked up a telephone on the picture desk on Monday morning around 9.30 and having said "Pictures…." listened, and then said "we've got a heavy breather" and put the receiver down.
The caller on the other end was Lloyd Turner (then editor) and when he spoke to me five minutes later had fire coming out of his nostrils.
The message is simple – don't let dumwits answer telephones and let's all be ultra-polite to callers, particularly the most important ones of all – our readers.
If I ever over-hear readers getting a hard time the jobless figures will increase by one immediately.'

Hitchen even invented a new time zone for the paper:

'Forget Greenwich Mean Time. From tomorrow we begin Daily Star Time which means I want each and every one of you to mentally turn your watches on ONE HOUR and to work like the clappers of hell.
Because of new production schedules we are moving everything ahead by 60 minutes and creating a whole new batch of deadlines. The message is simple – GET EVERYTHING SOONER AND FILE EVERYTHING AS SOON AS YOU GET IT – WORDS AND PICTURES.'

Hitchen's love of power made him interested only in those who had it. On his way up he had successfully emulated those who wielded it over him: his newspaper proprietors. Once at the top he interviewed those who wielded it over his proprietors including Prime Ministers Margaret Thatcher and John Major. Indeed Thatcher's press secretary, Bernard Ingham told Hitchen the Daily Star was her favourite red top and the paper which led her digest of news in the morning.

Hitchen reminded himself of his National Enquirer days by filling his office in the new Express Newspapers' premises :Ludgate House, in Blackfriars Road with US memorabilia. The Union Jack he had mounted on a standard with an eagle atop it like that in the Oval office. He also had a framed certificate which declared he was an honorary colonel for the State of Kentucky.

Ridiculed as the 'Kentucky Fried Chicken Society of Colonels', this 'non-political brotherhood' as one colonel describes it was created in 1931 by the then Governor of Kentucky to promote Kentucky and it's citizens. It is a charity-raising body which makes donations to good causes: a substantial donation was made to the US Red Cross after the terrorist attack on the World Trade Centre. For Hitchen, however, it was the 'rank' of colonel which appealed. That and the chance to purchase, via mail order, Kentucky Colonel clip-on string ties, gold-plated cuff links, T-shirts and caps.

Being a certified colonel was symptomatic of Hitchen's boyish love of soldiers and the military in general: he had never forgotten the soldiers who looked after him in Cyprus. The Daily Star's feature pages were regularly filled with yarns of derring-do carried out by the Paras, heroes of the Falklands War. The Paratroop regiments were delighted with their top Fleet Street friend. On one occasion a platoon of Paras turned up at the office, uninvited and rather the worse for wear, following a function in the City. With them came Pegasus, the Regimental Shetland pony. The commissionaires told the soldiers: 'We can't allow a horse in here'. But after a call to editorial, Pegasus used the lift and not his wings to ascend to the editorial floor where he was paraded around the newsroom.

The Falklands War was a very frustrating conflict for all newspaper executives. The news from reporters in the field was heavily censored by the military, and also delayed by up to a week. The bulletins read out daily at the Ministry of Defence were one-liners like: 'I can confirm that action was taken today'. By the time the war finished the Daily Star, along with many other papers was hungry for a story which could not be manipulated by the MOD. One of the ships bringing home the 'brave boys' was the QE2 owned by Cunard and the Chairman of Express Newspapers, Lord Matthews. founder of the Daily Star. As the editorial sat in conference Sutherland, said:' Why the fuck are we sitting here with the QE2 steaming home full of troops and nobody knows where it is?' He had a point and Hitchen called Matthews and asked him for the ship's position. The Chairman duly found out and called back with the coordinates. Bristol-based photographer Bob Barclay was despatched on a private plane and snapped the ship in the Western Approaches steaming homewards. Framed copies of the picture were ordered for the Chairman, and the captain of the ship.

The framing was carried out by a small business in Somerset, run by one Rosemary Barclay, wife of photographer Bob, a fact overlooked by Sutherland as a reward for a successful 'mission.' By the time the first Gulf War came round, Hitchen was determined to find a way around the MOD's news blackout and ordered Sutherland, to go and base himself in New York where, Hitchen was convinced, news would be less subject to censorship.

'All the censorship was done by HM Forces in Iraq,' Sutherland recalled, 'we were supposed to be saving money – cutting back on expenses at the time and yet it cost thousands to keep me there in an office in the Rockefeller Centre. I flew first class backwards and forwards across the Atlantic to come home at weekends and all because Hitchen wanted to be Generoso Pope who liked to say at cocktail parties "My man in New York and my man in wherever". I tried to talk him and Peter Hill (the night editor) out of it and got a bollocking.'

Hitchen was unimpressed with claims the censorship could not be beaten. He managed it –from the wrong side of the Atlantic. 'The only exclusives to come out of America came to me back in London via my contacts in Washington and caused the D-Notice Secretary to go apeshit. Sutherland's presence there was a complete waste of time and money,' Hitchen said. Sutherland's card was now marked.

The image which history framed as the defining moment when the Gulf War was over: charred corpses on the road to Basra, was not the one which symbolised the end of the war for the Daily Star.

Hitchen lined up the military superstars of the Gulf War to send video messages to the annual Daily Star Gold Awards at London's Savoy Hotel which was attended by Prime Minister Magaret Thatcher in person. Both Commander-in-Chief of the American forces, General Norman Schwarzkopf and General Sir Peter de La Billiere, Commander of the British forces, obliged. After his failure to beat censorship in New York, Sutherland at least managed to secure the attendance of de la Billiere's wife, Bridget and Schwarzkopf's wife Brenda and his sister but then only because his boss had done the homework. The pair were were promised Concorde flights from New York and the great warrior, Hitchen discovered, was a collector of silver figurine owls so Brenda was driven to a top jeweller's in Chancery Lane where she could purchase further precious birds for his mantlepiece aviary.

Hitchen did not give up easily and wanted Schwarzkopf 'on our news room floor'. He hoped there might be another opportunity and when Schwarzkopf later came to London he sent the man who secured the Elvis photo for one more try to get the American to Ludgate House. Sutherland went to Harrod's where Schwarzkopf was signing copies of his book 'You Don't Have To Be A Hero'. He bought Hitchen a copy but failed to secure the great man's presence at the Daily Star.

In classic Il Duce triumphalist style, Hitchen had bestowed his greatest decoration upon the 'hero ship' HMS Gloucester, the Type 42 destroyer adopted by the Daily Star for the course of the war. She was to receive the Daily Star Gold Award – normally reserved for plucky schoolchildren and popular sporting personalities.

Sutherland was ordered to fly out with the award and present it to the ship's commander in Gibraltar. The ship's company were as delighted with the role play as the editor. Sutherland was received with a guard of honour lined up on deck and armed with pike-staffs and was piped aboard.

At around this time Sutherland became interested in a red-haired Amazonian woman who worked on Horse & Hound magazine. Many men woud have left their wives for Patricia Elkins, who was good fun as well as looking like a raunchier version of Sophia Loren in fishnet stockings, but Sutherland got there first. The pair moved to a Sussex country house as Sutherland dropped the matey Jimmy for the more formal James, and appeared in the office with a dog whistle on a string around his neck. At home in his new bucolic role as a gun dog trainer he expressed his newly-adopted rural belief that dogs should be shot if they chased sheep. If Elkins, who kept horses, was unsettled by her boyfriend's violent ambitions to become a country squire, she didn't show it and was eventually rewarded with the much better paid job of picture editor on the Daily Star. But Hitchen, who wasn't happy with his Scottish subordinate's re-invention as a man of the Shires, was even less impressed with Elkins who he blamed for failing to get photographers up in the dome of St Paul's Cathedral for a fly-past of RAF planes celebrating Gulf War victory. The only people allowed up in the dome that day were security men, the long-legged Elkins, said, duly reporting what her snappers had told her.

But when Hitchen trained his field binoculars on Wren's famous roof and saw 'security men in kiss me quick hats and dresses' he blew a fuse. Hitchen had been promised by special reporter John Beattie – who had excellent contacts in the RAF – that the Red Arrows would all change route at Blackfriars Bridge, followed by Tornados and other military planes, so that a picture of Tornados flying past Ludgate House could be obtained. St Paul's was the best place to shoot the picture from. A picture Hitchen wanted to present to the Chairman, Lord Stevens, as a symbol of his, Hitchen's, power. This was known as an 'editor's must'. No staffer could fall down on a must.

At the flypast the planes were out of shot and down in the darkroom frenetic attempts at trying to join three pictures together were going on to make the desired snap. Alas the montage was in vain.

And so Elkins was in the doghouse. She had already blotted her copybook after another must had misfired. This was a story about a West Country parish council which had banned one of its residents from flying a huge Union Jack flag in her garden.

Hitchen ordered an even bigger flag to be erected in the main street of the offending hamlet and so Elkins commissioned a cherry-picker, at vast expense, down to the scene, complete with flags and a photographer.

When the image was eventually secured and brought to Hitchen's office he was incensed: the flag was upside down and there was no method of altering photographs in those pre-digital times.

Ironically Hitchen was appointed editor of the Daily Star because the paper had gone too far down market. The paper's Chairman, Lord Stevens, had done a deal with David Sullivan, who ran the Sunday Sport, a paper full of nude women and invented stories. At the time of the deal – September 1987 - the Daily Star was losing money and had done so for years: £90 million in it's nine year life, according to a Sunday Times report.

Yet there were plans to launch a Sunday Star to rival the Sunday Sport and when Sullivan announced he was to start a daily version of his Sunday paper to attack the Daily Star, a deal was brokered.

Sullivan was told he could have a halfpenny for every extra copy the Daily Star sold once it had been conjoined with the Sport. But what interested Sullivan more, was getting hold of a captive audience – one already peering at Starbirds – to introduce his other organs to. Once he offered cheap jewellery through the Star he would have in his hands a data base of names and addresses to which he could send out trial offers of his other journals. Journals like Asian Babes and Old Bangers.

Stevens took on Sunday Sport editorial director Mike Gabbert as editor of the Daily Star to replace Lloyd Turner. Gabbert had once been an award-winning journalist and deputy editor of the News of the World. But he had taken the Sullivan shilling and had produced increases in circulation on the Sport by packing it with naked women. This was hardly rocket science because the Sport never pretended to be anything other than complete fiction and soft porn. It was not, and did not pretend to be a newspaper. Would the same thing work on the Daily Star?

News of the deal was received in Manchester with huge enthusiasm as 'they threw their flat caps in the air in sheer delight' as one observer noted. In London the news was received in total silence. 'It was a different culture in Manchester,' said deputy editor Nigel Blundell. The north was where men put whippet racing, pork pie suppers and beer before the 'missus' and London was full of 'effete wimps' who went to wine bars, kept fit and ironed their own shirts. Women should be kept in their place: as wives. Wives in the kitchen preparing food or Reader's Wives bent over the kitchen table as magazine fare for husbands too unreconstructed to have a mistress. Affairs, after all, were for southerners.

Gabbert promised not to change things too radically: 'Say a couple of sets of nipples a day. We're not going to go mad,' he said, although in an interview with the trade press Gabbert was more forthcoming: 'The newspaper will be much more fun, and it will appeal to younger people. Even sex will be depicted as the fun activity that it is. I am an old wrinkly nowadays, but I have vivid memories of how enjoyable an activity this was in my younger days.'

At his first editorial conference he ordered the paper to carry at least two sets of the 'biggest boobs possible'. Then he asked women's editor Alix Palmer to run letters about 'really raunchy problems....the old man who tears his wife's knickers off five times before lunch and that sort of thing'. Palmer said she did not often receive such a mailbag and was told to re-write them to fit the bill. When she protested Gabbert said: 'Get me somebody in here next week who will make 'em up.'

The gloomy predictions made by one and all could not have prepared the Star staff for the first newspaper following the partnership: everyone was genuinely shocked. There were models wearing Star T-shirts with the slogan 'I get it every day'; a baker's ex-wife who claimed 'I go like hot cakes' and headlines such as 'Punter's pal beats the pants off Linda'; 'Girl's secret oats'; 'How Des keeps it up!'; 'Cabinet papers lost in a kinky brothel'; 'Get stuffed'; and 'Howls of lust drive neighbours bonkers'. The emphasis was not just on young women showing off their breasts, but 'illegally' young women. The drive was to find stories about girls below the age of consent wanting to reveal themselves.

The Daily Star started to make news everywhere: bad news. Director of Communications at Manchester University, Philip Radcliffe, claimed that the 'most revolting picture ever seen in a national newspaper' was that of a woman nestling a 'booby-trapped' mouse in her cleavage. 'Sometimes it wriggles free....and ends up in her knickers' the caption revealed.

A new word was invented so that headlines could be written with punch and not hobbled with asterisks. It was bonk. As in 'Bergerac Bedmate! TV cop to bonk Liza.'

The paper was dubbed the Daily Bonk by it's own journalists, a move countered by Gabbert who ordered a competition for a new word for sex to be found: 'Do you think bonking's boring and nookie is old hat', the 'story' asked, had not the word been around since 'William the Bonkeror' the competition asked. Readers were asked to send their ideas to 'Bonking, The Star, 11-12 Bouverie Street, London EC4Y 8AH'.

Daily Star London members of the National Union of Journalists passed a resolution stating: 'This chapel is dismayed and disgusted by the new editorial policies of the Star.'

Political editor David Buchan publicly and courageously described the paper as a 'soft porn rag' and was immediately fired. Blundell, also horrified at the transformation kept his head down. His subbing talents were put to good use on the Sunday Sport instead. He recalled Hitchen talking about a paper called the Weekly World News which was a 'repository for all the stories which were made up or even too wild for the National Enquirer.'

He decided to see what they had. Here he found stories such as 'Greyhound bus found at the South Pole'. He changed the vehicle to a Number 15 bus – one which trundles down Fleet Street – for the Sport version of the 'story'.

This lead in turn to the legendary 'B52 found on Moon' and another of his favourites: 'Aliens turn my love child into an olive.' He had single-handedly turned the Sunday Sport into a cult buy and circulation went up from 250,000 to 800,000 as it became a required tonic with those from binmen to bankers who did not want to miss out on what everyone was laughing at.

Meanwhile back on the editorial floor of the Daily Star's London office no one was laughing. Staffers sought jobs elsewhere. Some left with no jobs to go to. I took all time owing including holidays and managed to bodyswerve the mucky stuff. I had one run-in with Mark Bourdillon on the picture desk who asked me to write a caption about a schoolgirl whose breasts were too big for her school blouse. I rang her up and in the course of the 'interview' discovered she was 17 and a model.The desk did not want to hear this: they wanted to find girls who were prepared, for money, to pretend to be something they weren't: it would be hard to imagine how they could get away with publishing authentic stories about 15-year-old girls. I told Bourdillon to write it himself. About this time I moved house and when one of the removal men discovered I worked for The Daily Star he asked as people often do 'where did we get our stories from'. I explained that all the institutions of a great democracy provide daily fare as well as news agencies, local papers, freelancers, tipsters, etc. I then asked him which paper he read.

'The Sunday Sport,' he said without a trace of irony.

'But why? You know the stories are just jokes. There's no news in it.'

'Yeah, but at least with them you KNOW it's made up,' he said. But the new regime did not last long once the advertisers started pulling out: Tesco scrapped a £400,000 a year contract with the Star, just a month after the Sullivan link-up. Three weeks later Express Newspapers severed its links with the Sunday Sport. Gabbert left the company and Brian Hitchen was appointed editor. Under Turner and with Hitchen as London editor the Daily Star's circulation had hit a high of 1.75 million (though as Hitchen's deputy editor Nigel Blundell recalls this was on one day only when The Star had bingo and The Sun did not; The Star was undergoing a special cover price of 10 p, The Sun was not. And The Sun journalists were on strike and the Star's were not) But in any case The Daily Star's circulation had now plummeted to below 600,000.

Lord Stevens' money-making elan had been called into question and he had been made to look ridiculous. The word 'bonk' haunted him. It was like a red balance sheet to a bull.

On the occasional Sunday, Sutherland, who had hoped to be the first photographer ever to become an editor, was given the chance to prove himself, though he admits that when mobile phones first came out he used to 'edit the paper from the jacuzzi in the Portland Hotel in Manchester.' One such Sunday, after the disastrous Star-Sport link-up, Sutherland had gone home early and left Peter Sloan, the page editor, in charge and he had used the word bonk in a headline. The following day both Sutherland and Nigel Blundell, were called up to Stevens' office.

'It seemed to me the chairs were small to make him look bigger,' said Sutherland, 'and he appeared to be raised up behind his desk.' The pair were threatened with demotion if ever the word should appear again. But if bonking was out, there was still nothing wrong with sexual intercourse and nudity. Elkins used to count the nipples every day, the record count was 21.5, she estimated. And just eight months after the Star parted company with the Sport, Which? , the consumer magazine carried out a survey on national newspapers and the Daily Star topped the list for sex stories.

As a result the news editor, David Mertens, was dubbed the 'Prince of Porn' and picture editor Elkins, the 'Queen of Sleaze'. And whatever problems beset the world the Daily Star believed it's hired mammaries were the remedy: 'To every great story in the world we would send a Starbird with her tits out,' Sutherland said, 'it was the Starbird factor: that'll cheer 'em up was the philosophy. The thing is, though they had big knockers they were all dwarves,' he added thoughtfully.

Size mattered to Stevens who was now ultra-sensitive to accusations that his newspapers should be stacked on the top shelf. Every morning a copy of The Daily Star would arrive at Hitchen's office with hand-scrawled comments such as 'how silly', or 'what a load of rubbish'. Hitchen's secretary, Julia Westlake, screwed up the papers and threw them away until one morning Hitchen arrived early and noticed a Star cutting on Westlake's desk with the scrawled comment.

'What's Lord Stevens saying?' he asked Westlake.

'That's not Lord Stevens that's some nutter in the distribution department, they come in every day,' said Westlake.

'No it's not, it's his handwriting,' said Hitchen appalled.

Stevens would call Blundell to his office on a regular basis if he felt standards were slipping. On one occasion Blundell was summoned over the day's Starbird.

'Her bosoms are too large,' Stevens complained.

'Voluptuous,' Blundell defended.

'No – too large,' Stevens reiterated.

'I'll try and make them smaller,' said Blundell.

'Don't be impertinent.'

'But if we are going to have these girls in the paper they have to be attractive.'

'But they do not have to be pornographic.'

'Well they are smaller than The Sun's today.'

'No they are not.'

Stevens' concern, however, was too late – the damage to The Daily Star had already been done and it would take years, if ever, to restore its reputation as a proper newspaper, as the following ditty from a reader makes plain:

'Each day I see the "Daily Tit"
It makes me feel I want to quit
The kinkies, yes, may groan with glee
But the tits I see are not for me
You get 'em big, you get 'em small
They're never firm, they always fall
The reader added 'Seriously Mr Editor.....why not publish news not
abuse?'

Hitchen had arrived to save the Daily Star. His previous role was as editor of the Sunday Express, a job he had left his position of Daily Star London editor for. The former editor of the Sunday Express, Sir John Junor, was another of Hitchen's mentors. Junor was both a yachtsman and a golfer. Hitchen's first sailing experience had been aboard Sutherland's 26ft yacht on the Intracoastal waterway in Florida. The moon was out, the fish were running, it was quite magical. But the best bit was ordering the bridges to open with the blast of a foghorn. Hitchen liked the foghorn so much he later used one to announce conference at the Daily Star. He also bought Junor's ageing wooden yacht, called Outcast.

'It was full of holes and cost him bundles to repair,' said Sutherland, 'but it was JJ's boat, that's why he wanted it so badly: it was being John Junor.'

Sutherland also introduced Hitchen to golf at Ashford in Kent.

At the tee Hitchen asked: 'What club will I use?'

'Pick a five iron as it is your first time,' advised Sutherland.

When Hitchen unzipped his brand new white golf bag with red piping and his name on the side the clubs still had their polythene covers on with Hermans, New York printed on them.

'He had sent Stan Meagher to New York, at Express Newspapers' expense, to buy the clubs,' said Sutherland, 'but Stan was used to shopping trips, he once bought Hitchen and I monogrammed silk shirts in Hong Kong, although that time he was actually on an authentic story.'

The germinal of a daily newspaper is its news schedule which is the precis of that day's events gleaned from wire copy, Press Association - for domestic news, Reuters and Associated Press for foreign news, diary fixtures for staff to cover and running stories such as court cases.

It goes without saying that news editors are always looking for the exclusive line on a story, but so, too, are they on the lookout for the 'off diary' story, the unusual, funny or zany stories which give both tabloids and broadsheets some light among the dark. I can recall David Mertens getting desperate to find a story to put on the schedule for morning conference. First of all he attacked the 'wire clerk' whose job it was to tear off the news agency copy into readable sized sheets. He had clearly dozed off and Mertens was left with something resembling the Bayeaux Tapestry in length.

'It's like a bloody work to rule in a bog roll factory in here...sort this stuff out will you.'

Then as he started to read through it:

'Two Palestinians killed on the West Bank. Boring. Gulf tankers take down their flags of convenience. Boring. Hong Kong: what happens when Britain's time runs out ? Oh not another bloody feature on that. Boring. RUC man shot dead in Northern Ireland. No one gives a toss about Northern Ireland. Boring.'

Then he discovered a gem: the Queen, while on a visit to China, had eaten a sea cucumber. Mertens despatched a hack to Gerrard Street in the heart of London's China Town to sample one. That was more like it.

On the Daily Star the news schedule was a competition between the picture desk and the news desk to get their schedule lines published. If a schedule line became a headline, beer was bought for its author.

Sex, once again, was the subject matter most often sifted for such schedule lines:

'Sagging bra industry – three day week for workers'

'Cinema manager employs see-through nightie girl to boost falling attendances – now council probes complaints'

'Why women with perfect breasts have ops to make them even bigger'

'Sex shop half price for pensioners and dole customers'

'Peking: no sex or booze for the unemployed – by order'

'The sexy antics at school for scandal'

'Rumpty Dumpty. Roly-poly Navy wife's 50 lovers'

Such schedule lines resulted in stories like: 'I Want Lotts More Up Top' the splash headline followed by '36D Is Bust The Job' inside as we read that 'Lottery winner Sheryl Carthew yesterday vowed to splash out – on a huge pair of BOOBS'

One blue movie actress who hoped her story of sexual exploitation woud help others not to fall into the same trap would have been bemused by what actually appeared:

'Porn-Again Christian. Sexy Sharon ditches blue films for God. Porn queen Sharon Martin has given the dirty mac brigade the elbow for a missionary position – spreading God's word.'

'Britain's bathing belles are busting out all over', failed to 'make' the paper and so, on next day's schedule:

'Britain's bathing beauties are getting bouncier, says swimwear manufacturer (re submit)'

Animal stories were another schedule line favourite:

'Flying crab causes £80-worth of damage to a car – after being dropped by a seagull'

'Cool cat Millie survives 24 hours in a freezer – eating turkey pate'

'Monkey business is Big Business down on Frankenstein farm'

'No assing about in Britain's first donkey hospital'

'Starbird saves dog'

'Panda moni mum! Ching Ching is in the club'

Then there was 'human interest':

'Daily Star to the rescue of pensioner Evelyn Bradbury – she lost her false teeth leaning out of a taxi and now fears death from starvation'

'Disabled peer types book with his foot'

'Dog-bite woman dies of rabies. Seeking the tragic husband who took her on Indian holiday-of-a-lifetime after being made redundant.'

'The unkindest cut....vasectomy couple told they are expecting triplets'

'Woman, 81, eaten by pet dogs'

'Lightning Bolt Welds Dave To His Flip-Flops'

'Stew's A Lucky Boy, Then. Mo saved by his dumplings', was a story about a pre-cast concrete store boss Maurice Pilbrough's love of dumplings saving him from death when a one-ton steel sheet fell on him: 'Mo, 56, was flattened by the 19ft by 5ft metal sheet and his face turned blue as air was crushed out of his lungs. But it was his love of stodgy grub like dumplings and suet pudding that stopped him being crushed to death'.

Good old fashioned sensation still needed that news 'peg' thus when 3,000 Philippinos went down on an overcrowded ferry it was the fact that it happened 'The day after British TV viewers watched the film Jaws.......' that made it newsworthy for Star readers.

'JAWS 3,000 Dead In Sea

As many as 3,000 people were feared to have been torn apart by sharks yesterday after an overcrowded ferry sank in a collision.'

One of the major frustrations for Hitchen was the fact that although Express Newspapers were prepared to pay for stories and to finance editorial schemes, they were not in the same league financially as Rupert Murdoch and his News International, owners of The Sun, the Daily Star's direct rival.

This meant he relied heavily on the ingenuity of his editorial team to beat the big guns of the opposition. So keen was he to better the The Sun that sometimes Hitchen himself would dream up tactics which went beyond the pale. One such concerned the funeral of murder suspect Graham Sturley. Sturley was a 37-year-old property developer whose wife Linda an 'Avon lady' went missing from their home in Biggin Hill, Kent. Her body was never found and after police dug up the back garden of the Sturley home, although they found nothing, they had been preparing papers for the Director of Public Prosecutions with the intention of charging Sturley with her murder, when he died of a heart attack. The story had caused huge headlines nationwide and now the mystery would probably never be solved.

At Sturley's funeral, after all the press had departed, a woman in black turned up and laid a single red rose at his graveside. There was only one photographer there to capture the 'mystery' woman and secret lover of the man who 'cheated' a murder charge: Frank Barrett of the Daily Star. He had been briefed by Hitchen and the woman, was in fact, an actress friend of the man determined to have an 'exclusive' angle to the story. As it turned out Hitchen got cold feet and the Daily Star never published the article. Many believe this was Hitchen's plan all along: to stoke the Fleet Street rumour machine causing panic stations especially at the offices of The Sun.

Such stunts are considered 'gamesmanship' in the world of tabloid journalism, and as a master in such engineering Hitchen could smell a rat at a hundred paces and anything iffy about reporters' expenses was pounced upon as these examples demonstrate:

'The owners of Café Charco must be considering going into liquidation. Certainly they can't be doing too well if between 22nd April and 25th April they only managed to sell three meals or issue three receipts. You will notice that the receipts are numbered from 1891 to 1893. I am returning them.'

And:

'I am puzzled by your bill for £29 on 15ᵗʰ April for dinner at a Tandoori restaurant in Wimbledon with one 'Thomas Cooper' on the day of the death of comedian Tommy Cooper. Presumably this is not his son. I am returning your expense claim for your further consideration.'

Hitchen's aplomb at writing a withering memo to his errant staff was much admired and imitated by his lieutenants. Here is one time news editor Phil Mellor, with my hobby of sailing on his fevered brow:

'Dick,
You are a warm wonderful human being. All you ask from life is a bed for the night, a cosy book of knots and a healthy bank balance. All Lord Stevens, the Chairman asks is a fair whack at expenses. Do me a favour and look at these again.
Philip.'

If he memo'd Dick Durham, not just Dick, it was a mite more serious:

'As a would-be Master Mariner I would have thought even Captain Bligh would find it hard to navigate a job in London and end up having a meal in Luton.
Let's not bugger about, Park Street, Luton, Beds. had nothing to do with Cliff Richard, Captain Cook, the Young Ones or all points west. Reconsider, earliest.
PM'

Indeed Mellor began to relish his memo-writing as he discovered a flair for the witty attack. Here is one he sent to a colleague:

'I can find no trace on any schedule of a legless groom's stag night – if it were true!!
Oliver Reed died with his pants on – it was not on Monday March 3ʳᵈ.

*I can take the Saudi Prince background on March 6th – albeit your
contact Dr. Fagin has been used in a hit musical – and quite a
famous novel.
I am sick and tired of being quizzed by Struan Coupar about
rubbish expense claims.
If as much originality went into stories as expense claims – we
would all lead a happier life.
PS I return your expenses for another try.'*

Reporters tried the same method to justify their expenditure,
here is one of mine written to David Mertens at the time of the
gunman Michael Ryan who ran amok shooting several people
before turning the gun on himself:

*'Re: expenses
Not since Hungerford have so many figures been cut down in cold
blood. Ryan must have had a reason but he didn't leave a note.
Nor did you, what's the problem?'*

The long-suffering managing editor, Struan Coupar, had a
reputation as a tough, but reasonable man. It was the reasonable
side of his character I decided to appeal to when we had a little
memo skirmish over a £50 valeting bill I submitted for my
company car. I recalled how Express photographer, Tom Smith,
always keen to let nothing stop him getting to the story, threw
sandwich crusts, apple cores, and half-eaten pies over his
shoulder while driving his company car. The resultant mulch,
after many months resulted in mushrooms sprouting from the
rear resulting in his Ford having to be fitted with new back seats.
Coupar was having none of it this time and so I decided to
explain why it had been necessary:

*'Memo From Dick Durham To Mr Struan Coupar
Although the man and his machine had been in perfect harmony
for the many hundrds of miles covered over rugged territory, the
bodywork had taken on a five o'clock shadow of airborne fauna.
No longer could coralis mocha – Ford's description of beige – be
used to categorise my Sierra. She looked like a flying wedge of*

pepper Boursin. Three car washes could not shift the gnats and bits of gnats which had fused onto the alloy. Nor could Tesco's special enzyme biological wash, although it did take a layer from my palms.

If that wasn't enough, on another occasion she was driving in very fine rain when a squall passing over a badly stowed cement lorry, applied a overcoat the Mafia would have been proud of. I wanted to keep the car up to the standard I received it in and therefore ordered this valet, which includes a protective coating of wax.'

He replied:

'To: Mr R. Durham   From: Struan Coupar
Much as I admire your vibrant prose style, I am inclined to the view that it conceals, intentionally or not, the plain, unvarnished fact that had you cleaned the car more regularly it would not have become so encrusted that valeting was necessary.

A "full valet", incidentally, involves cleaning the inside of the car as much as the outside – had the gnats managed to insinuate themselves there as well?

Keeping the car in reasonable condition is your responsibility. I suggest that you pay this bill.'

I paid the £50.

5. THE ANIMAL KINGDOM

Human beings can be slaughtered wholesale in a far away war without causing the British public to pause for long over their cornflakes. But maltreat a cat and they will call for the reinstatement of the death penalty.

The photograph of a man with a baseball bat swung back over his shoulder, his trunk half-turned ready to release a powerful blow on a puzzled looking, white-furred, seal pup looking innocently up at its assailant, remains unsurpassed as the greatest animal 'cruelty' picture of all time. It made the career of Kent Gavin, who survived as a staff man for 40 years on the paper that published it: the Daily Mirror. Most newspapers in Britain and some in other parts of the world have sent photographers back out to the Arctic Circle trying to emulate Gavin's scoop. The Daily Star was no exception and photographer Tom Stoddart and I flew to Halifax, Nova Scotia in 1980. It was here Stoddart and I were introduced to clam chowder in the Bluenose restaurant, which I did not enjoy, but worse was to come later when I got back to London and Hitchen was signing off my expenses.

I did not know he had been to the very same restaurant years before and famed for his 'steel trap' memory did not recall the place selling wine. He called them up and confirmed that it was as he remembered: a diner with no wine or spirit licence and which had five dollar hamburgers as the most expensive dish on the menu. My expenses were signed but only after the dinner at the Bluenose had been omitted. He later told me 'That's the problem with having a boss whose been around the track a few times. The upside was having a boss who didn't fire you for duplicitous expenses.'

In Nova Scotia, Stoddart and I joined the Greenpeace ship Rainbow Warrior for a voyage north to the Gulf of St. Lawrence where the crew were to stage a protest over the annual Canadian seal cull.

Stoddart and I decided to try and talk to the sealers before Rainbow Warrior left harbour. We wandered the frozen streets of Halifax where old, dirty snow had been piled up off the highways into grubby, frozen head-high embankments on the sidewalk until we found the seal hunters' depot. We explained we wanted 'their side of the story' an age-old method of getting a response. A response which would provide the 'balance' to enable a pre-conceived, biased and inflammatory story to be published. The sealers were surprisingly accommodating and one even posed on the dock-head with his club swung a la Kent Gavin. The only trouble was the lack of dewy-eyed seal waiting to receive the blow.

I asked the burly sealer how he felt about bashing the brains out of the cute little creatures and he said the first one or two made him feel sick.

'I felt really bad on the first day – I hit them as they were weaning – but after a few days the seals just looked like 25 dollar bills to me.' The fact that unemployment is very high in Newfoundland, that the seals breed like rabbits and are in no danger of extinction, that their oil is used for rubber products, tanning and margarine, that when the sea is frozen over boats can't fish and that using guns on slippery ice would be dangerous to the sealers, is ignored by the antis who have their own industry to think of: raising considerable funds from sentimental animal lovers who are 'sickened' at the slaughter 'just for fur coats'.

Such arguments don't sell newspapers either.

The Rainbow Warrior took three days pushing north as ice-floes lifted eerily, like undulating white fields, in the growing North Atlantic swell. We tried to cut the corner off into St. Lawrence Bay, but the ice sheet got thicker and the old Hull trawler got trapped. Then a blizzard encircled us and that night some of the hippy crew broke out the marijuana and played Beatles tapes as they partied. Next day conditions were no better and, trying to sound unabashed I asked the radio-operator, a laconic bean-pole of a man with straight waist length hair and pebble spectacles, where the nearest helicopter-base was. It wasn't.

'You gotta think warm Dick, you gotta think warm,' said the Tennessean, 'We've gotta "vibe" our way outta this.'

Stoddart, a Geordie lad, had been in his bunk for two days, sick to the core of lentil soup and teeth-cracking home-made whole-grain bread, and dreaming of egg and chips.

That night, passing the galley, I saw a row of oven-ready chickens. I dashed to Stoddart's bedside: 'Tom, great news, there's chicken tonight. Roast chicken I'll bet – I've seen them all lined up.'

He smiled weakly. At supper time we joined the queue to be confronted by two huge stainless steel tureens.

'What's that?' I asked.

'Meat or vege' came the reply.

'Where's the chicken?'

Chef bashed the first tureen with her ladle. I looked in and it was full of brown gruel. The one next to it was full of red gruel – the vegetable course. They had liquidized the lot. Stoddart went back to his bunk, unfed.

Eventually we re-traced our passage through the ice-floes and – much delayed – reached the Harp seal nursery. We were too late. The sealers had already done their gory job. They had left an open air mortuary of skinned seal pups on ice. Mothers flapped about growling at us – still guarding the perfectly formed but skinless corpses.

We were too late for the award-winning picture. Instead Stoddart had to make do with a Greenpeace activist, Patrick Wall weeping over the steaming meat still staring with glistening eyes. His picture made the front page even so and inside ran my story: ' There was one bloody stain as big as the ship. Like a spider's web the red trailed out from it......like highways of blood made by the pelts.'

Having filed the story I checked in with the London newsdesk via the ship's radio.

'Any problems?'

'No it's fine but Manchester have come up with an idea.'

Stoddart and I looked at one another ominously.

'Can you bring a seal home with you?,' crackled the voice of Peter O'Kill on the London night desk.

They wanted 'Lucky' the seal saved by your caring Daily Star to live happily ever after in a UK zoo.

I turned to the Greenpeace project leader. 'Give me three good reasons why I can't bring a seal home.'

Fortunately it was against Canadian law to take a seal off the ice. In any case they only stay white, furry, little things for about four weeks before they begin the transformation into very heavy, unlovely, and exceptionally hungry, bald mammals.

I was with Stoddart on another occasion in Rennes, France having lost a UK lorry we had followed from St. Malo in pursuit of an 'Evil Veal Trade' story. Not speaking French I was obliged to put my forefingers to the side of my head and 'moo' at passers by in a bid to find the slaughterhouse. Incidentally the only cruelty to the young heffers that trip was when Stoddart took his pictures. He and I crept among the creaking trucks aboard the Portsmouth – St. Malo overnight ferry trying to find one where the beasts were 'packed so tight they can't sit down' as we had been told. Eventually in the dark we found a cattle truck and climbed up it's sides.

Stoddart's flashgun unnerved a dozen or so small cows which had so much room they were laying on their sides in blissful slumber. Their subsequent lowing sent us scrambling back out of the rolling car deck.

Despite the tabloid newspaper lack of appetite for publishing stories about foreign war, famine and disease, Stoddart decided such subjects required less artifice than working with animals, left the Daily Star and went off to cover conflict, as a freelance, in the Balkans, Iraq and The Lebanon. He also covered famine and the HIV crisis in Africa, earthquakes and flooding elsewhere.

After a quarter of a century riding as the fifth horseman of the Apocalypse he was reduced to getting a show in Amateur Photographer magazine and told them : 'I have risked my life getting these pictures but all papers are interested in is Posh, dosh and Becks' referring to newspapers' obsession with celebrity and money.

But the seal he and I had been ordered to rescue that day on the Newfoundland ice floe was fortunate. For any creature deemed worthy of Express Newspaper's deliverance had an unnerving habit of exiting rapidly to the knackers yard.

There was the time when a polar bear lost its mate at Chester zoo. Then, too, Manchester had 'an idea'. It was to replace the pining bear's mate with a new one to be called Twinkle, the Daily Star polar bear. Manchester-based reporter Tony Brooks recalls: 'They wanted to find one on an ice-floe off Vladivostock.' The plan to provide a mate for the bear incarcerated at Chester had overlooked the findings of a study by Oxford University, namely that polar bears enjoy an 'average territory' in the wild of 79,482 square kilometres and travel, on average, eight kilometres a day, But the logistics of darting a polar bear in the wild were abandoned and as Brooks recalled: 'I think the bear was bought from Moscow Zoo.' Unfortunately the zoo's new inmate did not survive. Some have it that the giant bear mistook some glass-fibre ice effect over the cage plunge pool for the real thing.
When it came up from a dive after feeding time, ready to head butt it's way through the 'frozen water' it found the fibreglass wouldn't give.
Whatever the truth, when news reached the desk, panic set in and reporter Brooks was despatched direct to the zoo.
'It's closed' he complained.
'I don't care how you get in. But get in and remove that sign from the bear cage!,' his desk ordered.
'What sign?'
'The sign that says – "Twinkle" courtesy of the Daily Star'. The duty editor said.
Fortunately the newspaper was then in its pre-launch phase and all stories produced were run only as dummies, and so the outside world and more importantly The Sun, never did hear about the caring paper's match-making. Years later when the world became 'enlightened' about the ethics of zoo-keeping the great Arctic bear was to come under the Star's scrutiny once again, this time as part of a campaign to return a bear to the ice-cap from its squalid concrete pen in another British zoo. It was only when Phil Mellor pointed out that the poor creature suffered from alopecia as a result of some vitamin deficiency that the mammal was spared freezing to death in its 'natural habitat'.
If it is axiomatic that humans should never work with animals and children it is equally true to say that animals should never

work with tabloid newspapermen. It's definitely bad for their health. Chris Boffey, a reporter who began his Fleet Street career as a Newcastle-based reporter on the Daily Star had the job of interviewing the owner of 'Britain's Most Talkative parrot'. The bird was kept in a heavy-duty cage and the owner was reluctant to get it out. However the photographer could not go back to the picture desk sporting a snap of Polly with bars in front of it's beak. So the proud owner was persuaded to lift the heavy lid of the cage which was held open with a prop while Polly was encouraged to raise it's head clear of the bars.

When the flash popped the startled bird flinched knocking clear the prop jam and was instantly beheaded by the falling door. As Boffey ruefully remarked: 'We were left to interview the former owner of Britain's most talkative parrot.'

Another idea was to adopt a stray pooch from Battersea Dog's Home which had been abandoned over Christmas and make it a celebrity dog. A dog which might even meet the Queen's corgis. A photographer, Stanley Meagher, was ordered to give it a home. Meagher, who, for the Daily Express, had literally ducked bullets in the Cyprus Conflict, and who had been the first photographer to walk across the Sinai Desert in the Six Day War, was incapable of getting near the snarling dog without getting bitten. Just to add insult to injuries the hound gave Meagher's own family pet distemper and both had to be put down.

'What shall we tell the readers?,' Mellor asked his editor.

'Just forget it,' Hitchen decreed and no more was ever heard of Lucky the Christmas dog.

Another unlucky hound was accidentally run over by a photographer sent by the Daily Star to interview a UK disco-dancing queen.Tony Brooks was the reporter on the story: 'It was a yappy Yorkshire terrier which had a habit of sitting under cars. Unfortunately the gate was left open and nobody noticed it had got out. The pet lover sued the paper for causing distress and the loss of her pet.'

Surprisingly dogs are not exactly in plentiful supply for rescue purposes in the UK and so The Daily Star couldn't believe its luck when it got a kennel load of beagles from an experimental centre which had closed down. Mike Housego – who had once been a top showbusiness reporter with genuine contacts in Hollywood, counting names such as Kriss Kristofferson, Johnny Cash and Willie Nelson as personal friends – had fallen on hard times and so desperate was he to get a staff job again he jumped at the job of coordinating the supply and demand of beagles to safe homes with Star readers. He was taking hundreds of phone numbers a month mostly from telephone boxes near the potential pet owner's home, as it would seem there is a correlation between poverty and pet owning.

People were left hanging around the phone booths for hours while Housego tried to match hound with home. When they eventually got their beloved dog Housego was then the recipient of many more calls from public phone boxes as complaints poured in from owners at their wits' end as the hounds went mad tearing up carpets ripping down curtains and biting children in a bid to reduce their surroundings to something akin to an experimental kennel.

When news came through that an 'animal welfare park' in Bedfordshire was closing down and flogging its menagerie, reporter Sue Blackhall was briefed to go and cover the story of how creatures great and small were being traded illegally as the centre had no licence to cover such a sale. She firstly had to delicately negotiate her way around the then editor Phil Walker who had excitedly called her in and requested she bought 'Quilly' a porcupine for his wife Sharon Ring – herself a former News of the World hack. He even handed Blackhall a plastic dustbin so she could avoid injury. Blackhall had to diplomatically explain it might not be a good idea to be involved as a purchaser in the 'evil trade' they were about to expose.

Even after the taxidermist had been at work, animals were always the downfall of Daily Star teams. When reporters Gerry Brown and Mike Parker decided to prove how easy it was for people to smuggle their pets in and out of the UK, breaching quarantine laws, they used a stuffed cat. With the moth-eaten relic in the boot of an Express Newspapers pool car they drove to Calais for lunch. It was a long lunch and upon their return to Dover they were disappointed when it appeared Customs were not interested in them. They also began to realise that writing about taking a stuffed cat on a day trip to Calais was not a very good yarn.

'Hey look what we've got in our boot,' Brown announced. The Customs man took a look.

'Ah yes, a stuffed cat.'

'But it could be real.'

'But it isn't.'

'Do you mind if we take a picture of you looking at it?'

At which point the Customs told the pair they were over the drink limit for driving and confiscated the car. They had to trudge round Dover drinking coffee before they were allowed to drive back to London.

After a while the newsdesk became so wary of animals that the next time a creature was thought worthy of national attention a freelance was given the job. If it went wrong the paper could then distance itself from the job by 'firing' the hapless hack. Freelance hack Syd Breman wrote some glowing copy about 'Bambi' a small Roe deer which vandals had attacked with a cross bow. The arrow, which was still in place, had pierced it's neck from one side to the other, but the beast lived on in time to give our readers a tear-jerking Christmas. This time the story back-fired when the RSPCA criticised the paper for cruelty – they said the deer should have been immediately put down.

Most times, of course, the tabloids work in tandem with the RSPCA. One such case was the bizarre will left by one Mary Mirehouse, 85. Another 'animal lover' she could not bear the thought of leaving behind her pony, donkey, four pigeons, two canaries, seven red setters and two swarms of bees. She had ordered their execution before her funeral. Already the red setters had been put down before the RSPCA tried to contest the will in court and the Daily Star and The Sun arrived on the woman's bucolic 'doorstep' in the wilds of a hamlet called Hawkesbury near Bristol. The Sun had arrived first with a horsebox and had backed it up to the gate which gave access to the paddock where the pony and donkey were innocently grazing.

The Star's Bristol area man Dave Newman, not to be outdone, had parked his company car across the horsebox and when I turned up I added my own to the blockade. Afternoon turned to evening and both teams from the rival papers agreed a truce to go and dine: leaving a pair of freelancers to cover for both newspapers. A sumptuous feast was produced in a nearby pub before we returned to the scene after midnight. To our dismay we found both cars had been bounced out of the way and the horsebox had gone. As we stood in the moonlit lane debriefing the freelancers a cacophony of EE-Aws came from the paddock as a second Sun team leapt out from behind the hedgerow. Newman and I heaved a sigh of relief at the wind-up. The following day the RSPCA won their week-long court battle and the other animals were saved. It was lucky for them that the Star was not obliged to come to their rescue.

From donkeys to dolphins the Daily Star has acted like a kind of inept Noah's Ark, hoping for a deluge of circulation.

Some of God's creatures have been luckier than others. Probably the most famous was Blackie the donkey saved from being ridden to death by the fattest man in a Spanish village during it's annual fiesta.

Or was it?

Don Mackay competed against Hugh Whittow, then on the Sun, to be the first paper to secure the dusty prize. There are of course many donkeys in Spain and many donkey owners who are only too happy to re-christen them especially for large injections of cash. Not surprisingly both newspapers claimed to have saved Blackie. But only one, The Daily Star, had a receipt which we published as the ultimate 'proof'. The Sun, furious at having been beaten to the prize, then tried a different tactic and published a story saying it was cruel to bring a donkey to Britain – where Blackie ended up – because it could not understand English.

Such was the furore over Blackie that we had to employ an extra temp to answer all the mail and the calls which poured in. I myself was on the night desk during the unfolding story and was offered Clive of India's reins by a patrician-sounding old gentleman who had probably never read the Daily Star before in his life.

Every other call to the desk was from another animal lover offering a stable, a field or in one case a lifetime supply of hay. It became impossible to operate the desk and when one call came through from a chap in Manchester I tried desperately to bounce him over to the Manchester news desk to get them to take part in donkey salvation.

'This is urgent.'

'I know,' I said patronisingly, 'but if you are in Manchester then the best people to talk to are in our Manchester office'.

'For Christ's sake do you want to hear this or not?' came the frustrated reply, 'a ferry has sunk with 200 people onboard.'

It was the first call we'd taken about the March 1987 Herald of Free Enterprise ferry disaster at Zeebrugge and I took his point. Blackie was making headlines in foreign newspapers as editors in US and Europe, fascinated by the tabloid war, were following the saga. This meant that other British papers which had loftily ignored the story now felt obliged to mention it, though grudgingly. The Daily Star's stable mate, forgive the pun, the Daily Express, found a way of covering the story and at the same time rubbishing it:

'Donkey in 'cruel farce' row

As the Star newspaper arranged yesterday to bring Spanish donkey Blackie to Britain, the RSPCA branded the wrangling over the animal's fate as farcical and cruel.

"Blackie is just being used in a circulation war," RSPCA spokesman Mike Smithson said.

"It has been reduced to the level of farce."

He added: "He would be better off left to spend the rest of his life in Spain."

He appealed to the editors of the Star and the Sun to stop wrangling over who saved Blackie from the cruel death he was alleged to have faced at a fiesta in the Spanish village of Villanueva.

Last night Blackie, who was bought by the Star, was given a clean bill of health by Spanish vets. But before he starts a new life in Devon he must endure 30 days quarantine in Spain, a long journey in cramped conditions and a further six months quarantine in Britain.'

Farce it undoubtedly was, and as such meant that poor Whittow earned the ire of his editor, the maverick Kelvin MacKenzie on the bigger, more powerful and much richer Sun. To this day Whittow, who regularly canters through the countryside on horseback with his equestrian wife Lesley, is reminded of the Star's scoop every time his mount shares a field with a donkey. However it didn't do his career any harm, Whittow became editor of the Daily Express, although in recent years the newspaper has carried so many page one leads about the weather, one could be forgiven if the paper has a new area man based in Exeter, home of the Met Office.

Such was the status The Daily Star enjoyed among the animal-loving British public, that calls came in from many folk who wanted the paper's help in saving animals. Most were ignored, but one mysteriously caught the then Editor Lloyd Turner's attention. It was a call from a gentleman in Lagos, Portugal who wanted a cat saved.

From what grisly fate was never explained but hack Allan Hall and photographer Tim Cornall flew out to save the moggy. Unfortunately it turned out that Perdido (Portuguese for 'the lost one') as the creature was quickly named, by the team, was completely feral. It was bald, had few teeth and hated humankind. Hall had to buy a pair of leather welder's gloves to handle the beast and also a cage to fly it back to the Daily Star sanctuary. Unfortunately it soon became evident that Perdido had only one lung and would therefore not be allowed to fly. 'Drive it back,' came the newsdesk order. So Cornall flew home while Hall hired an expensive car and spent three days in fine hotels feeding Perdido his Michelin meal leftovers while he drove to a vet at Wimereux just south of the French ferry port of Boulogne. Here the creature was left while quarantine stipulations were entered into and Hall returned to London. Hall was later informed the man-biting cat had 'escaped' and the story was consigned to the litter tray of history.

It was my own duty to journey to Belgium to 'save' Green Kilt, one of the Queen's former race horses, from the dinner table of 'greedy' Belgians. The fate of all horses in Brussels, once their racing days have ended, is to be served up as Dobbin burgers as neither the Belgians, nor the French for that matter, are sentimental about their mounts.

Unfortunately the Daily Star in their enthusiasm for the story, published news of the nag's deliverance before I had managed to purchase the beast:

'He Won't Be Kilt. Daily Star rescues the Queen's horse from dinner table.

Our caring Daily Star readers are winners. For we've bought the Queen's racehorse Green Kilt....to ensure that the colt NEVER ends up on Belgian dinner plates.'

The owner was keen to snatch the £2,000 we were prepared to pay – not bad for a load of horsemeat – but his colleague was suspicious. Why did we want the beast? Who would pay such a sum? Could he see a copy of the paper?

I told him the British were very sentimental about animals and that as it was the Queen's former horse we simply wanted to bring it home to an 'animal sanctuary'.

He tried very hard to get a copy of the Star but fortunately the little town of Ritie was miles from any major city or ferry port. And in any case the owner was keen for the cash, he didn't really care what we wrote, so his colleague's skepticism was overlooked.

Once I'd secured the nag and – remembering Whittow's fate – pocketed the receipt, I had to wait for some ancient former jockey and his passportless mistress to turn up in a horsebox from the UK. The 'illegal' made it out of England but, ever nervous on the dreaded animal story, I insisted she get in with the horse on the way back in case she was stopped coming through immigration and the whole tale went pear-shaped.

Once safely at the Newmarket Horse and Pony Rescue Centre: 'There's Neigh Place Like Home', all the desk required was a good snap of Green Kilt 'laughing' with joy. That morning I collected some sachets of pepper from the hotel I was staying in and then waited to get the horse rescue centre proprietress, Julie Elliott, out of the way.

Briefing photographer Tim Merry to stand by for the shot of Green Kilt expressing relief at his new lease of life – I had heard that if nags sneeze they have their dirty old teeth in the caricature of a grin - I lured the great creature to the stable door with a bucketful of oats and palmed the pepper toward it's damp, quivering nostrils.

Green Kilt reared up like Trigger on a photo-shoot for Roy Rogers' birthday. It then, in one skip, reached the back of the stable and wouldn't come anywhere near us. The creature had been ill-treated in Belgium – painful operations to keep it racing had crippled it's legs and the thwacks of an ash shovel had been used by the owner to drive it into our horsebox. Perhaps it felt it was about to get more of the same. The problem I now had was the fact that Green Kilt's long snout had pepper dusted down it and there was no way I could get near him to brush it off. Merry and I made our excuses and left. We later discovered Merry had secured a perfectly focused shot of Green Kilt's throat.

Once again the Daily Star mailbag was full to bursting because of the, for once, successful rescue. One reader from Hull, wrote: 'I was heartbroken to read your front page article......you have pleased your readers again with your prompt action....I hope Green Kilt's spirit has not been broken.'

I once chased a dolphin all round the Ring of Kerry in Ireland because it had 'fallen in love' with a local female scuba diver, Caroline Hussey: 'Dolphin Flips For Girl Diver'.

The other theory: that a harpoon wound to it's cranium made it swim round in circles always missing the outlet to the sea was judiciously overlooked by those of us covering the 'story'.

Whatever the truth of the matter Daily Star executives did not consider the mammal for rescue and it therefore survived.

For many years Fleet Street had been very keen to 'stand up' a story on dog-fighting. Everyone knew it went on, but only the results had been photographed – the RSPCA would release pictures of scarred pit bulls occasionally, and there had been second and third hand accounts. But no one had gone in undercover to get words and pictures. So when we took a call from a man in Kingsbridge, Devon who said he could supply what we wanted I was sent down to interview him and try and organise an undercover piece. It soon became clear that the money we were to pay the man for his services was to be used to sponsor the dog fight itself and this I reported back to the desk.

Hugely disappointed that their exclusive was so compromised they sent down Neil Wallis 'Britain's no.1 Reporter' as the paper then billed him. But even Wallis' contortions to get the story, but to keep the Star's part in it camouflaged, failed and so the dog fight went ahead somewhere, but we were not part of it. Animals grow fur to protect them from the elements but they'd be better off bald when it comes to the adoration of the public and the attention of the media.

No one loves scaly-old fish, nor do newspapers compete to save them. That is unless European fishing fleets are after them. When the UK threw a new fishing exclusion zone around it's coast, Danish Euro MP and trawlerman Captain Kent Kirk vowed to sail into UK waters and drag his nets.

He invited the British press to sail with him to witness the deed and therefore caused a bun-fight on the quayside at Esbjerg between reporters trying to get a berth. ITN's camera crew – sound man, camera man and reporter were taking up three berths and as such their right to sail was contested by The Sun. The tall bouffant-haired reporter for ITN, Michael Cole, tried his greasy charm on the hardened old hack, George Lynn, who told him" "Fuck off you pompous ass" and that was it – settled. ITN were relegated to a following boat.

Aboard Sand Kirk were the Daily Express and the Daily Star, The Sun, and BBC Radio among others. Among our number was legendary Express snapper Tom Smith, who rescued a wounded paratrooper in the Falklands war and whose dead-pan Cockney humour was equally as legendary as his exploits. Before we boarded he commented on his reporter', Ian Black's hastily purchased royal blue wet weather gear, thus: 'Are you doing a shift for Dyno-rod?' My personal favourite Smith one-liner was about Daily Star photographer Mark Bourdillon who was off sick with a broken leg after a horse-riding accident. On hearing the news Smith said: "Hasn't he got a company car?"

The voyage was rough and Smith was the first to be sea-sick and took a Mogadon to knock him out for the voyage across the North Sea.

As an old hand at sea I was the only member of the press not to succumb – at first. Instead I remained on the bridge with Capt.

Kirk – he of lantern jaw, Beatle mop-top, matinee idol looks and great charm. He relayed interview after interview over the ships VHF to various radio stations around the UK. As Sand Kirk wallowed through the stormy night., He had his back to the wheelhouse window as he sprawled his torso over the chart table which faced aft while hanging on to the curly-cord receiver of the radio telephone. Sand Kirk was under automatic helm. It unnerved me that no-one was keeping a look out and so I did and eventually spotted the lights of what appeared to be a large ferry. They shut off as we dropped in the troughs of the waves, they flared at us once more as we went up the crests. The ship appeared to be on a converging course and I opened the bridge door and went out on to the exposed wing for a better look. Spray soaked my head in an instant. Yes it was a ferry and yes it was on a converging course. I alerted Kirk, who lager in one hand, radio-phone in the other was on his umpteenth interview. "Can you hold one moment?" he said and swung round to look at his radar.

"Oh yes, it's a ferry for sure" he told me in his sing-song voice, and proceeded to adjust the automatic steering to put us clear. Then it was back to his interviews. Soon afterwards I shared a meal of fried plaice with Kirk's crew but then joined the casualty list for mal de mer.

The following day an RAF Nimrod buzzed the trawler providing a photo opportunity – except for Smith, who was still comatose. Being a member of the 'gissa-neg club' that did not present him with a problem however: another photographer provided an image. Kirk eventually got to break the law by trawling a couple of miles off Middlesborough. Nobody told him the waters here were among Europe's most polluted so he was surprised that there was literally only one small fish hooked up in them…. plus a condom. But he'd proved his point and we'd got our story.

6. FANCY DRESS

Red-top newspapers regularly entertain their readership with
first person stunts which require the hack on duty to dress up
and make a fool of himself. Being the news is a humiliating
experience but my cuttings book is full of the performing arts –
once you make a good job of something in Fleet Street you are
quickly categorised as a particular horse and your course is,
from then on, pre-determined. It all went back to my job as
elephant boy with Roberts Brothers' Circus – I was marked

'first person' expert. So when It was announced that
Edward was joining the Royal Marines, I was ordered
to his commando base in Lympstone, Devon to experience
Edward had coming: 'My Royal Commando performance,'
the headline.
til then no more had been demanded of my abdominal
muscles than that they held in place a stomach regularly
stretched from a plentiful Fleet Street lunch. But on that first
afternoon I was bullied, and bawled at until I managed to bend
my midriff double 80 times in one sitting.

The Physical Training Instructors were unimpressed with the
result even though I threw up. The next part of my sedentary
anatomy which came under military scrutiny were my puny
arms: as limbs to work a typewriter they were adequate but as
tools to haul my flabby torso skywards up a rope they failed
miserably. I collapsed in perspiring humiliation on the gym floor.
Then came the running. In standard army hobnail boots – just
don't do it.

'Christ,' I thought, 'don't they know who I am?'

They did not. That evening in the officer's mess the huge joke
was finally revealed to me: the base Commander had told his
number two to put me in for the preliminary RMC training even
though at 32 I was too old, the closing date is 25. The PTIs later
told me they thought I was the son of an officer who was trying
to work the system.

'We could see you were too old and not fit enough,' one
cheerfully told me, 'so we decided to prove you weren't going to
make it!'

Though unsuitable material for HM forces, as far as HM Press
was concerned I had set myself up as clothes horse for the Daily
Star.

When the film Batman, starring Jack Nicholson, was released in
Britain, I was ordered to the streets of Gotham, a village in
Nottinghamshire, dressed as the Caped Crusader. My other prop
was a broken down Robin Reliant car – Batman and Robin,
geddit?

My role play invited only this response from two old men on a
bench: 'Eh 'oop it's Batman.' However this caper inspired the

makers of the BBC TV programme Only Fools and Horses. The only time in the long running series history when the characters were shown reading a copy of the Daily Star, was following publication of our story when Del Boy and Rodney dressed as Batman and Robin for a fancy dress party. It was art copying, er, life.

Donning a pith helmet, and armed with a butterfly net I went off as 'Spider Man' to try and trap an escaped tarantula in Middlesex, actually we did the pictures outside Mother Bunch's wine bar off Fleet Street, where some dusty flora struggled for survival in a rare patch of unpaved City.

Posing as a beggar I sat in the streets of Winchester where vagrants had been banned and received not one penny all day: 'The Miserable Beggers of Winchester' was the headline. I donned a furry rodent suit and posed as a giant rat with my head sticking out of manhole covers all over London for a piece on the capital's collapsing Victorian sewers. When Accrington re-opened its canals and was dubbed 'The Venice of the North' I dressed as a gondolier to punt a canal barge through a lock with some bemused bargees as customers.

I once went jogging with Madonna in London's Hyde Park, in a bid to secure an interview – she never uttered one single word – for the story headlined 'Marathonna', but at least I got a designer track suit and trainers out of it.

'A Word In Your Ear, Petal' ran the headline over a photograph of me in a white coat, and stethoscope around my neck and a megaphone in hand to 'talk' to the buds at a nursery in South London in order to depict the Madness of Prince Charles. The Prince of Wales had said on TV that he talked to his plants at Highgrove House in Gloucestershire to encourage them to grow. The nasturtiams I was chatting to had the temerity to ignore me so I ate them. A reader from Folkestone, Kent wrote in:

'We are now programmed to believe any daft sick mania – plants have ears, eyes, hearts, brains and take language courses in English. Charlie knows we can all become a lot of CHARLIES.'

Dressed in top hat and tails, dress shirt and bow tie, but also green wellies I tried to get into London's Connaught Hotel for a drink because Lord Lichfield had recommended it as being the third best in the world in a guide book adding that one must 'dress suitably.' The rather poorly contrived idea was that I should act ingenuously: I was trying to emulate 'top people' by wearing all the all the right nob's clothes, but – not being a nob - getting it slightly wrong, representing our working class readers' 'aspirations', as the desk thought.

The hotel manager didn't get the joke either and I was pictured by photographer Ken Lennox being refused entry: 'Posh Off' was the headline followed by 'No Room At Toff's Inn For Dashing Dick.'

After a run of these stunts I met my old friend Tom Merrin on a doorstep: 'I refuse to do all that crap. They don't ask me to do those kind of stunts anymore. Not after I pulled out my union card and said: "See that? It says NUJ, not EQUITY".'

I decided to put the ridicule to good use however and when Stan Meagher came up with the idea of going to New York with me dressed in a John Bull outfit to woo back windy Americans who had cancelled holidays in Britain following the US bombing of Libya from English-based USAF airbases in April 1986, I embraced the concept warmly. After all it was a 'foreign'.

Brian Hitchen was enthusiastic too, though he made a refinement: "Go as Shakespeare Dick, and remember – ONLY if you can get the airfares paid for!"

A quick ring round secured two return flights courtesy of British Caledonian and when I met their PR at Gatwick and rather bashfully explained our 'assignment' he said: 'We had a man from Surprise Peas once. He went over to the Big Apple dressed as a giant pea.He rolled himself along Fifth Avenue and no-one took any notice – to them he was just another sidewalk freak.'

So I was pictured with a backdrop of Manhatten for the headline: 'Bard of Broadway' with the byline 'By Star Scribe Dick Durham.' As tabloid fare is a relentless serving of shock and horror, it is felt that such light stunts are a 'bit of fun' – something that will cheer the readers up and help to avoid them cancelling their delivery in a fit of depression. Another hardy annual, guaranteed to warm the cockles of sentimental hearts, are the tedious RSPCA dossiers on creatures they have brought back to good health. The donkeys with uncut hoofs like scimitars, dogs with lobster-pot rib cages and cats as bald as eggs, are always guaranteed to boost their donations and sell newspapers.

When the Daily Star ran a story about a mongrel dog, dubbed 'Lucky' found by the RSPCA tied to a tree with head wounds and 'left to die' letters poured in from readers offering the pooch a home. One from an 88-year-old in Wisbech, read: 'We lost our dog about six weeks ago and desperately want another. We have a large bag of dog meat here ready. He will never have to be tied up. Plenty of fields to hunt rabbits. Ride in cars. Our other dog was named "Lucky." Please let us have him.

PS We live in a lonely place. We want him to keep the burglars away. The other one did.'

Another offer came from a woman in Luton, who had taken in a dog from a kennel for strays. She wrote: 'We had a dog, Sherri, which by your picture was so much like Lucky's face. Unfortunately after weeks of nursing she died of distemper.'

The apogee of what is described as infotainment - both dressing up 'stories' and working with animals – came together for me in Dorset where I had been sent on a yarn which involved both. A Lyme Regis sub aqua club diver had discovered a 'seven foot lobster' in a wreck off the coast and the Daily Star went to 'rescue' it. From what threat no one had stopped to think, but as a former diver myself with a corroding set of aqualung tanks in the shed – I secured a new wet suit, demand valve and twin air tanks for the dive, headlined 'Claws Encounter'. This was finally too much for the accounts department and I was called in to see the managing editor, Struan Coupar.

'You've spent a lot of the company's money Dick?'

'That's true but the desk wanted me to dive on the wreck and you can't be too careful with equipment.'

'You are a diver aren't you Dick?'

'I was, not anymore.'

'Well perhaps you'd like to bring the equipment into the office then.

We'll store it here in case it's needed again.' Coupar said giving me withering look.

'That's fine' I said and went on to explain that the wet suit would need to be regularly aired and dusted in chalk to prevent it perishing: the demand valve would need to be kept in a dry place and regularly checked – just supposing it failed when used by another member of staff? Also the air bottles would need to be carefully stored, they sometimes exploded.

Coupar then suggested I buy the equipment from the company. That seemed reasonable and they accepted a cheque for a fifth of the purchase cost.

Sometimes we got others to engage in stunts. When the Star, in the course of covering the UK's relationship with Europe, unfavourably compared Darlington with it's twin French city of Amiens, the local mayor was infuriated and, securing the Northern Echo as an ally, wrote a letter of complaint to the Daily Star's editor. He said he could show us the real Darlington and all it's delights. So back north I went with photographer Bob Aylott. On the way we tossed a few ideas centring on the local railway museum which the mayor had listed in his dossier of attractions. A few hours later we had him dressed in his full mayoral regalia tying me to the rail tracks in front of an ancient train at the transport heritage centre, "Going Loco" I wrote.

But I was not alone in being recruited for dressing up. Reporter Joe Clancy was once obliged to wear shorts with his suit jacket, collar and tie and then walk about Fleet Street, after a report came out which advised that city gents in Sydney, Australia were less likely to suffer from prostrate problems in later life because they wore shorts to work.

Reporter Rab Anderson was once briefed to dress in a skirt and walk past building sites to gather stories of the kind of sexist remarks women were then complaining of.

Even the health correspondent, Charles Langley, had to go out looking like one of the Flowerpot Men dressed from head to foot in traffic cones because disc jockey Terry Wogan had said on his radio show that there were so many cones on the roads they must be breeding somewhere during the night. Passing motorists were unfazed and treated Langley as a human contra-flow.

During all the domestic turmoil surrounding Princess Diana, including publication by The Sun and The News of the World of recorded telephone conversations between her and alleged suitors, the Daily Star decided her honour was at stake and sent reporter Gareth Morgan, dressed as Richard the Lionheart to defend her reputation by standing outside Buckingham Palace. Then there were the Daily Star T-shirts, all photographers were obliged to carry in their camera bags. If, at the end of a story – especially one concerning anybody who appeared on the television - the subject could be persuaded to don one it helped build up a library of 'Star" support.

One of the earliest victims was Terry Wogan, who must have been relieved he eventually escaped to radio.

The tabloid year follows the conventional calendar starting with Easter and April Fool's Day running through the summer recess of Parliament which produces 'silly season' stories then on through to Christmas. Editors and their deputies are forever trying to dream up new and novel ways of marking the year's milestones. An so it was that one Easter time photographer Bob Aylott and I found ourselves briefing a mother of four, Lynn Linkin, on how to hatch duck eggs in the cleavage of her ample bosom. Aylott went to an Oxfam shop and bought a £2 white lacy cotton dress and a straw boater with which to dress our subject. Our subject was being paid £200 a week for this exercise, an arrangement organised by the editor and so never questioned. The two young sons of the 'mother hen' had been having a claw-hammer throwing contest in the front room when we arrived so research into her suitability as the subject of the story had not been extensive. We draped her in the farmer's wife outfit and drove her out to the nearest barn where she posed on bales of hay with the eggs in her cleavage.

"If it doesn't work out we can always run it as an April Fool's Day stunt" said news editor David Mertens, ever the pragmatist, but he had no need to worry, for 10 days later Lynn 'QUACKED IT!' and: 'Mother Duck Lynn Linkin finally heard the patter of tiny webbed feet yesterday.After 10 days in the warmth of her ample bosom, Quackers the orphaned duckling hatched out. Mother-of-four Lynn, was eggstatic.

Quackers was just another duck egg when his mum Jemima was killed by a fox.' Aylott himself was a daily source of tabloid stories – he had a never ending stream of potty ideas which kept the Daily Star's pages filled - and conveniently kept him out of the office and 'on the road'.

His inventiveness was highly valued and had taken him around the world while on the National Enquirer. With him had gone the family laundry and dry-clothing, which he dumped at each hotel he stayed at. His first wife, Heather, had thought it a great wheeze to get Aylott's expenses to cover the cost. For the Enquirer he had gone to South Africa, hunting aliens, South America to find Shangri-la and all over the US on various hare-brained assignments. He only got caught out once when on arrival at some mid-western town he discovered none of the addresses he had been given, checked out, nor did any of the protagonist's names. It turned out that the reporter, an alcoholic, who had gone there before him, had made the whole thing up. Aylott tried to cover for him but after three days had to tell the desk that the whole brief he had been given was a mirage.

The silly season, when the Palace of Westminster is in recess, the time of high summer and with it a serious drought of stories, was created for Aylott. One such summer he had spotted a statistic – that 320 people are killed on UK roads every week. He then ploughed through a Gazetteer until Eureka: he found a village, Drewsteignton in Devon, which had exactly 320 residents.

We hit the road to Drewsteignton, a charming hamlet with a unique pub – the landlady was an old crone in her 80s – who left customers to serve themselves from tapped barrels and afterwards to drop the price of each pint into a plate. A couple of regulars made sure no-one short changed her. In her establishment we organised all the inhabitants of Drewsteignton to turn out in the village square next morning. Aylott meanwhile, had hired a cherry-picker for the day which also turned up at breakfast time. I then had to persuade every resident to lie down in the main road at the same time. Kids kept standing up larking about, dogs wandered around.

But in the end all Drewsteignton posed as corpses. At least so I thought, but any reader looking closely enough would have seen one young boy lying on his back with his arms sticking up at right-angles.

'WIPED OUT...EVERY WEEK.'

The news-desk were happy with the result though, and as Christmas approached Aylott was back looking through his gazetteer. This time he found a hamlet called Christmas Common. 'I know,' he said 'Why don't we re-enact the 12 days of Christmas. It would make a great spread!'

Nervously I agreed, but organising all the constituent parts proved nightmarish and cost the Star over £7,000. Not only that but the 12 swans a swimming proved an insurmountable problem for Aylott's direction. He was busy enough trying to keep villagers, who had been drinking mulled wine all morning to keep off the winter chill, to remain in one place for the picture. When the swan-less results were shown to the deputy editor, Nigel Blundell, he went beserk, this was a man who once fired the whole sports department and reinstated them the next day, so one had to tread carefully. He severely bollocked both of us. Needless to say the picture was never used – April Fool's Day was no time to run the Twelve Days of Christmas.

Elections were also a problem for the tabloid executives who assumed they were boring to the red-top reader. Thus in the 1997 General Election, the then editor Phil Walker, decided on a gimmick which would, he hoped, keep readers buying the paper. This was the "Pole of Polls" quite literally a £1,000 worth of aluminium pole with ribbons and boards on it which was transported outside Westminster by scantily-clad Starbirds who kept a tally on the totem of each party's varying progress.

Apeing the success of television programmes was another way of keeping circulation up. When the children's series The Teletubbies started causing controversy among child psychologists over its primative dialogue, the Star newsdesk's man in charge of forward planning, Stuart Winter, asked me to find a man with the name Terry Tubby and ask him if his life was being made a "living hell" by people mocking his moniker.

I spent three days trawling through telephone directories until I did indeed find a Mr. Terence Tubby who had not the slightest idea what I was talking about when I asked him if his name caused him any grief.

Winter, loath to let his idea drop, then said: 'Can't you put a few calls in to him asking for Mr.Telly Tubby?'

The European Union soon replaced 'loony left-wing councils' as a target for tabloid ridicule.

When British sausages were found not to comply with EU regulations An enraged Brian Hitchen mobilised an 'invasion' team, hiring a landing craft, a flock of 'Starbirds' and top sports writer Peter Batt. The pictures taken of Batty storming ashore in 'France' waving a large frying pan and the Starbirds draped with bandoliers of sausages were in fact shot in Sandbanks, Dorset. Later, having caught the ferry, Batt and his Starbirds set up a barbeque under the Arch de Triumph, Paris and offered British sausages to war veterans on Armistice Day.

Hitchen who had a Union Jack draped over his office wall, and a portrait of Margaret Thatcher on his desk, found his dander up again when French farmers started torching our exports of live sheep. He ordered scores of polystyrene shapes of sheep to be delivered to the new Blackfriars HQ where all the Star staff were deployed painting eyes and mouths on the cut-outs. The flock was then put on a lorry and driven towards Dover bound for a cross-channel ferry. Quite what the hapless reporters were to do to provoke the militant farmers into attacking the sheep once they arrived in France nobody had yet decided. But before a suitable briefing could be devised an unplanned for gust of wind swept much of the wool-less flock off the lorry as it crossed the M2 bridge in Kent and into the River Medway below.

Then there was the time the Daily Star was invited along to witness a game of 'Strip Darts' in an Essex pub: 'Get Yer Double Top Off!' The organiser set up his dartboard and then offered the 'punters' – girls and boys, the chance to play darts against each other. The player with the lowest score having to remove an item of clothing. The fact that the female 'competitors' were expert dart players and also plants in the pub audience was not grasped by many of their inebriated male counterparts.

One middle-aged man, who fuelled on by much drink, became the most determined to see some of his opponents' flesh the more naked he became himself. But by the time he was down to his underpants his ill-aimed arrows had become a hazard to the non-competing customers and he was persuaded to end his play. His libido running riot the poor fellow now made hopeless advances to his fully-dressed opponent before giving up and driving home followed by a police car who watched him turn his car over in a field in a bid to escape their attention.

I illegally parked my own company car in North London on the day that Meta Davies retired. She was the traffic warden who booked Beatle Paul McCartney's car, 19 years earlier, near his Abbey Road studio and inspired the song 'Lovely Rita Meter maid'. I got her last parking ticket.

During the 1998 Paris World Cup we received a tip about a student from Kent, of Turkish origin, whose French girlfriend had won a ticket for the final. She was not a fan of the game but he was, and according to the news agency report I received, was planning to dress as a female in order to be able to get into the stadium. When I spoke to Cem Mustafa myself, this turned out to be only partly true – hardly a surprise as most local agency copy is either mind-numbingly parochial and not worthy of national attention or stretched so thin you can see straight through it . It was something, said Mustafa, that he had only joked about. Without him dressing up I had no 'story'.

Now the student was in a predicament – he wanted cash for his yarn but did not want to wear women's clothing. I suggested he could say he was 'planning' to wear a frock and we settled on that. When the picture desk got the words they wanted an illustration to go with it. Not surprisingly the picture they wanted was the subject in his skirt. But Mustafa refused, posing only in his England football strip. The days of computerised imagery had recently reached the Daily Star, however and the resulting story about a 'footie fan' who was going to 'turn tranny' for a ticket came complete with our man in wig and frock...

'The Girled Cup' ran the headline with a picture of Mustafa waving an England flag with the caption In-Girl-Land and another picture of Mustafa in long black wig, and a low cut dress showing a female cleavage. This picture had the caption: 'Ticket Tart: This saucy shot shows how Cem might look dressed as a woman.' In the copy the picture desk had inserted a paragraph to explain why he HADN'T actually dressed up himself for the shoot: 'Cem, a business student from Eltham, South London, refused to dress up for a picture in case French soccer chiefs recognise his disguise.'!

Never mind being ridiculed by secular friends, as a Muslim, he claimed, it was doubly shaming for him to cross-dress. A bit of extra cash, as is nearly always the case, ironed things out. If there was anything in the Koran which ruled out such personal gain our subject was unaware of it.

I covered the King's Cross fire in the London Underground system in 1987, which killed 30, seriously injured 12 and provided much copy, though it was shifted off the front page after day one. With the next day's paper to feed, the news editor wanted answers quickly. But what factors caused the fire and why, were not immediately forthcoming. So to 'keep the story moving' the picture desk told photographer Frank Barrett to get a snap of somebody laying a wreath at the smoke blackened entrance to the Underground station.

When he asked 'Who ?' he was told 'Get Durham to do it.'

There was no way I was going to pose up for such a stunt and for once I refused point blank to be a picture desk prop. Batman and Shakespeare OK, but even I drew the line on posing as a non-grieving mourner.

I told Barrett I was happy to find a railway worker who would do the honours instead. He whinged that it would take too long and that no self-respecting railwayman would get involved in such bad taste...

But indeed I found a sympathetic-looking ticket supervisor, Warren Levy, and explained that many of our readers had sent in money to buy a wreath for the fireman Colin Townsley who also lost his life in the blaze and wondered if he would mind placing it for us at a suitable ,i.e. poignant, location. To our relief he was more than happy to oblige, so off we trotted to the nearest florist.

'When's the funeral?' was a question we had not anticipated.

'Er, now' I said to the suspicious florist who looked me and Frank up and down taking in our doorstepper's garb, which did not include black ties.

'You'll have to pay for it' announced Barrett, as photographers do, always on the bludge and for ever trying to body-swerve costs.

'I'm certainly not paying for your props,' I said.

'But I haven't got any money!' whined Barrett, who as the Daily Star's chief snapper had more foreigns than anyone else on staff, and had to be ready to go to Heathrow at the drop of a hat.

'Use your company credit card.' I said. We wrangled over the bill as

the bemused florist finished weaving together the wreath and Barrett was obliged to pay and we departed.

Then, as an after thought he ran back into the shop, chased her through the lillies, ivy and yew clippings into a back office.

"Could I have a blank bill?,' he pleaded.

7. CRIME

Time was when the act of homicide was so rare and therefore shocking that it was guaranteed to sell newspapers. Today murder has to be most foul to get a 'good show', in fact the fouler the better. Even local newspapers need a 'good angle' on a murder for it to make more than just a few paragraphs.

When gay murderer Colin Ireland – sensitively dubbed 'nature's pruning fork' by Hitchen - started leaving the bodies of homosexual men across London, a fevered tension gripped the Daily Star's news room, as this was something novel.

Everyone was waiting for the next corpse to turn up – where would it be and when? After a week with no new victims Hitchen demanded to know in conference what the latest developments were. When told that all had gone quiet and no more bodies had turned up he bashed his desk and stormed: 'Call himself a fucking serial killer?,' in frustration.

His anger uncannily matched that of Ireland who had read in an FBI handbook that to become a serial killer a total of five victims was required. He eventually succeeded and was sentenced to five life sentences in 1993.

The Metropolitan Police have their own grisly emporium which exhibits many of the most gruesome 'angles' of remarkable murders. Hacks are occasionally invited to Scotland Yard's Black Museum on the understanding that they do not to write about it. A decree which has traditionally been ignored in the past. So as I describe it to you now I am following a dishonourable tradition.

I was the guest of a former Press Bureau Chief, Bob Cox, an engaging and intelligent Irishman. On my tour was Chris Fields, Home Affairs correspondent of the Sunday Telegraph and Sylvia Jones – formerly of the Daily Star newsdesk but by then staff on the Daily Mirror.

The museum is sometimes used as a confessional by ambitious young detectives to air, in confidence, any difficulties they have with the press and to size up the 'opposition'.The rule of silence, given gravitas by the grisly contents, is used as a way of ensuring coppers can off-load their grievances in confidence, after a few drinks. It is also used to show the new intake of cops their horrific heritage.

Cox poured me a couple of large whiskies and quizzed me about Jimmy Nicholson, the aforementioned Star's crime reporter. It seemed he wanted to know whether Nicholson had an anti-police agenda. But the Prince was getting long in the tooth and needed his police contacts more than ever before. He was not about to 'turn them over'.

The Daily Star's editor was trying to find a younger reporter to step into his shoes. One such hack – Allan Hall – who went on to run his own news agency in Berlin supplying British newspapers with news from the German capital, had refused: 'I was not going to stitch Jimmy up,' he said.

After Cox put the whisky away I was introduced to the 'curator' of the Black Museum. Our tour started with the well-known tale of the condemned man being taken to the gallows at Tyburn.

The victim was taken in an ox-cart along Oxford Street then up Tottenham Court Road to a pub called The Halfway House where he ate his last meal and was allowed a skinful of beer to sedate himself. Apparently the routine was that the condemned man would then stand on a table and announce to the landlord: 'I'll pay you on the way back!'

At Tyburn, for an extra sixpence, the unfortunate soul could have his 'leg pulled' by the hangman's assistants thereby ensuring he did not choke away his last minutes on the end of a rope given an insufficient drop.

The museum holds the last noose ever made before the abolition of capital punishment. It is one that has never been used in anger but instead is placed around the neck of visitors, as it was around mine to demonstrate how the running eye-splice tightened the noose up under the chin to ensure the breaking of the neck.

Photographs of Jack the Ripper's victims are on display as are the forearms of a British murderer who was tried and condemned to death in Germany. The Metropolitan Police requested fingerprints from the German authorities to confirm the identity of the wanted man in order to close the case. The corpse was butchered and his arms sent by post: 'with Teutonic thouroughness' observed the curator in his well-rehearsed patter.

From the arsenal of the Kray Twins came a suitcase with poisoned needles and a crossbow: they were to have been used against the witnesses for their prosecution. And from the weaponry of their great rivals – the Richardsons – came the electrical box used to torture folks south of the river. Also on show is the microscopic pellet which was stabbed into Bulgarian dissident George Markov's thigh by his umbrella – wielding KGB assassin.

The famous telegram – the first sent across the Atlantic – which convicted Dr. Crippen, hanged for poisoning and dismembering his wife, lies in the gloom, faded under glass.

There is the stove and pot used by gay serial killer Donald Neilson to boil up his dismembered victims, as is the bath he used to cut them up. Stiletto knives concealed in ball point pens, rice-sticks used by Chinese gangs to crush their victims' larynx were shown to me and demonstrated by our guide from Hades.

The large kitchen knife used by a shop raider to stab one P.C. Hammond - an attack which necessitated him receiving 300 pints of blood – caused me to halt as this was a crime I had covered myself. I stared dumbly at his blood-stained, white Metropolitan Police shirt.

Our curator slowly started his own proselytising. He was clearly a red-top reader. He told us that parents were not teaching children the difference between right and wrong anymore and to reinforce his belief showed us a golf-ball studded with nails then screwed onto a chain and affixed to a cosh – a mini chain-mace. It had been made by an eight-year-old.

There was a riot shield melted into a misshapen blob from a firebomb thrown during the Brixton Riots – I had covered the aftermath of this event, too. Our guide told us the Met were now using shields which could withstand much higher temperatures.

Most fascinating exhibit of all is the 9mm automatic pistol sent to the Met from Field Marshal Bernard Montgomery. His 'gift' was inspired by the 1966 slaying of three police officers in Shepherd's Bush by Harry Roberts. What is astonishing is the letter on show from Monty who expresses the naïve hope, knowing that bobbies on the beat are unarmed, that his handgun, also on show, could be used covertly to help the police fight crime!

Our guide said 'In the future more policemen are going to get killed!" Capital punishment would eventually be re-introduced in Britain, he told us.

The curator ended the shocky horror show by announcing that MPs, even those who had campaigned against ever-rigorous policing, had changed their sympathies after a visit to the Black Museum. He told us one magistrate had refused to enter the museum in a bid to maintain objectivity on the bench, but which the curator saw as a dereliction of duty: 'And there he is s'posed to be judging criminals!' For my part I left the museum knowing how to stab somebody properly.

An item of evidence not on display in the Black Museum is the lock of hair torn from the scalp of John Bell the lorry driver convicted of the murder of a young female hitch-hiker from Colchester. Bell had refused to give a hair sample to investigating officers for DNA analysis so one of the detectives investigating the case lunged forward while interviewing him in a police cell and plucked a few strands from the burly driver's luxuriant thatch. But even armed with this evidence police investigators feared he'd be aquitted.

In October 1993 as I watched the jury return a verdict of guilty in Chester Crown Court, I noticed DI Colin Seal hidden from the rest of the court by a wooden panel, drop down on one knee and give thanksgiving to the Almighty for the conviction.

I had been sent to 'mind' the family of the slain girl, keeping them away from rival newspapers. But by then the Daily Star was under a new cost-cutting regime, and news editor Graham Jones, had taken the economy of Express Newspapers to heart and had sent the following memo to all staff:

'Recently I asked you if you could show voluntary restraint in your expenses claims because of a big over-run on the Budget.
I regret that I must now take firm action to redress the balance.
The depressing position is that on home expenses alone we need to save £25,265 or £842.16 per week until the end of the year just to break even. This represents a reduction of 35 per cent in the weekly home expenses budget or a saving of £25.52 per person per week.'

Jones promised his new expense regime would 'not be imposed in Draconian fashion if you co-operate' and yet I was told to find this murdered teenager's parents bed but let them pay for their own breakfast!

This was an order I ignored – I was not going to prise tear-jerking copy on the girl's life from her family and then ask them for the money to pay for their toast and coffee.

While covering the court case I had wandered into Court 1 – notorious for being the stadium for the Myra Hindley and Ian Brady trial. It was a hideous, dark, Victorian ante-chamber to Judgement Day. Old stained wooden panelling surrounded the walls, deep pit-like pulpits for witnesses and defendants. If a room could be given a 'make-over' to be made suitable as a studio to hear the tape-recorded evidence of a child being tortured this was it. Now over 30 years later the ghostly place was imbued with the spectre of Hindley.

In Hindley's case she was never allowed to even try and forget. Never would she be forgiven, and never would the tabloids allow her to forget. Two generations of readers have been introduced to the hellish crimes as the tabloids have raked up the yarn every year since the convictions.

In 1998 when Hindley was moved to a new jail in Suffolk I went up to talk to prison officers living locally. You can always find them – just ask around and soon you'll stumble across their pub. Before long I had the stereotypical Hindley yarn: how she had a luxury cell, with special en-suite facilities, a telephone, colour TV, so she could 'entertain her lesbian lover' : Myra's Prison Love Suite, was the headline.

When I contacted my Manchester colleague John Mahoney - Hindley had originated from that city, as had her victims – for some reaction, he told me the mother of one of the children, Winnie Johnson, whose son 12-year-old Keith Bennett's body was never found, had given permission to be 'quoted' whenever a story regarding Hindley cropped up. Deadlines had to be met and people were not always available for reaction. But so strong was the desire to keep Hindley in jail – the victim's parents willed her to stay in custody and die before they went to their own graves, a prayer that was eventually answered, - that this wretched mother was happy to have 'rot in jail' quotes attributed to her whenever the news story required 'reaction' to a Hindley yarn.

So if Winnie was unobtainable on the day the reporter was making enquiries she could be verballed at will.

Mahoney said: 'Your only worry is that you don't make the "quotes" evil enough. Winnie has told me she will refuse to talk to me ever again if they aren't!'

Child abduction, rape and murder is the dark territory where tabloids excel. The obvious sensational nature of such hideous crime is the tabloid's natural domain, and no moral judgement can plausibly be laid against them from the 'unpopular papers', to use the former Sun editor Kelvin McKenzie's neat touche. For it is most definitely in the 'public interest' to expose all the details to help apprehend the miscreant. Once the suspect is in court the reporters will be working on backgrounds, collecting photos, getting interviews with the defendant's families and friends. There will thus be a vested interest in a guilty verdict. Conversely innocent men, who are convicted, will have to wait years, if ever, for redress and hope they come to the attention of a dedicated investigative journalist.

Exposing paedophile rings can hardly be described as anything but journalism in the public interest. However one is left with the uncomfortable feeling that such coverage has a prurient side and undoubtedly the sordid details are eagerly scoured both by perpetrators of child sex crimes and the more harmless but equally seedy seekers of thrills vicarious.

Two crime reporters Cockney Paul Henderson, who having told the Daily Mail's Charterhouse-educated news editor, Jonathan Holborow, that his father was a docker, received the reply: 'Oh, really, which hospital?', and Barry Gardner, had amassed impressive evidence about a huge syndicate of men who were procuring young boys for sex. They had everything, pictures, statements, names of perpetrators, and much damning evidence against them.

They had everything except an account from a victim. I suggested to Henderson that we go down to the graphically named 'Meat Rack' – the railings outside the Wimpy Bar in Piccadilly Circus, where young rent boys gathered to sell their bodies and procure a couple ourselves.

We did so and in our reporters' raincoats looked the part. We immediately attracted the attention of two youths. One looked like a diminutive and underfed James Dean. The other was taller, plumper and altogether more queenly.

Revealing our intention to interview them rather than sleep with them we took them to a restaurant for a decent meal. I asked the questions, Henderson took the notes.

The route to becoming a rent boy was laid out before us. They were sexually abused as a child by an adult, either a parent or 'uncle'.Ever after the violation they found it 'natural' to offer their bodies up for the pleasure of others. After abuse from his uncle the queenly one had then become convinced he was gay and in Sheffield, from whence he came, could find no outlet for his sexual inclination and so drifted to London, where, after failing to get work, he went on the game. He tried to 'love' his 'punters' –that word again - and his affection was often taken advantage of by customers enjoying sex then, disgusted at themselves they would assault him and rob him of the fee for services rendered.

The tinier, tougher James Dean – a – like, gave oral sex to commuters before they caught their train home. But he told us he had a steady relationship with a man who loved him. This man had a bed with silk sheets, was wealthy and used to stroke him with a glove made of ocelot fur. Why, with such care and affection lavished upon him, he felt obliged to take £30 a time for meeting men in lavatories he never explained satisfactorily, but when I spoke to a detective later on he astonished me by saying before I finished my account: 'Yeah and don't tell me, he's got a sugar daddy who really loves him. He's got silk sheets and strokes him with a fur glove?'

I nodded in disbelief.

'There are a lot of those about. It's a ritualised make-believe world they hang on to, to stay sane,' said the cop.

In 1983 when six-year-old Marie Payne was snatched from a council playing field in front of her home, then raped, murdered and buried in Epping Forest the nation was understandably appalled. When the Daily Star newsdesk got a tip that her elder sister had been admitted to hospital having taken an overdose we were understandably intrigued. Photographer Frank Barrett and I were sent down to the Payne's Dagenham home where Mrs. Payne, still in a state of shock and disorientation, let us in. She revealed that Marie's elder sister, a 13-year-old, had been left in charge of the tot while mum and dad popped out. This had not been a regular occurrence: the parents were decent, responsible guardians but it had been a dreadful, fatalistic day to choose to leave the house together. Little Marie had been playing happily in front of the house and when her elder sister turned away for a few minutes she was snatched. The shock of her brief lapse of attention had driven her to attempt suicide. Fortunately the child had recovered. Mrs. Payne herself was mildly sedated when she let us in and told us the story. Once outside again Barrett said: 'You're not going to use that are you?' There was a moment – and this was before I had my own children – when I weighed briefly the thrill of the scoop against the sensitivity of the circumstances. But in those days it was a weigh-in that was fleeting. 'Of course I am' I said. And the next day 'Torment of Marie's Big Sister' was splashed all across the front page with an exclusive tag.

Newsdesks are reluctant to let a good exclusive die too soon and Barrett and I were sent back to the Payne's house. This time both parents were there and they hadn't liked the story. It was an emotionally charged moment on the doorstep and one which – as always – can go either way. Either you are left staring at a door, it's slam still ringing in your ears and mentally, imagined headlines crashing all around you in big, black letters, or the crack becomes a threshold into an Aladdin's Cave of tabloid glory.

We entered the house once more. The family were concerned that the outside world now knew about their surviving daughter's guilt. She had enjoyed horse-riding. 'Let's tell the world she's fine, she has these interests...' I said. 'It would help if we had a photograph,' This time we secured what we had failed to get the previous day, a collect picture of the sister enabling us to run the whole story again.

The 1998 murder trial of Lewes headmaster Sion Jenkins also sparked Fleet Street newsdesk speculation about under-age sex.

Jenkins' adopted daughter confusingly called Billy-Jo Jenkins – her real father's surname - was a very pretty and highly-spirited East End girl.

Through various petty and tragic circumstances – the jailing of her mother for credit card fraud and the subsequent jailing of her father, a petty criminal and former alcoholic - left the child in care and finally fostered and adopted by the superficially well-to-do Jenkins. Although he was found guilty of her murder no evidence of sexual misconduct was offered at the trial, indeed it was difficult to find any motive from the evidence barring a brief mention of Jenkins' loss of temper. However, after lengthy interviews with her real father, the late Bill Jenkins and her Aunt Margaret, it appeared Sion Jenkins was obsessed with Billy-Jo. He spent money Billy-Jo's real family could not afford, on fashionable trainers for her, he promised to spend more money on acting lessons. He even, according to Aunt Margaret, followed her out to the disco, concerned she might find a boyfriend.

When he turned up at his home to find Billy-Jo painting the French windows and slopping paint over the patio, he may have been irritated at the loud music she was playing at the same time.

Whatever really happened next we shall probably never know, but Billy-Jo's head was stove in with a metal tent peg. Watching Jenkins in court I was struck by his demeanour. He was totally impassive and in control – for a headmaster perhaps that was only natural. But it didn't seem natural. I warmed to Billy-Jo's father however. He was rough, had not had a good time of it generally, yet was highly intelligent and struck me as a very genuine and compassionate father. He had lost his daughter because of a kind of societal diminished responsibility. He had lost her to 'respectability'. I believed him when he told me that Billy-Jo, shortly before her death, had said she had something to tell him about Jenkins' behaviour. She had been due to visit her father just days before she was murdered. Whatever it was she wanted to reveal she took it with her to the grave.

One of the reasons I got past Bill Jenkins' door was that he was still in shock over the approach made to him by a News of the World reporter.

Jenkins told me: 'After the murder you can imagine the state I was in when the News of the World called the following week. The reporter seemed a bit frustrated, he said: "It's a pity she wasn't killed a day earlier, we would have had it in time for last week's paper and we could have paid you more money."'

Six years after being convicted of Billy-Jo's murder, Sion Jenkins' won an appeal against his conviction in July 2004. He was formally acquitted in 2006 following two re-trials upon which neither jury could reach a verdict.

Good copy and stories which appear to have instant analysis are occasionally published thanks simply to good timing. I, along with other Fleet Street hacks, had been invited by Scotland Yard to attend the Metropolitan Police basic firearms course at Lippitts Hill in Epping. Neither the police nor I could have known that just a couple of days later Inspector Douglas Lovelock, in pursuit of a dangerous suspect, would shoot dead an innocent woman, Cherry Groce in Brixton, South London.

The Daily Star had yet to run my feature on the Lippitts Hill visit and I had the chance to re-write it: 'A policeman has 3/8 of a second to make up his mind' 'GUN LAW' yelled the headline. 'Starman Dick Durham finds out how easy it is to shoot and kill'. 'Inspector Douglas Lovelock would have been gripping his model 10 Smith & Wesson 38 calibre revolver with both hands as he kicked down Cherry Groce's front door. But before he even plucked the weapon free from his leather press-stud holster he knew he had only three-eighths of a second to judge whether he should shoot. Only on Wednesday I faced the same nerve-racking decision. Suddenly in front of me stood a black woman dressed in jeans and holding a shot gun. I hesitated, and academically, I was dead. Police Sergeant David Chambers switched off the slide viewer at the end of the shooting gallery and turned on the lights.

"It was the fact she was a woman that put you off, wasn't it?" he said. I should not have hesitated. I should have shot to kill. That was the chilling message which came through loud and clear!
' ....

This was a PR nightmare for the poor old Met. But I had no doubt it was perfectly timed copy ...... 'Douglas Lovelock would have been wearing body armour stuffed with reinforced rubber and padded with feathers on that morning in Brixton.

It will stop the bullet from a 'Dirty Harry' magnum .44 revolver ......

The police rule is that they must protect firstly the public, then themselves and then in the words of Sergeant Chambers, "The health of the bad guy!"

'At Hogan's Alley last week PC Clive Rew told me: "You shoot to stop, not to kill, at least that's what we say. It's a useful play on words. If as a result of a shooting a man dies, that's an unfortunate by-product!" PC Rew did not need a holster. He drew his revolver from his trouser pocket as he demonstrated how to put two plastic bullets through the plywood chest of an armed robber. Under Section Three of the Criminal Law Act 1967, the policeman can use reasonable force to make an arrest. In the case of somebody with a gun, you simply shoot first and ask questions later. Inspector Alex Moir put it this way: "Don't put yourself on offer." And I was told it was "Perfectly legal" to shoot the following targets: -

A man with his back to me holding a shotgun with barrel skywards and facing a police officer.

A man threatening a police officer with a knife.

A man holding a woman hostage with a gun.

As Sergeant Chambers said: "I've got to be first, I've got to be accurate. If there's no time to issue the challenge: 'Armed Police' if I'm in immediate danger, then it is a waste of time to make a warning. So I aim for the chest, the largest part of the target. We shoot to stop, not to kill, but we accept the fact that by shooting them in the chest, they may well die."

Physical training inspector PC Tom Tanner said: "You don't want a sympathetic introvert who's going to hesitate."

Commander Bill Skitt admitted the police were warned about their image. This weekend it did happen again but at Lippitts Hill the targets don't bleed and the bullets are made of plastic.' Understandably the police were not over-happy that their open-day held among D11 officers behaving in a macho fashion, should have predated the shooting dead of an innocent mother by one of their men – an experienced inspector – by 3 days. But then the police get good service from the press most of the time because press coverage is a big help to them when they are fresh out of leads. Immediately after a crime the police will give you every last detail of what they know and if that doesn't lead to some phone-calls from eye-witnesses, family or friends of the perpetrator,then the police will be open to further suggestions from the press to 'keep the story going' There will be the obvious line up of bereaved mum, dad or partner for a tearful press conference.

That will give good coverage for two days. Day 1: The Crime. Day 2: Relatives' reaction. After that the story has got to be kept running with either fresh evidence:murder weapon found or in-depth interviews with the officer leading the investigation – his pet theory as to who the killer is or why he did it. Finally the hack pack might even turn up something themselves from banging on doors.

As soon as the police have a really strong lead all co-operation goes out of the window and the press, are given nothing. This is partly because legally they can write little after an arrest and virtually nothing after a charge, but it is also because the police no longer need the press.

After the trial, when a not guilty verdict has frustrated police officers, a police spokesman may finally add:

'We are not looking for anyone else!'

When a new and powerful drug, crack-cocaine, started making headlines in the US, I realised it would only be a question of time before it made good copy this side of the Atlantic. But where to find it? It was fortunate for me that the West Midlands Constabulary had been so deeply mired in corruption scandals that they were receptive to getting the press on side once more and when I rang their press office to ask if Birmingham had a problem with crack-cocaine, they openly admitted they did because they wanted to show off their street-wise drug squad who already had the SP on crack and were determined to beat the dealers. They would give us all assistance in publicising the new scourge.

To put this offer of help in context let me say that I had contacted police press offices in cities with large inner city problems:

Glasgow, Edinburgh, Manchester, Bristol, London, Newcastle, Liverpool, but not one of them had a single piece of hot crumpled silver paper in its resident's pockets according to the respective public relations department of each area.

Photographer Aylott and I drove to Birmingham to meet a Detective Inspector whose press officer, herself a former reporter on a large regional newspaper, had arranged for us to meet him over lunch – at The Daily Star's expense, of course. Over the next three days it dawned on me that the DI was a man with a very healthy appetite, but one which, once sated, produced lengthy post prandial patter, that increased in newsworthiness with each bottle of fine wine. And so it was after the first lunch I had a notebook full of pertinent observation on the crack problem, of compelling statistics which would add perfectly to the gravitas of the piece and buckets of background on how the West Midlands Constabulary were going to combat the problem. When he learnt that Aylott and I needed pictures of crack being bought and sold on the streets of Handsworth, he was horrified.

'That means going to a Blues nightclub. They are all black faces in there – you start popping off cameras you'll get shot!' An under-cover cop had indeed been shot in a Blues just weeks before.

However it was suggested by the constabulary's PR girl that if we would like to meet our policeman friend over dinner, one of his undercover informants would be summoned to help us. That night as the hungry inspector finished his fourth course, ordered port with his coffee, and helped himself to Aylott's cigarettes he at last gave us the contact number.

Next morning Aylott and I drove out to a council estate in Handsworth and were met at the door of a state-owned flat by Darryl, a large, athletic Rasta with dreamy, unfocused eyes and an unnervingly distant manner. He seemed pre-occupied and puzzled as to our presence on his doorstep, and appeared to have forgotten the telephone conversation we'd had the night previously. But Aylott and I were ushered inside and soon found ourselves the audience at a lecture on racial misinformation. Apparently Bach had been black – our host showed us a book which 'proved' this – he was concerned, also, by the claim that Victoria Falls had been 'discovered' by David Livingstone. 'Did he think that no African before him had ever walked past them?'

'No,' Aylott and I both readily agreed, 'how could he have done, it's ridiculous' It took us some time to get Darryl back round to crack and his part in helping us acquire some.

But when he was ready and not before, he stood up and showed us to the door, on the way stuffing a sheathed 12 inch Bowie knife down the back of his trousers.

It had been decided that the 'Blues' were simply out of bounds to white blokes on the score. Even an armed Darryl would not take us into one. Instead in broad daylight he guided us around an area of Handsworth where drugs were being bought and sold on the street.

But there was no crack. Next he took us to a bar. Before entering he asked me: 'Do you play pool?'. Although I had spent many a long afternoon in the Snooker Club under the shadow of St Brides Church, the hours had been so mis-spent that I had never even picked up a cue, let alone learned how to play.

'Yes,' I said unwilling to jeopardise our transaction. So it was decided that we would play a harmless game of pool while Darryl worked out a strategy for us to witness a crack deal.

Once at the pool table Darryl immediately pulled out a £20 note and laid it on the baize surround – he invited me to do the same. He had not previously mentioned ours was to be a gambling game of pool. I broke and immediately sent a coloured ball into a pocket, I then looked for the next ball nearest a pocket – I sunk that too. Suddenly activity in the bar stopped.

People who had been rolling joints put them down. Others who had been supping sarsaparilla and vodka stared. I had pocketed a circled ball. Realising my error in time I then said: 'Oh bollocks I'm not playing you for cash you'll beat me anyway,' and proceeded to pot all the other balls in a fit of sham pique, I hoped was convincing. By aborting the game I hoped to cover my ignorance of it's rules.

Fortunately the occupants of the club accepted my tantrum as genuine and Darryl meanwhile had found us a crack dealer.

With our 'rocks' in the hand we left the place without more ado.
Now I needed an addict. Darryl knew of a chap who regularly
took crack-cocaine.

'Would he give us an interview?,' I asked. 'Yeah, if you give him
the drugs,' Darryl, the West Midlands police informer said.

The fellow was summoned and turned out to be a reporter's
dream. Intelligent and articulate he was able to describe in
graphic detail the effect of the drug, why he craved it, and the
reason it was so much more powerful than anything else on the
hop-head's menu.

Now we needed a picture. Our subject had been given one rock
for his interview. Would he pose-up for the rest? A guarantee of
not identifying him, secured the shoot and we found a suitable
graffiti-sprayed lavatory in a local park to add a little
atmosphere if not authenticity to the picture.

The following day, at lunchtime, of course, we met our gourmand
DI again to arrange interviews and pictures with his crack-
busting team.

Over the hors' d' ouvre I explained that we had been obliged to
acquire some crack for the purpose of the article and that I
would have to write about this. Would I be leaving myself open
to prosecution? The inspector shook his head as he fought to
masticate and after fighting down a gobbet of sirloin reassured
me that no police action would be taken.

With our story and picture complete Aylott and I returned to
London.

We were very pleased with ourselves, for crack was making
many headlines but had so far been an American problem. No
newspaper had found it being dealt in the U.K.

Just to add cream to our exclusive a U.S. top cop had recently
arrived in London to warn of the crack threat.

And then it all went wrong. Day one of our 'investigation'
showed the crack addict in full glory inhaling his stimulant.
Nobody had taken the trouble to obscure his face which was
down to the incompetence of the picture desk. I had a furious
Darryl on the phone. The police had identified his contact from
the photographs and he had been obliged to 'leave town' before

facing arrest. Images of the 12 inch Bowie knife floated before me like Macbeth's dagger.

Next on the phone was the hungry DI.

Was there any chance of changing the next part of the series?

'Why?'

'Because I may be forced to arrest you.'

'What?'

Our pay off line on day one, a 'come on' as it is known in the trade, for day two read: 'Tomorrow: We buy crack on the street'. This had fanned the flames of competition in one of Birmingham's evening newspapers – they had sent a reporter out on the streets where he'd also bought crack and then published his story to beat our part two.

Quite understandable but unfortunately this had obliged West Midlands Constabulary to consider prosecuting the local reporter.

What is good for the goose ....

Our well fed DI appeared to have lost his appetite for helping the Daily Star and now also wanted to know what I had done with the crack – I told him we'd flushed it down the lavatory.

However, our day two story showed how responsibly the West Midland Constabulary were facing up to the crack threat and the problem, like newspaper stories themselves, faded away.

As for Darryl's drug addict, with the promise of some cash to feed his habit he faded away too.

Working on one's own in a big city is preferable to the demands of working against the pack in a small village. But the latter was the case in Coggeshall, Essex, the village, where lived one Dr. Robert Jones whose pregnant wife Diane went missing in July 1983 after a boozy night out which had culminated in a domestic row.

Three months later her body was found in a Suffolk field. It had been a big story when she went missing, when her remains were found it became a huge story. Coggeshall is a small, intimate village, the sort of place where the local G.P. is admired and respected by everybody.

It was certainly the case with Jones and the villagers loathed us, the press, who turned up in droves.

One hotel – The White Hart – had actually put up a sign 'No Press'. Every national newspaper plus local news agencies and national T.V. had reporters there. Some had two, but we were lucky as there was one villager who was also an outsider. He had recently moved to Coggeshall and opened a wine-bar, The Musketeers, and because he was yet to be accepted by the Coggies, it was here that Fleet Street formed it's H.Q.

Mine host could not believe his luck, he had expected to make a slow start within the incestuous confines of this middle-class village. Instead he had moved to a boom town. He made a fortune over the weeks that Jones became first the target for the national dailies, then the Sundays, then T.V. and radio, then the women's magazines and finally a couple of true-crime style authors. The happy proprietor, who had to order more receipt books in his first week, had driven into Coggeshall in a Citreon 2CV and by the time we left was purring through the village in a Mercedes saloon.

Because of the hostility we all faced from the Coggies we gave up trying to outwit each other and instead formed a coalition. It was us and them and slowly but surely we began to feel as much antipathy for the scowling residents of this place as they did for us. Seeing us marching around their manicured gardens, past their listed buildings and down the streets of their conservation areas reminded them that murder most foul had happened in their midst. They were suffering from a kind of psychological Nimbyism. They wanted to quickly tidy away such a sordid matter, to move on. For me that mutual antipathy reached it's zenith in the hotel I was residing in. After a long, fruitless and frustrating day trying unsuccessfully to get folks to talk, I retired to the upstairs lounge of my hotel where I sat at a table supping beer.

Hardly had I a chance to read despairingly through a notebook full of asinine quotes when a barman said: 'I'm afraid you'll have to leave sir, this is a private party.'

'No don't worry I'm a resident,' I said pleasantly.

'No sir, that doesn't matter, this room is pre-booked, I'm afraid you'll have to leave!'

'O.K. then,' I said trying to muster an equanimity from an ebbing supply of rictus courtesy after a day spent in his stifling, unfriendly town, matched only by a hectoring, inflexible newsdesk, 'When I've finished this beer, which incidentally I was served in this room at that bar over there, in this hotel at which I am residing, I will leave.'

'I'm afraid I'm going to have to ask you to leave now sir.'

'I'm afraid I'm going to have to drink this first.'

Next thing a large man arrived in a suit. Now there's two of them badgering me. But when the burly figure put his hand on my shoulder and I knocked it off, I then discovered the bloody party was for the local masonic lodge, attended by the Chief Constable for Essex, who had just tried to man-handle me, and whose man-handling I had rebuffed! Remarkably somebody rang the police – more police – and the whole idiotic situation ended up with yours truly surrounded by cops in the foyer. Colin Bell of the Daily Express and Howard Foster of the Daily Mail acted as my sponsors. They did a good job as I remained in the hotel.

The next day all three of us had more of the same ill-luck trying to scratch something out of Coggeshall, so we thought we'd punish our newspapers for keeping us there for so long and so fruitlessly by dining at a 16th pile, Woodhall Manor, near Woodbridge at exorbitant expense.

Queen of this time-honoured tradition was Ginny Hill, now a successful TV producer, who travelled nowhere without her Good Food Guide when on an 'out of town story'. This she used to help her locate suitable accommodation: the nearest five star hotel to the story, however far away it was. Once when the news editor asked if anyone had heard from Ginny, a wag yelled: 'She's eating her way across Hampshire as we speak.'

The day after our dinner at Woodhall Manor we went on an excursion to charming Aldeburgh for beers, then on to Orford for a seafood lunch. By now the Coggeshall doorstep had become a loathsome and tedious task.

Then they took the doctor's front gate away. For the police to lift off and remove a five-barred farm gate must have meant something so back we went into seething Coggeshall – making the rounds of calls yet again. Foster started making headway.

He had at last managed to lure out an acquaintance of Diane Jones to the Musketeers.

Foster had a masterful touch on the doorstop. Articulate, and plausible with a quiet delivery, which obliged the interviewee to stick his head further and further out to hear what he was saying. So far out in fact that a hidden snapper could benefit or one of Foster's Church brogues could act as a door stop.

Foster quietly reassured the potential interviewee and was proffering a second glass of wine down him when Bell burst in. 'Fucking hell!,' he said 'these fucking Coggies give me the shits, want a drink Howard?'

It wasn't Bell's fault – all week we had secured no more than a frosty glance. He was not to know the man getting up and leaving Foster's table was a potential story, and Foster took it very philosophically.

The police were delighted we were giving Jones and his neighbourhood a hard time, but after a week of Coggeshall and very few page leads I was summoned back to Fleet Street. The pack had momentarily been called off. This was before accountants ran newspapers but even so newsdesks had budgets to meet and the paltry page leads coming in from Essex were not justifying the overnights, lunches and dinners.

But Dr Robert Jones was a cursed story, for me at least. In October 1985 I was at the Old Bailey engaged on the background of Nicholas Boyce who was convicted of manslaughter after strangling then butchering his wife Christobel – one of Lord Lucan's child minders.

During my enquiries I came across a detective who told me how they had taken a call from a man who had listened to reports of Diane Jones' body being found and had recalled seeing a figure dump a carpet in the same area six months before.

He had been outraged at what he thought was a litter lout and had made a note of the car's registration. He had left the note behind a clock on his mantlepiece and forgotten all about it until the news report.

Then he tried unsuccessfully to find it, even questioning his cleaner to no avail. Officers then put the man under hypnosis, and he recalled something close to the registration number of

Jones' car. It meant nothing as prosecution evidence and the fellow could have noted the registration at any time, but was a fascinating story. Unfortunately not only was I listening to it, so, too, was The Sun's reporter.

It was a Friday and we both agreed to sit on the story until we had time to make further enquiries the following week. The Sun published the following day leaving me scooped and feeling foolish.

It was always much easier to go out on a story with a preconception: preferably the preconception of the newsdesk. This is known as a 'briefing'. Basically it is a headline already written in the news editor's mind which you are obliged to go out and 'stand up'. One of my early tasks in this field was 'Mugger's Mile'. That was the headline dreamed up by the then news editor Phil Mellor, famed schedule-line writer, who had 'come over' from the Daily Mirror. Clapham, a district of South London had a street which seemed to fit the bill – it was very long and ran through an area of high unemployment. At first we were going to

look at it over the course of a Saturday night. When that only produced one or two robberies we extended the period to a weekend. When that, too, failed to produce the requisite number of crimes, it was extended for the week. This was going to have to be the street because the Daily Star had 'flown on it' – taken an aerial shot. In the end once we included some house break-ins in adjacent streets we eventually had enough material to run our 'Muggers Mile' spread.

The article touched a chord and many readers wrote in, one of them offering this doggerel:

The Mugger

The mugger he was lurking
Lurking in the night
Amongst the seedy alleys
In the places not lit bright
For a victim he was waiting

Waiting with his knife
For the foulest way of earning
Was his chosen life
He saw the policeman walking
Walking down the street
He oozed into the blackness
Like a snake down its retreat
His evil mind was fuming
Fuming at that tread so slow
For two old age people scurried
In the safety of the tall shadow
He slipped away still cursing
Cursing that uniform blue
It's no place for the likes of a rat like him
Near a man with a job to do
So if you go out strolling
Strolling where lights aren't bright
Take care that you're not lurked upon
By a mugger in the night

Another reader did not beat about the bush:

'This letter I am writing to you is, I know, a waste of time, talking is no good, action must be taken, now I am going to tell you the answer and believe me it is the only deterrent: birch and cat-of-nine-tails and whip them hard, this will cure the bastards.....I am not a man of words but I know human nature.'

Covering stories at the Old Bailey meant that the pack gathered in the bowels of the Central Criminal Court to meet up with the agency reporters who worked there full time: St. George, Joe Wood and his son Tim and two Press Association reporters, Sue Clough and Pat Clarke. They would provide national hacks with a verbatim account of the trial to date, which was useful for briefing yourself on the case but no good as background, as most of it had already appeared in newspapers as the case unfolded. The reporter's job was to dip in and out of court mainly to talk to the police officers in the case or identify witnesses and to try and second guess who the people were in the press gallery. Among them would be relatives, loved ones and enemies. It was they who held potential stories and photographs for background. The late Jimmy Lewthwaite of the Sun had developed a healthy loathing of life in the new Murdoch headquarters at 'Fortress Wapping' and had therefore convinced his newsdesk it was worth the newspaper's while having him permanently stationed at the Old Bailey. So he was usually one step ahead of the rest of us when it came to background. That in turn required lunching with Lewthwaite to get a steer on what he might have, which was fine as he was excellent company, a good reporter and a generous sharer-out of 'lines'. He in turn relied on Jimmy McCleod of the Evening Standard who had a perfect shorthand note and who covered the story up to early afternoon – after that it was too late for the Standard's deadline. This meant we could lunch in safety and McCleod who was an old hand, would always help you out with a 'fill' or account of the proceedings you might have missed – but who only gave you that fill if you were suitably impressed by his dramatically delivered analysis of the morning's hearing and with the significance for the morning newspapers, ie ours, which he bestowed upon what he was about to impart.

Covering the background might take the reporter away from the court for a day or two, but once the jury are out to consider their verdict the pack get their heads together. As the time ticks away the tension grows because the background has been written anticipating a guilty verdict. If the jury returns a 'not guilty' verdict then the reporter's work is in vain – the background has to be scrapped entirely or hastily re-written. In some cases backgrounds are prepared which can run once the first few lines have been adjusted for the verdict, thus:-

'Sick pervert John Smith who murdered children in cold blood, having lured them to his torture chamber with sweets and comics,' on a 'not guilty' verdict becomes:-

'Innocent father of three John Smith, walked free from a child murder case yesterday and vowed to continue his work with underprivileged kids.'

Newspaper sales at such times are, like the defendent's fate, in the hands of twelve good men and true.

Knocking about the Old Bailey is a good way of making police contacts. They are at the end of their hunt. The quarry is in the dock and they are, on the whole, in an expansive mood. Months of leg work has left them ready over a few glasses of beer, to talk about the inside story of the case. They are, some of them anyway, only human after all and want to share their insights like anyone else.

Sometimes, though illegal, they seek payment. Mostly they are happy it's a curry and pint of beer, if fact several pints of lager, all rounds on the hack. I once had the great fortune to come across a Customs officer who was part of the investigation branch and who saw the job as a great game. He loved conspiratorial meetings over expensive lunches and had a fascination with the press. In his front-line fight against drugs he gave me some great stories. One - that Colombian drug barons were using submarines to export cocaine out of the South America, literally under the noses of the US DEA cutters - was too fantastic for even the Daily Star, who refused to run it. Later on the story, like the subs, surfaced anyway in another journal. His first tip was of a raid by Scotland Yard and Customs & Excise officers on central pubs and clubs in NW London, to seize gaming machines whose owners were not paying VAT. Of more interest to our Fenian-hating editor was that profits from the fruit machines, all in 'Irish' pubs, were believed to be going to the IRA. Because of his information we had photographers in place at the time officers came out carrying the seized machines and the following day the picture and story were splashed on the front page: 'IRA' Pub Racket Busted, Cops swoop on 'terror' bandits, but to cover my contact I referred to him throughout as being 'police sources'. My source hinted that payment to him to cover his 'expenses' would help him work towards a future story. The newsdesk sanctioned these expenses which were paid to his mother.

Following the acquittal of jeweller John Palmer of fencing gold bullion from Britain's then biggest robbery, £26 million from Brinks-Mat, in 1987, it became clear that an attempt had been made to 'nobble' the Old Bailey jury. It was a sensational story and one which was unwittingly aped by a reporter some years later. I was then working as the Daily Star's 'area man' covering East Anglia and Kent and Sussex and Cambridge and Huntingdon – in fact every time I checked in with the newsdesk I got another county to cover.

As a result I was obliged to use other agencies and freelance reporters to cover parts of my patch, or when a story moved off my patch like the prosecution for the Rettendon slayings, for instance, which was heard at the Old Bailey. It was close to Christmas 1995 and I was watching my youngest daughter's school Nativity play when my pager started bleeping. Three men had been found shot dead in a Range Rover down a snow-covered farm track in Rettendon, Essex.

The gangland shootings of drug dealers Patrick Tate, Tony Tucker and Craig Rolfe eventually led to the arrest of Jack Whomes and Mick Steele. Their Old Bailey trial was long-winded and as the court was no longer in my 'patch' I sent a keen young reporter along to cover the day-to-day events. Steve Klein had Essex stamped all over him.

Dyed blonde highlights, a French crop, big flashy car, designer clothes and a winsome braggadocio. Klein continually told the Sun, for whom he also worked, and myself how he had lots of 'dodgy' mates in the underworld. He had also sold his indispensability to one of the London television companies, warning them that to send one of their 'townie' reporters into the villainous jungles of Essex would prove fruitless. And indeed he did make successful inroads with several of the murdered hoods' relatives, from whom he secured 'collects'. After the arrests of the two men eventually convicted, Klein also proved as good as his word and used his pushy charm to great effect with their families. But that was his undoing for as Klein's confidence grew he treated the mother and other relatives of defendant Jack Whomes like his own family.

During the trial Klein was standing on St.Paul's Underground station with the pair at the end of the day's hearing when he noticed an attractive member of the jury, who were hidden from view of the public gallery. Klein who also fancied himself as a ladies' man, proceeded to point her out to the pair. There was nothing sinister in it – just Klein behaving in his normal 'I'm a tasty geezer, all the girls like me' manner. But I was horrified when I found out, especially having covered the jury nobbling story of Palmer all those years previously.

Klein was arrested and held for 22 hours at Snow Hill police station. He was told he faced charges of perverting the course of justice and intimidating a witness and could do 14 years in jail. With him was Linda Christie, another young reporter and aspirant-crime-book author from the Basildon Evening Echo, who had put her faith in Klein's bravado. As part of the Palmer legacy Scotland Yard had formed a Jury Protection Squad and they claimed Klein had intended to push the jurer on to the railtrack! Fortunately such ludicrous claims were seen for the nonsense they were as Christie and Klein, obviously interviewed separately, gave innocent and complementary stories. They were let off on police bail.

A month before the Rettendon shootings, as the gangland slayings were dubbed locally, the parents of a girl who died from Ecstasy, Leah Betts, decided to turn their daughter's fate into a nationwide anti-drugs campaign by releasing a dramatic picture of the 18 year old on a life support machine. The picture became a poster with the coarse colloquial phrase for realising one's desires as the sole legend under the photo: 'Sorted' It became therefore a national story and when the trio of drug dealers were found, shot dead only a few miles from Leah's home, The Sun linked the dead gangsters to Leah, saying they had supplied her Ecstasy. It was an obvious and brilliant stroke and I was sick I hadn't thought of such a flyer myself.

Next day I spent most of a valuable interview with the detective leading the murder hunt, in getting him to knock down the Leah Betts link. I knew he would knock it down, the last thing he wanted was to give any justification or sympathy to the men who shot Tate, Tucker and Rolf and he wanted them, the killers, to be fingered not supported. So of course he knocked it down but what did his categorical denial mean a day after The Sun's masterful news management? Not a lot!

It's not an easy task to get one over The Sun and therefore sweet triumph when the 'Current Bun' cannot say of itself 'well done my Sun'.

After Michael Stone was arrested and charged with the murders of Josie Russell's mother and sister and the attempted murder of Josie herself, in July 1997, the pack descended on Chatham Magistrates Court to witness Stone's first appearance in the dock, and also to start the clean up on background. The Sun had it's usual team of three reporters against the Star's one. But by a stroke of luck I bumped into Stone's old girlfriend, Rachel Marcroft, who needed money for cigarettes, which I duly gave her. I then took her to a local pub where after an hour and a further tug of £40 I got a good interview describing Stone's unconventional foreplay, namely how he liked to strangle his sex partner, to within minutes of expiry, before interrupting his coitus. A further tug of £20 sent her looking for pictures of the heroin/methodone ingesting lothario but to no avail. Fortunately I had already alerted Frank Barrett the Star's photographer, to take a picture on a telephoto lens and so we had a background in the bag.

Of course, once she realised newspapers would pay serious money for her story she contacted The Sun and they got almost as good a story as I did but it was rumoured on Fleet Street that The Sun had coughed up £20,000 for it whereas the Star had to find £60 to reimburse my morning's work: 'My Hell with Josie Fiend, by his lover' was the splash the day after Stone was jailed for life.

The Russell murders were a gruesome case. The sheer grisliness of the attack was somehow made more nightmarish by happening in a part of Kent which until then had been considered an Arcadia. Down into this rural idyll came young Tom Keenan, 16-year-old son of a Catholic Boy's School headmaster, Frank, OBE, who had sought out work experience for the lad who wanted to be a journalist.

Tom's mother, Tina, a God-fearing woman looked a little bewildered when I rang to hurry Tom up on the morning of the crime, and it was only upon reflection I understood why.

'Tell Tom to get his skates on, we've got a bloody good murder on in Kent,' I'd said as I picked him up that day. And young Tom rose to the challenge slotting into the reporter's life with gusto. He got on well with all the other hacks, especially Bob McGowan of the Daily Express. McGowan and I traced an eye-witness of the man who turned out to be Stone, to his home. He gave us what sketchy details he had but did not want to give us his full name. Young Tom stood on the doorstep with us and when the interview was over he said: 'His name was Trevor.' 'How do you know that?' demanded McGowan and I. 'He had it tattooed on his arm,' said Tom. That night young Tom's rite of passage continued. He got roaring drunk with us in the pub, recounting his day's sleuthing seemed to give him a thirst beyond his years. He also stayed with a local photographer, Phil Houghton, whose house in Faversham was only 30 minutes from the murder scene. Houghton introduced the lad to a Reader's Wives blue video, before he turned in that night.

When I dropped him back to his parents the following evening his initiation was complete. 'Dad, I want to be a reporter'. Fortunately he came to his senses and went to Reading University instead and is now a school teacher.

In 1987 it was the Daily Star's turn to appear in court charged with defaming the character of Lord Jeffrey Archer, former Deputy Chairman of the Conservative Party. The Star had been snared by it's own 'Sunday for Monday' desperation. Sundays are always quiet news days and also the days when the garish and now folded News of the World,People and Sunday Mirror arrive to titillate and excite the hungover populace with scantily clad women, naughty goings on and prurient investigations. Try following that for Monday. On this particular Sunday the now defunct 'screws', News of the Screws, as the paper was affectionately known among the press pack, had a story about Archer paying a prostitute, Monica Coughlan, as an act of benevolence. A tipster had spotted Archer with Coughlan and called the press, she was then taped telephoning Archer to say she was with him.

Tantalisingly they never actually stated he had met her. So a week later the Star did, having sent two hacks out trying to find hookers Archer may have known. Archer sued and once the libel trial started, every crumb of potential evidence was sought out. During a night shift I was ordered to accompany Deputy Editor, Nigel Blundell, to Luton. We were driven there at high speed by freelance photographer Ian Cutler in his Range Rover. The job was top secret and only when we arrived did I discover the purpose of our journey.

A reader had been on holiday in the Mediterranean and claimed to have taken photographs of Archer on the beach with a semi-naked group of women. Quite what this was supposed to have added to the Daily Star's case I never discovered, but on seeing the picture I knew immediately it was not Archer. The potential doppleganger was indeed with some attractive women but that was because he was younger, better looking and more hirsute than the baggy-faced peer.

Blundell, understandably, did not want to hear this, however, and took the picture anyway for further examination. Sadly it did not prevent the Daily Star being found guilty of libelling the slimy Archer and being faced with £1.3 million in costs and £500,000 in damages.

Archer's solicitor, Lord Mischon, let The Daily Star's legal team – Lovell, White & King – dubbed Lilly White and Clean by Blundell –know that Archer would settle out of court for £16,000 and an apology, but Lloyd Turner, the editor, had the bit between his teeth and decided to fight on. It was an expensive mistake.

Poor old Turner had to be held up by Blundell and Mertens after the verdict. Back at the office Lord Stevens was waiting with the champagne to celebrate winning the case. 'We have done our best we might as well drink it anyway,' he said. But for once not even a good drink could revive the tabloid spirits. Blundell was ordered by Turner to go through a transcript of the trial, which was covered by a trusted hack Allan Hall, who by then was chief reporter, and look for anomalies – to find a loophole and later when the News of the World had to fight their own case against Archer the transcript was handed to them. After Turner was fired he decided to write his own account of what happened in his autobiography and he came to Blundell for the transcript. That's when Blundell found out it had been left by the NOW executives in the Printer's Pie - Blundell had been on holiday at the time - for his collection. When he retrieved it he discovered the pages had partly rotted away with the two forgotten trout at the bottom of the supermarket bag it had been delivered in. Many believe Turner went to an early grave because of his High Court defeat.

In July 2001, 14 years after the High Court defeat, Archer was found guilty of perjury and perverting the course of justice at the 1987 trial and sentenced to four years' jail.

The Daily Star preferred 'proper' criminals and at one time started a debate to air the unfairly extended imprisonment of Reggie Kray, notorious twin brother of Ronnie. It was said Hitchen wanted to groom Reggie to get hold of useful underworld contacts. The campaign proved fruitless however and the only time Reggie saw the outside world again was to attend the funerals of his mother Violet and that of Ronnie's. I covered the latter and there was more scar tissue than Kleenex along the Bethnal Green Road the day London's East End turned out to 'pay their last respects' or gawp in macabre curiosity depending on your view, when he was buried. I had kept a letter given me all those years before by Canon Richard Hetherington when I was working on the Ealing Gazette. It was from Ronnie and interestingly was his first confession of being a villain. In it he pleads with Hetherington to try and do something to help Reggie get a softer prison or one nearer their mother's East End home: 'Father, I hope Reg can go to Portsmouth if and when I go to Broadmoor Hospital, as I am the one who was the BAD one out of the two of us and I want to see Reg, get a chance in life. 'Father would you phone the prison, here is the number, it would make me very happy if you would .....' the sinister missive ended. We splashed the story of Ron's confession. His efforts to pull strings on behalf of his brother from within his cell proved fruitless. Reg was only released so that he could die of cancer in hospital five years later.

All Fleet Street watched the pall bearers carry Ronnie's coffin from the horse-drawn hearse. They included Charlie Kray, Freddie Foreman, Johnny Nash and Teddy Dennis, each one representing a 'gangland' area of London: North, South, East and West.

The old gangsters then surrounded the coffin for a 'minute's silence'.

In 'a message from Reg.' During the Kray order of service he wrote:- 'My brother Ron is now free and at peace. Ron had great humour. A vicious temper, was kind and generous. He did it all his way, but above all he was a man, that's how I will always remember my Twin brother Ron. God bless – Reg Kray.'

During the funeral John Burns of the Daily Express recounted a story told him by John Jones, another Express hand, about how Jones had gone to the Grave Maurice pub in the Mile End Road back in the early 60s to talk to an informant about a fixed boxing match.

Apparently the challenger had been paid to lose the fight. The problem was, as Jones learnt, so had the defender of the title. Throwing his head back in mirth at the revelation, Jones knocked into somebody and spilt their drink. The pub went silent. Jones turned and apologised to a bulky well-dressed man. But the pub remained silent. Jones tried to continue his interview but nobody spoke, he turned back to the well-dressed man apologised again and offered to buy him a drink.

The swollen-faced man whose black eyes glittered menacingly behind semi-rimmed spectacles refused but asked Jones what HE was drinking. It was gin and tonic. The man in the Prince-of-Wales cheque suit then ordered Jones a triple gin but told the barman to hold the tonic. Next he 'persuaded' the hapless reporter to down it in one. After three such drinks Jones was reduced to throwing up in the gutter. That's when he found out he was drinking with Ronald Kray.

Another yarn told me by a former Smithfield meat market porter had the twins as young lads on holiday at a caravan site in Allhallows near Rochester in Kent. Here the pair practiced their newly discovered boxing acumen by trying to knock out a tethered horse. An arresting photograph of a murdered underworld figure, Patrick Onione had me on an unenviable doorstep in November 1982.

"Paddy Onions' as he was known was shot in the back of the head in London's Tower Bridge Road and a snapper got a picture of his corpse before the cops arrived. The rumours were that it was a gangland slaying: a revenge attack for the stabbing to death of one Peter Hennessey at a charity boxing match in Kensington's Royal Garden Hotel. Photographer Stanley Meagher and I were sent to Onione's family home in Blackheath, where the front door was opened by a red-eyed fellow we took to be his son.

'I' m very sorry to trouble you at this time,' I stuttered, to the poor fellow who appeared to appreciate the respectful approach, 'er, was it a vendetta?' It was then we discovered he was not alone. Two fellows who resembled Conan the Barbarian and his Siamese twin came through the doorway. One of them had a head like a huge Malteser chocolate: not a hair blemished his shining tanned dome.

He threatened to use my body as an outside lavatory having first of all removed my own head. Whether this was confirmation or not was impossible to say.

When Meagher checked in with the picture desk he was told by Sutherland: 'That's the picture…Durham getting beaten up.' But I didn't hang around to ask the question again.

During a lacklustre 'campaign' to help disabled people get wheelchair ramps at public buildings, Hitchen ordered me to sign up a crippled police officer to the cause. Traffic cop Philip Olds had been paralysed from the waist down by a gunman's bullet in a bungled London off licence raid in 1980. He had been awarded a Queen's Gallantry Medal and used a giant rubber ball to roll around on in a bid to keep his upper body fit.

He declined the chance to help the Daily Star with their campaign explaining that he had too many demands upon his time and that he was desperately trying to concentrate on re-building his life. When I reported back to Hitchen he said: 'Offer the cunt some money.' All tabloid men believe there is no-one who cannot be bought.

I went back to Olds and explained that although I knew he was very busy we would very much like to help him with his schedule by covering all his expenses…

'I am offended by your offer. I have already explained to you why I cannot help. Do not ring me again,' he said.

Olds' strength and integrity were impressive, but sadly not enough to save him. Six years after his life was ruined this good-looking young man was found dead in his home, an empty bottle of pills beside his corpse.

During the harvesting of Yorkshire Ripper background in 1981, Daily Star reporters had a successful yield by 'buying up' the brother of Peter Sutcliffe, the convicted slayer of 13 women. They then had the unenviable task of 'babysitting' Mick Sutcliffe, who was kept out of harm's way – and rival newspapermen's gaze - at a secret hotel location for many weeks until the trial was over. Sutcliffe was not used to such luxury and during his first meal in the hotel restaurant reduced the waitress to tears when she lost her footing and threw soup over his chest. She had tripped over his hobnail boots which, following some atavistic northern ritual, he had removed before supper and left neatly placed beside the table. Fresh soup was proffered along with an extra bread roll which Sutcliffe saved until the coffee arrived. He then made a sandwich of it using his After Eight mints as the filling.

8. FOREIGNS

'Foreigns' confer prestige on the reporter. The hack who is sent away on a 'foreign' is more important than the hack who is not: the number of boxed, hotel room, shower caps in a reporter's overnight bag is a measure of his status! Foreigns can occasionally be a perk vis-a-vis the junkets put up by holiday companies, and are handedout for good work done. But mostly hacks go foreign when the story goes foreign.

To that end the cunning hack will push the desk into the commitment of air tickets. He might say he understands The Sun are 'sending' to Thailand to investigate the Bangkok end of a sex crime currently running at the Old Bailey. In most cases, however, the story will be overseas in toto and the desk will send whoever is flavour of the month. Not only does that mean an exotic trip for the hack, he has the opportunity for running up an equally exotic expense bill and is away from the office and clocking up time off in lieu: a couple of overnights - nights spent away from home - are rewarded with a 'day owing' to say nothing of weekends.

In this manner, with the seven weeks holiday allowance to take into account, plus the month-long sabbatical I had accrued after five years employment, there was one year -1985 - I worked for only six months – legitimately!

Another part of the reporter's foreign 'fieldcraft', explained to me by 'old hands' was to get as big an advance as possible, and change a minimal part of it at a bureau giving a poor exchange rate for the currency required. If Thomas Cook were selling Pesetas a 220 for the pound, the hack would change a small part of it, keeping the receipt of purchase, then change the bulk of the advance in Madrid where the rate might be 250 for the pound. The second receipt, as an example of the rate, might not always find itself attached to the eventual expense account presented to the office.

By its very nature, news meant that the hack never knew when the call would come to defend democracy overseas, and so he kept an 'overnight bag' in the boot of his car and a current passport in his suit pocket.

Some of the more enterprising hacks, seeing the way the wind was blowing - say in a fledgling war - would start applying for the necessary visas long before their newspaper had considered sending anybody.

When the time came for 'our boys' to be involved, the newsdesk would be racing to get reporters accredited to various fighting units, or just to the country in question. A hack who had prudently got himself 'visa'd up', a process which can take weeks, was going to be first in line for the coveted foreign. You don't need a visa for Iceland as I discovered one night in 1986 when the phone rang in the 'office' pub, The Old Bell.

'It's for you Dick – the Desk!,' yelled Paddy the landlord over the hubbub of hacks swapping notes.

'Have you got your passport?' said the duty nightdesk editor, Gordon Gregor.

'Of course'

'Go to Heathrow, the tickets are waiting.'

'What's on?.'

'The Gorbachev-Reagan summit.'

'Very funny.'

'I'm not joking, Blundell's on the rampage and has bollocked us for not sending .... he's had a good lunch.'

Nigel Blundell, as deputy editor, had joint 'ownership' of the John Bull printing set with Brian Hitchen.

Blundell, or Dingly Dell as he was affectionately known, was in fact only away with the fairies after lunch. A hugely talented tabloid man who had been a maverick influence over on The Sun and the Daily Mirror, he was the production expert upon whom Hitchen, an editorial man, relied. Blundell, Hitchen would incantate, 'can do no wrong.'

When Hitchen had brought his deputy on board, after the Sullivan debacle, he had promised him a huge salary, Rolls Royce, a two-year contract and it was all in writing.

When neither the salary nor the car materialised Blundell said: 'This contract isn't worth the paper it's printed on.'

'I know,' said Hitchen, 'I forged it.'

Over this particular lunch, Blundell had been out with top executives from other Fleet Street titles who were boasting about 'sending' to Reykjavik. He was a deputy editor, he, too, would send.

Gregor, that rare thing, an executive who was the 'reporter's friend' used a messenger to send me over sheafs of torn-off Reuter copy on the events running up to the summit. As I sat on the plane leafing through acres of print on multiple-independent, re-entry, vehicles, anti-ballistic missile systems and the high tech of playing chess with pilotless nuclear warheads I turned despairingly to Star photographer Ken Lennox. 'I don't know how the fuck I'm going to get THIS in The Daily Star.'

'Don't worry,' said Lennox unzipping his camera bag, 'Look at these' he pulled out two rubber masks one of Gorbachev the other of Reagan.

Saved by a stunt.

At the Hotel Borg in Rekjavik we arrived just before the Icelandic authorities threw up a security cordon. Inside we soon discovered a conference room where the two leaders were to hold one of their meetings. They even had little US and USSR flags ready on the tables.

Lennox deftly set up his camera to work on automatic and we pulled on the masks. I played Gorbachev, Lennox, Reagan and we sat at opposing ends of a table and engaged in a mock arm-wrestling contest. Pop, went the remote flashgun.

Next morning I checked in with the daytime news desk. I started to explain what we'd got, but was cut short.

'Just come back, Blundell wants to know where you are.'

'Well, why don't you tell him?'

'We're working on it.'

Eighteen hours on, lunch was forgotten and Blundell, a well-built fellow, and as unpredictable as a dehydrated wildebeeste on a waterless Savannah, was irritated.

The Gorbachev name was to feature in foreign places the following year when I was among a hack pack in Cyprus after the Archbishop of Canterbury's envoy Terry Waite, who was seen in Fleet Street as a missionary seeking martyrdom, went missing in the Lebanon. Beirut, even East Beirut itself was considered too dangerous for Fleet Street's finest to base themselves while awaiting developments on the bearded egotist's fate.

Cyprus was the nearest place. So we holed up at a hotel in Larnaca and days, then weeks went by as we 'analysed' the various military stalking the streets of the war-torn Beirut via news-cuttings and correspondents with larger experience in the field: the BBC's Keith Graves – for example spent time explaining Shi'ite and Sunni, Hezbollah and Hamas, Jihad and Jumblatt to us. But after a while the tabloids tired of Middle Eastern roguery and then so did the broadsheets, leaving only radio and TV to cover daily events in the Lebanon. To make use of the time in Cyprus I got the hotel secretary to type out a letter from the

Daily Star to a Geordie who had joined the Palestine Liberation Organisation and was serving a prison sentence in a Nicosian jail for his part in the murder of three Israelies on a yacht. The prepared letter was left for me at reception and as I read it to check for errors Jon Hampshire of the Daily Mail read it over my shoulder and had the hotel staff draft his own version. As it turned out the killer from Sunderland did not want to see either of us. But now a game was on. At Larnaca airport a press room had been laid on for all the British national dailies. The airport was our 'doorstep' as anything happening in the Lebanon would start with air traffic of one kind or another in Cyprus. Hampshire's phone rang while he was not there and I answered it.

An Eastern Mediterranean was muttering an apology for postponing a meeting with the Mail hack. I said that was quite OK but could he tell me the address of the rendezvous again. I had 'forgotten' to make a note of it. The poor fellow's English was halting and he seemed relieved at the opportunity of spelling it out using the VHF radio operator's code, A: Alpha, B: Beta etc. so that I could make sure of the rendezvous. So credulous was Hampshire's informant that I was even able to glean from him the 'story' he was setting up! I explained that working for the Daily Mail and the Mail on Sunday I had so many different lines of enquiry on the go that I wanted to be sure of the story in order to assign the correct photographer.

"Reemember Jon, eet is the aunty of Gorbachev you want to meet"

Of course it was!

Detailing Frank Barrett the Star's Cyprus photographer on the case, we actually brought the story forward to that afternoon "To get the right light" and photographed and interviewed the new Soviet leader's aunty on her memories of the young Mikhail before the film was sent directly to London in the pouch of a colleague: another Fleet Street photographer who had been 'pulled out'. Exposed film is sacrosanct: no one ever breaks that particular code. That evening in the bar Hampshire was looking very smug and revealed his 'exclusive', thinking it was too late for us to match it.

Yet hacks can work with each other abroad as well as against each other. And so it was when a trip to the World War I battlefields became an assignment for reporters on both the Daily Star and the Daily Mirror. Allan Hall, Chris Boffey, Peter Welbourn and I – all from the Daily Star had been touring Flanders Fields with Murray Davies of the Daily Mirror, when Hall, a concientious reporter checked in with the newsdesk even though he was on holiday.

Could we immediately drive to Brussels they urgently asked? Missing estate agent Suzy Lamplugh had a mystery name in her contacts book, a Mr. Kipper, and for some reason a Mr. Kipper living somewhere in Belgium had become of interest to the Metropolitan Police. We immediately saw the benefits of scrapping our holiday to go back to work, namely that we could write off the travel and accommodation so far incurred by us to the company.

The office were delighted, they and the Mirror were going to have reporters on Kipper's doorstep before any of the opposition. All we had to do was await an address.

We chose a top Brussels restaurant and gorged until late evening when the address came: it was in Antwerp. Dressed in our trench-walking wellington boots and sheepskin coats we burst on to the doorstep of Mr. Kipper, spelt Kyper, and got a brief interview. Then we checked in to one of Antwerp's finest hotels and turned in.

Next day we split the job up. Hall and the others concentrated on getting 'talks' with the Antwerp police, Davies and I set off in Hall's company car for Knokke Heist on the Belgium coast, where a vehicle linked to Kyper had been found. En route Davies and I decided that Knokke Heist was a lot further away than it looked on the map. Everyone in Belgium speaks English so we decided to 'cover' our end of the story by telephone. We turned off the main highway to search for a suitable lunching station.

Comfortably settled at the bar we discovered we'd driven into Holland. Still it made no odds, their English was even better. We gathered the information required and after copious draughts of fish soup and even greater quantities of muscadet, we drove back to Brussels, delighted with the number of blank receipts

we'd gathered to share out with the others. That was until
Murray suddenly stared fixedly ahead.

'Shit.'

'What?'

'We can't use these bills.'

'Why not?'

'Wrong country!'

And try as we might later, with the Belgium cops, we could not
find a Dutch angle to justify use of said receipts.

On the way back to Brussels we got lost and made a detour
through Ghent. Eventually the car ran out of petrol on the
outskirts of the Belgian capital. I walked to a garage got some
gas and returned to the car. Unfortunately the container had a
neck which allowed me only to decant a small amount of the
petrol into the tank. But it was enough to get the car going.
Later, after we had all reunited and enjoyed a sumptuous supper,
Davies decided to provide some cabaret by pouring the left over
petrol down a drain and then attempted to light the sewer
cocktail with a dropped match. The trouble was he was doing so
while standing on the drain grill. Fortunately the matches failed
to work and we spotted him and tucked him up in bed.

Sometimes the call of duty requires a hack, while in foreign
parts, to forego the luxury of five star hotels and instead 'rough
it' to get the story. To this end I slept in the cab of a lorry
travelling through France and Italy while on a mission to expose
corrupt practices within the French highway police and Italian
border customs. The Daily Star had become the 'Truckers
Friend' in a bid to increase circulation and coverage of big unit
lorry races had invited a full mail bag of complaints about French
police blackmailing truckers who had infringed motorway
regulations, by taking goods off the back of their lorries. Almost
as many complaints had been received about Italian customs
using false and time-consuming bureaucratic demands to extort
'quick passage' payments: 'Highway Robbery' was the headline.
The spy-in-the-cab tachograph demanded that our first night's
stop was at Auxerre, France. If I was not to bed down in a
comfortable room I at least was going to dine in a top Burgundy
restaurant, and invited the driver to join me.

'No thanks mate,' he said.

'The Daily Star are paying,' I told him, 'You can have whatever you like!'

'No ta mate,' he said and to my horror unpacked a portable gas stove on which to prepare fried egg butties, 'I don't like that foreign muck.'

'Well at least let my bring you back some wine,' I rejoined, 'white or red?'

But the dutiful soul would not take a drink either and once across the French border and down in Como, where we spent three days loading and unloading, I still could not persuade him to dine out. So while I lay soaking in a bath in my hotel, happy in the knowledge that Italian fare was being prepared for my supper, my companion lay freezing in his cab with congealed egg yolk in his moustache. I eventually got him to leave his lorry, but only at a Les Routier truck stop where the excellent fare, thought still 'foreign', was eaten by other truckers.

On our way home across the English Channel my driver made up for his self-imposed xenophobic fast and he ate well in the ferry canteen. I carelessly forgot to mention on my expense sheet that I was paying for the driver's meal as well as my own and received this memo from accounts:

'The accounts department believes you are pregnant – in that when claiming dinner of 7 February (at 3.46 pm) you consumed fillet of cod, plus the chef's steak pie, plus a pudding, plus two teas, plus two bottles of water. Please explain…. In the meantime, I have deleted your claim from your expenses.'

Apart from being briefed to drink beer at the pub nearest the Australian Embassy in London on the day in 1983 a Perth-based yacht won the America's Cup thereby breaking an event held by the US since 1851, 'Fair Drinkum' as the Daily Star saw it, yachting was not high on the priority of Daily Star coverage, but the then editor, Lloyd Turner was an Australian. He ordered the news desk to get a case of Australian 'champagne' from El Vinos to toast his country's success. Bon viveur Brian Hitchen was appalled that anyone could believe Australia could produce champagne and glued a fresh lable made from Daily Star headed note paper on the bottles before they were passed round. It read: 'Kangaroo Piss'.

When yachting did once become high priority for the Daily Star, such coverage was motivated not by securing potential new readers, but by some nepotistic urge. Such was the case, in 1993, when I, being a longstanding 'weekend messer about of in boats' was told to go and interview Lord Wade in the House of Lords about the entry he was keen to promote in the Whitbread Round The World Race, Hitchen had already laid the groundwork with a letter to Wade which read:

'Dear Lord Wade,
Our mutual friend, Geoffrey Ampthill, spoke to me about your Dolphin project to finance a yacht to take part in the Whitbread Round The World Race and crewed by people who have overcome a physical handicap.
I am particularly interested in endeavours of this nature. Money is tight, to say the least, but I will be delighted if my newspaper could help you in any way to publicise what promises to be a tremendous adventure.
With this in mind I have asked one of my staff, Mr Dick Durham, to contact you.
Mr. Durham is an ocean racer and a lone yachtsman. He has written several books on sailing and the sea and I know that he will write a first class feature.
Please accept my very best wishes.
Yours sincerely,
Brian Hitchen, C.B.E'

On reading the letter I began to feel rather good about myself. I dug out a chart of the Thames Estuary and checked it to see if there were any oceans within its boundaries. Alas there were none. As somebody, who until then had never raced on any ocean nor sailed further single handed than a few creeks in Essex, I was relieved when I did eventually meet Wade at the Peers entrance of the Palace of Westminster, that he clearly knew little about the Seven Seas himself. Soon I was listening to his enthusiastic support for Dolphin & Youth, a boat crewed by those with a partial disability. Wade, I later discovered, was a mate of Lord Stevens, chairman of the Daily Express, Sunday Express and the Daily Star. The resulting piece secured me a five-day 'foreign' to Florida, where I met the boat during one of the race stopovers at Fort Lauderdale. I had to out-manouvre one of the Daily Star sports correspondents who had got himself down on the promoter's list for the trip. Kevin Francis remained on bacon in Manchester while I dined out on lobster every night, was showered with free gifts – leather deck-shoes, sailing shirts and shorts, and was feted with tours of Florida including a deep-sea shark fishing trip on which the correspondent for the Guardian, a paper noted for its worthy environmental coverage, hooked and landed a 200 lb. hammerhead. The five-day trip, which cost the sponsors thousands secured seven paragraphs in the Daily Star on the only theme possible to wedge yachting into the paper: 'Love On The Ocean Wave': Britain's Round the World yachtsman Matt Humphries has found love on the high seas...........'

Foreigns are one of the 'perks' no longer enjoyed once the reporter becomes an executive. That's not to say that editors never get trips, the travel department will see they are kept happy. But the day-to-day chances of visiting exotic parts is no longer part of the editor's diary. Brian Hitchen, the editor who presided over the Daily Star for its halcyon years was no exception. As a reporter on the Daily Mirror and National Enquirer he had travelled widely, and still yearned for the produce of foreign parts. My trip to New York dressed as Shakespeare was sanctioned, in part, by Hitchen's desire to purchase scarves from Bloomingdales for his wife, Nelli. I duly acted as his shopping proxy. It was not long before I had the chance to act as foreign purchaser for the Hitchen wardrobe again, this time in the Far East. Hacks exploited Hitchen's interest in anything military to get 'foreigns' and I was no exception. Tony Poe was a former CIA operative living in the jungle of Thailand, who had once paid his ethnic hill tribesman to cut ears from the heads of dead communists as proof of the 'body count' strategy employed by the US in Viet Nam. Poe was a man with a fearsome reputation earned in the backwoods of Laos. John Hayes, my old colleague from The Sunday Post had found his way out to Thailand, where he had been working on the Bangkok Post for many years. Through a friend, Al Dawson, who had been in Saigon with the Associated Press agency when that city fell to the Vietnamese Army, Hayes had met the late Tony Poe. He was said to have inspired the role of Marlon Brando, as Kurtz, in Apocalypse Now. Dawson was a friend of Poe's and Hayes was a friend of Dawson's and also of mine. A meeting with Tony Poe could be arranged. Hitchen was very keen and sanctioned the trip. The night before I was due to fly out I had a call at home from Hitchen. It is a rare event to get calls at home from the editor.

'Dick?'

'Yes?'

'It's Brian!' .... I knew it was, his rich authoratative and unnerving, slightly menacing voice was unmistakable.

'Dick you're going to Bangkok tomorrow. I wonder if you could do me a favour?'

I took down an order for an assortment of silk polka-dot ties, both straight and bow, and matching handkerchiefs. They had to come from Jim Thompson's emporium.

With this foreign I fell foul of newsdesk realpolitik, dictated by the Machiavelli brothers: Phil Mellor, news editor and his deputy Dave Mertens, who were furious I had secured such an exotic trip and were already moving to rubbish the story. So when I arrived in Bangkok and discovered that both a connecting flight and Dawson, who was to take me to meet Poe, would not be available for five days I knew they would take great delight in making as much mischief as possible. Mertens said: 'Oh yeah, Durham in Bangkok for a week waiting to start the story. I don't fucking believe it!'

"Well there's plenty of background to be getting on with" I said judiciously not mentioning the editor's shopping list, how they would have loved spreading that one around.

As it turned out, as always, there was some background work to do: calls to the American Embassy to get their perspective on Poe and also to discuss the possibilities of US servicemen still alive, living in Viet Nam. There was also 'Lucy's Tiger Den' a seedy bar where US oil workers, some of them former US marines, hung out drinking Mekong whisky and watching Hollywood movies on the Viet Nam war – Apocalypse Now was the favourite.

The more people I met in Bangkok the longer the list of anecdotes I got about Poe.

One thing they all had in common was a respect for this man and astonishment that he had agreed to see me: 'You are honoured,' 'You are privileged' were the phrases tripping off the tongues of those who knew of his legend. They included an Australian TV crew I ran into, among them some of the first western journalists to uncover the Khmer Rouge genocide in Cambodia. Even they were impressed I was to see Poe. And so his status grew in my mind, not unlike that of Kurt in Joseph Conrad's novella Heart of Darkness on which Apocalypse Now is loosely based. However, what they didn't know was that Dawson had sold me to Poe as a hack doing a story on MIA's (Missing In Action). Dawson, knowing that the repatriation of US servicemen's remains from Viet Nam was a subject close to Poe's heart, had correctly guessed that the great man would see me on that pretext. We then hoped Poe would open up on his own role in Laos and more specifically methods which made him a 'satanic killer' as one report in the Washington Post had described him.

On the way up to Udorn Thani where Poe lived, I asked Dawson the best procedure for interviewing, should I take notes, ask questions, or should I use a tape-recorder?

'Don't do any of that,' said Dawson, 'just listen.'

We met Poe at Udorn Thani airport. He had driven there in his incongruous canary yellow, custom built MG sports car. On the windscreen was a sticker which read: 'Jane Fonda Fucking Commie Bitch!'. Poe, then 62, a big man, who did indeed bear a passing resemblance to Brando, even his head was shaved, still wore combat boots. Quietly spoken and courteous he drove us to his home as my ears started burning. Poe had once kept a sack on the porch of his jungle house in Laos. Into it would be tossed the ears of Pathet Lao soldiers brought home by 'his boys' as he described the Hmong tribesmen who fought for him.

That afternoon we started drinking Mekong whisky, and continued drinking Mekong whisky through the night and most of the following day. I was glad of the binge, otherwise what other excuse would I have had to make repeated trips to the bathroom where I feverishly scribbled out my notes?

Not unnaturally Poe started off by discussing the politics of his war in Laos and his deep loathing of those who, he alleged had benefitted from it, including a Laotian general, Vang Pao, who, Poe claimed, had used US money set aside to mobilise, feed and clothe Hmong tribesmen to instead feather his own nest. Pao eventually fled Laos for the US where he settled in San Francisco. Fascinating stuff but none of it much good for Daily Star readers, and one Daily Star reader in particular, namely Brian Hitchen.

Poe wanted to know from me what I thought of the miner's strike in the UK. I had a lot of sympathy for them, it was just another nationalised industry the Tories wanted shot of and instead to support it with cheap foreign imports of coal. Less jobs, emasculated unions.

'Those bastard miners are holding the country to ransom,' I said meeting with a large jowly head and beady eye nodding in approval. I did not require a briefing on where Poe's political sympathies lay.

Dawson and Poe talked and we covered the MIA issue, Poe had received reports from Laotians living in Thai refugee camps on the border, and, suspiciously during my visit, was told that bearded US servicemen had been seen working a plough somewhere in North Vietnam. They were kept manacled in a hut and used as forced labour in the rice paddies. All good stuff, but I still hadn't got the personalised accounts of slaughter that Hitchen wanted to hear. He had got his silk ties coming but would not be too happy if I did not produce the story I said I'd get.

Eventually I think Poe got irritated that I HADN'T asked him about the things that had made him the legend, all passing reporters wanted to meet.

Throughout the haze of Dawson's cigarette smoke and the blur of Mekong whisky and the strange haze of an eastern dusk, my drowsiness was suddenly arrested by the phrase:

175

'That's when I started on the ear thing.' I was now 'all ears' myself and listened, gripped as Tony Poe at last told his own story.

He had indeed paid one US dollar per communist ear to his boy soldiers and collected them in a sack on his porch. His CIA bosses became disturbed by his unorthodox methods when Poe sent a report down to Vientien, the Laotian capital, complete with one ear stapled to it. Thus the legend of the operative who had gone 'native' and who was working to an oriental set of rules was born. Poe had become Kurtz. That was the received wisdom. But the reality was that Poe still worked with compassion and concern for his own troops. He simply spared his barbaric ways for the enemy. When, on inspecting his boys one day, he noticed one had an ear missing (the lad was hard pushed for cash and had had no success in killing communists), Poe took a different tack.

'That's when I decided on heads,' he told me.

Collecting heads had other uses too. In his Dakota, Poe had flown over Laotian villages he suspected of harbouring communists, he banked over the village square and allowed severed heads to roll from the open belly of the plane. He would alternate the heads occasionally with jam jars filled with primed grenades.

His own injuries were many, but the most obvious were the missing two middle digits of his right hand, blown off by a booby trap, leaving him with a giant hand that looked like a grotesque croissant.

There was only one person Poe was scared of, his wife, a Hmong princess, Sheng Ly, whom he had married to get even deeper 'in country' but who he shared a successful domestic life with. However, Poe's occasional sexual transgressions – another aspect of the South East Asian culture he had absorbed while 'going native' - caught up with him when she surprised him in flagrante and pulled a Derringer pistol on him.

I had my story. I needed a picture. Poe was not the sort of man to pose up for media shots, but by now Dawson explained I wanted one for my own album, of me with Poe and his wife. Poe duly obliged.

176

Back in London I wrote the story up, planning a news piece on the missing US soldiers and a follow up piece on Poe and his operation for the inside pages. Hitchen was off on the Sunday that I wrote it up and this allowed the Mellor faction to poo poo the story which eventually appeared as a one page piece under the moronic headline 'The Real Rambo', Hitchen was furious, he had to justify the expense of the trip and a single page was not going to do that. The only good thing was, much to my surprise, Poe loved the piece.

I had developed a taste for the Far East and though I knew little about sport and cared even less, I did enough research on the upcoming Seoul Olympics to discover that South Korea had a repressive democracy and the students of the capital were not averse to charging lines of riot police dressed like modern day Samurai Warriors wielding shields against Molotov cocktails. There was also the threat of terrorist action from the communist North Korea, a state not included in the events. I drafted a sufficiently lurid memo to the editor to secure my five week sojourn at the 1988 Olympics. I flew out of Heathrow with my sports reporter colleagues to cover news, and found myself sitting next to Kevin Francis, one of the Daily Star's Manchester-based sports hacks and a most respected 'operator'. My few pints of Welsh blood have left me with an atavistic feeling of great comfort when my feet are on the ground and consequent feeling of great loathing when they are not. Therefore before being hermetically sealed in the flying toothpaste tube, I had downed a few large gin and tonics at the airport, and swallowed 1/2 a valium. Suitably drugged into a state of courage I read with interest that day's Sun splash on 800m runner Tom McKean who they alleged had been seen with a prostitute in Glasgow. 'This is a great story,' I said to Francis, 'we should get a chat with him during the flight and be ready to file when we land.' Many of the British athletes were on the plane with us and the Sun had failed to get a reaction from McKean in their piece.

Francis seemed reluctant to get involved, sports reporters are loath to actually cover anything about the athletes which is negative, for fear of being ostracised by them later. It seems puzzling to me because in my experience the big name athletes don't talk to them anyway. The sports reporter is left, like the common hack and the encyclopaedia salesman, standing on the chilly doorstep of hard sell.

Anyway, I badgered Francis to at least identify McKean. He would only take such a risk, when he was happy he was not being observed, and waved in the direction of the gathered athletes, a gaggle of whom were standing at the back of the plane.

I approached them with my copy of The Sun and identified myself and asked to speak to McKean. A large, lean athletic fellow stepped forward and said:

'We don't want the fucking Daily Star asking us questions.'

'Are you on drugs?,' I asked.

The large man suddenly seemed to shrink. He'd gone from towering inferno to damp squib.

I made the most of his disappointment to explain quickly that this story was a matter of record and that McKean would be badgered throughout the games by hacks like me until he made a response. Surely it was better to give his side of the story now and have done with it?

The large chap then stepped aside and a slightly built man, also in a track suit, stepped forward and identified himself from the gaggle as being McKean. He said the story had caused him a lot of pain and that the first thing he was going to do in Japan, where the athletes were going to acclimatise themselves, was contact his wife and reassure her that it was not true. He went on in this conciliatory vein, as I took notes.

I sat down again with Francis and took great delight in telling him of my 'exclusive' but Francis seemed unmoved.

'That wasn't him,' he said.

'Wasn't who?'

'That wasn't McKean.'

From The Sun's photograph it was not possible to identify McKean, and as I have not the slightest interest in sport myself I had been reduced to asking the gaggle which one of them he was. They had put forward a swimmer to stand in for the elusive McKean. Who can blame them if they stitched me up?

Francis seemed anxious: 'You know who that big guy is?'

'No'

'That's Linford Christie, Britain's greatest runner!'

'Well he certainly runs away at the mouth,' I said.

Now I urged Francis to identify which of the athletes McKean was. I then returned. There ensued a chase around the plane. If Jumbos fly at 500 mph then I was making 510 mph through the air, trouble is McKean was a little faster than me and in the turbulence of the chase a First Class passenger's drink was spilt into her lap.

I never did get the interview, but when the plane landed the man I now knew to be Christie cornered me behind the bulkhead at the back of the plane where neither of us could be seen. Shaking me by the hand, he said: 'No hard feelings?'

There certainly were none. To me this was all part of the job, though I would have liked to have got that interview, but for the time being I was puzzled as to Christie's climbdown.

Wandering the ugly, concrete city of Seoul, I noticed a number of shops selling artificial limbs. This was a legacy of the Korean War. Because of the build up of fear over a fresh attack by North Korea, who considered themselves still at war with the US-backed South Korea, I made a few enquiries of these prosthetic workshops to see if they were making longer limbs for potential athlete victims. Unfortunately they weren't and a 'Sunday for Monday' bit the dust.

My billet in the 'Press Village' was several stories up in a tower block where I shared an open-plan apartment with Kevin Francis, Bill Elliott a sports writer and John Dawes, the chief sports photographer for the Daily Star.

Dawes, a hugely overweight, and perspiring man, the very antithesis of anything approaching physical jerkery was nevertheless one of the finest 'operators' to capture sportsmen on 35 mm film. He was also a veritable jackdaw of freebies. He collected, stored and hoarded all the paraphernalia showered upon journalists at such events. But he made the mistake of also hoarding the tea, coffee and powdered milk which had been left for the communal usage of the Daily Star team. I had assumed we had to purchase our own and asked the charming Korean woman who came in daily to clean, where I could buy the necessary items. She explained that we had already been allocated tea and coffee.

It was then that Elliott and Francis, who knew Dawes better that I, speculated on the refreshments' whereabouts and the fact that Dawes, unlike the rest of us, always kept his bedroom under lock and key. We persuaded the cleaner to unlock his room. It was an Aladdin's Cave of T-shirts, sweat-shirts, shorts, trainers, badges, belts, press packs, Olympiad pins and there on his table was our unopened coffee, tea and powdered milk. To teach Dawes a lesson we re-stored all his material wealth around our own rooms, put back the tea and coffee into the kitchen and gave the powdered milk, which none of us enjoyed, to the cleaner who was over the moon with such a 'luxury'.

After Dawes had blown a gasket we gave him his goods back. He had doubles and trebles of each freebie, and later as we came to depart and the usual mad scramble was on to 'upgrade' into business or first class I incurred Dawes' displeasure once more by asking if he was 'upgrading' to freight.

Most evenings we gathered in the Press bar to discuss the day's events before seeking out a good restaurant, not an easy task in Korea, where the national delicacy is rotting cabbage disinterred from a six-week burial.

In the bar at nights was the then British Prime Minister's daughter, Carol Thatcher, a freelance journalist and general good egg. She was one of us, we argued, and therefore all agreed to ignore the fact that she kept a vodka bottle zipped up in her handbag with the neck just proud of the zip. She thus provided her own spirit for the mixers she bought at the bar. But there is always one hack more ambitious than the rest and the Daily Express's Paul Thompson broke the agreement and alerted his paper's diary to the story. It landed poor Carol in a lot of hot water poured from the boiling kettle of Mrs. Margaret Thatcher, who could have ignored the Daily Express diary story, but who could not ignore the fact that many Australian newspapers picked it up and ran it big.

One morning Evening Standard hack Colin Adamson and I got access to the local university and witnessed petrol bombs being made by militant students: 'I saw the loony Lefties filling hundreds of rice-wine and Coke bottles with petrol poured from teapots…,' I later wrote. We interviewed several who started getting a bit edgy around us. Outside Adamson exclaimed: 'Christ, no wonder they didn't trust us, what are you wearing that for?'

I had completely overlooked the fact that I was wearing an old T-shirt I'd been given by one of the Viet Nam vets in Bangkok, depicting a pair of crossed M15 rifles it also carried the slogan 'Kill Communists'.

I had been filing stories surrounding the games quite happily and the newsdesk seemed content so I was completely taken unawares when the phone rang at my Press Village bedside and I heard the stentorian voice, that confident diction laced with menace, which I recognised at once as being Brian Hitchen's.

'I've had a letter, Dick, from some cunt at the British Olympic Committee. They want to take your accreditation away. What's been going on?'

I told him what had happened on the plane out.

'You're doing a great job Dick, keep up the good work. I'll tell this bloke to fuck off.'

You never knew with Hitchen what he was thinking. You could certainly never tell from what he said. So with mixed feelings I carried on, but my accreditation stood.

About a fortnight or so into the games Christie failed a drugs test. Now suddenly I realised the impact of my words. Chris Boffey, who had by now moved to the Today newspaper said: 'File the story – it's a belter'

'What story?' I asked.

'How you challenged him on the plane, It's a world exclusive.'

Given the full context of the 'challenge' I decided against such action. In any case a day or so later the Olympic Medical Commission confirmed Christie's claim he had been drinking ginseng: 'Christie drugs storm in a teacup,' as the Daily Star ran the story.

The big event being the 100 mts sprint, many hacks were betting against the Canadian Ben Johnson. The Yank Carl Lewis was the favourite to win but in my lack of interest I had a bet with John Jackson of the Daily Mirror that Johnson would beat Lewis.

Jackson affected an avuncular stance among the hacks. He had covered every Olympics since the year dot and took great delight in recounting them, whether the recipient did or not. He knew I knew nothing about sport and was as sick as a parrot when Johnson sensationally 'won' the race and created a new world record.

However, when it was established that Johnson had also been taking drugs, although something a little stronger than herbal tea, he was disqualified. Jackson came to get his money back. I asked him, if with all his sporting experience, he honestly could say that he would go to a bookmakers and expect to get a refund. Johnson had won the race upon which we had bet. The wager did not include a caveat on how he won it. Jackson was not as sporting about his loss as the great names forever issuing from his lips. But I refused to budge.

As soon as the closing ceremony had closed, nay before, the whole press corps excluding the Guardian and Observer, whose sanctimonius hacks love to write about their colleagues, gathered for the most important duty of the foreign, especially one which had gone on for a month: collating our expenses. The endless nights of drinking with tedious mini-sports officials, the meals, the lunches, dinners, now all had to be accounted for, and needless to say in the scramble to get stories, remembering to get a receipt for each and every expenditure, was often overlooked. In Seoul this was not a problem for one of our number had got several receipt books especially printed with Korean restaurant headed paper.

At the Press Village each tower block had been allocated a team of Korean students to look after our needs and also act as security. They had become our pals and more importantly they all spoke English. A platoon of these young Koreans were now set to work at our desks on an upper floor of a pre-selected tower block. Not for nothing are the South Koreans world famous for production line prowess. They clocked in at 9am and worked throughout the day as though turning out Hyundais until our lunch receipts, dinner receipts, taxi receipts, receipts for interpreters, receipts for entertainment, and receipts for guides were finished. The aforementioned Adamson, known as 'Animal' by his Fleet Street colleagues because of the way his 6ft, 15 stone frame reacted to being sated with lager, had surprised us all. He had found a blind wood carver who sat on a street corner in Seoul chipping bamboo canes into figures for tourists. From him was commissioned a bamboo stamp, which in Korean read 'Paid With Thanks.'

The hacks racked their memories as they marched up and down between the feverishly scribbling Koreans, dictating their previous month's existence: 'Lunch with British Olympic Official £25.70' 'Taxi to Panmanjum £12.63' 'Dinner with Korean Police Inspector £32.80' The students knew the proper exchange rate and the bills were then passed to a sorting desk where they were branded with the bamboo stamp.

The banging could be heard from dawn to dusk.

Looking back on my own dining at the Olympics I realised I had only eaten out once on my own. That was when news editor David Mertens had called up and briefed me to go and dine on dog. The dog restaurants of Seoul had been cleared off the main streets by Korean government decree, knowing that westerners were dog lovers, stories about hounds being hung up by their back legs and whacked with sticks so that their muscles became saturated with adrenaline, a delicacy which apparently improved male potency, would not go down well.

However, the seedy carts cooking tortured dog still carried on their business in the back streets and, I have to say, the dish may have been psychologically hard to swallow, but in fact tasted good: 'The diners, brown juice staining their chins, guzzle unconcernedly and wash the mixture down with gulps of strong rice wine,' my despatch ran. Having digested a plateful I was not immediately blessed with a record erection. For both the poor dog's sake and my own I pondered that it had been a blessing that the desk only wanted me to eat one and write about it rather than 'rescue' one and for the Daily Star's zoological sanctuary.

Not even dogs were available to eat in the grim streets of Bucharest in 1990, a year after despot Nicolai Ceausescu had been overthrown by revolting Romanians. Photographer Frank Barrett and I had flown in to witness the privation after 12 months of non-communist rule, or rather the legacy of Ceausescu's style of communist rule. Our interpreter, a rotund, frumpy woman who had worked for the BBC, kept telling us we must be 'objective'. We explained that on a tabloid we had not got time to sit around soaking up the atmosphere and hoping that fate would arrange something newsworthy and plant it in front of us. We had to make it happen. And by that I mean we had to either witness first hand the dire straits people were finding themselves in or get them to recreate it for us. She refused to help us arrange a family of five around the table for a dinner of one chicken leg, a story she herself had told us. And she proved very reluctant to help us find a food queue. In the end we found one ourselves but she refused to join us to help out with interviews. It was not long before I realised why.

About eight hundred people had formed a queue which went around three sides of a warehouse. They were lining up for a few chicken bones. Among their numbers were professional queuers, people who for a few lei, queued all day on behalf of their employer.

Barrett took up a pitch on the corner of the street from where he could focus on two sides of the building, and therefore two lines of queuing people and then unpacked his lightweight aluminium ladder. Before he had got three steps up in the air, the crowd broke, within seconds we were running for our lives, chased by a half-starved proud people who were not going to be recorded in such humiliating circumstances. Whether or not they would have resorted to cannibalism, we did not stop to find out. Both being well fed and with just enough of a head start, we outran them.

The Romanians might have been sensitive to losing face in adulthood but they had no such reservations about letting us depict the plight of equally hungry children in the mass orphanages of Bucharest. For once our interpreter was prepared to actually work for the dollars we were paying her and escorted us to an orphanage in the city. Admittedly it was one the authorities were allowing us access to and therefore unlikely to be anything other than a 'model' but even so it was shocking.

Barrett and I took a huge bag of chocolate bars with us which I handed over to the orphanage manager to distribute. When his back was turned the interpreter told me he would keep the confectionary for his own use, either to sell or give to his own family. I then made an excuse to get the bag back from him and he meekly handed it over. We entered a caged area full of boys aged from about seven to twelve and shook the sack out on the ground, a pack of about 40 boys fell upon it. At the end of the scrum one little boy, paler and more sickly than the others and wearing ladies' summer sandals, which were too big for him, stood weeping and without a single candy bar.

A tough young lad with a vivid scar across his nose had managed to fight his way to ownership of the last four Mars Bars. Appealing to his better nature, which didn't work, we then demanded he give the snuffling boy a bar, and that was when I noticed the bigger lad's footwear, he was well-shod in boy's shoes of the correct size. Clearly anything in the orphanage was fought for and the fittest prevailed, either with a fight in the case of the orphans or a con in the case of the manager. Passers-by even stuck crusts of bread through the cage and the boys massed around to snatch them. Through the interpreter we discovered that the tough lad had earnt his scar in a street fight over a restaurant rubbish sack with a dog. On that occasion the boy had lost.

Back in London, Barrett brought some old chicken bones from his Sunday lunch and got me holding them outside Ludgate House in the parking lot, wrapped in a Bucharest newspaper. We had our picture of the average Romanian Sunday 'roast'. We had visited a Romania which had suffered becoming a satellite of Soviet Russia because of it's pro-Nazi stance during World War II.

Another foreign saw us in Normandy for the 50th Anniversay of the D-Day Landings, the beginning of the end of the Third Reich. Our first target was the Mayor of Arrowmanches, Dr Jean-Paul Lecomte who had banned drinking in the afternoon, forcing hundreds of old soldiers to commemorate their reunion with milk.

He had been keeping a low profile, aware that he had invoked the wrath of the tabloids. Arrowmanches was grid-locked and I had to walk for several miles along the coast road to get to it. I had with me my Canon Sureshot camera, a piece of equipment which focused itself and required no more expertise than the pressing of the tit. I eventually found the mayor and engaged him in chatter about the wonderful atmosphere Arrowmanches was enjoying, bustling with veterans, warships gathered off the coast, tourists flocking to see the old soldiers and the Queen about to arrive. Because his town was in the news he'd brushed up his English no end and he warmed to the subject of his town's ambience. Prattling on I mentioned the fact that my mother's partner, Clifford Pace, had fought at El Alamein but unfortunately could not be here today. The Mayor was most sympathetic and agreed to pose for a snapshot so that I could show Pace later. He even posed happily in front of the Union Jack, Click!

Camera safely packed away I then asked him about the booze ban.

The apogee of all foreigns came for me when the Daily Star wanted coverage of the annual Fleet Street fiesta of 'Sick Senor' bashing stories which pitched cruel foreigners against poor 'innocent' creatures. All the tabloids tried to outdo one another with tales of bestiality towards creatures great and small. I was assigned Bob Aylott, the aforementioned National Enquirer photographer, as my partner. David Mertens, news editor, was very keen to start kicking Spaniards. He cited the previous summer's coverage of the town where donkeys were lobbed from church spires as part of a fun festival. Manchester-based reporter John Mahoney had 'earned his spurs' stitching up a bull breeder whose animals were also used as fiesta fodder, tormented by crowds before being despatched in the bull ring. Mahoney had requested an interview with the Spaniard and had been invited to his villa for a superb lunch where the Rioja flowed freely. They got on like a house on fire and Mahoney's donkey page spread began "I looked into the sick senor's face and watched the wine dribbling through his teeth" or something similar.

Now it was my turn and I had to top Mahoney's story. I contacted an eccentric animal 'rights' outfit in the UK, hoping to find the most horrific fiesta of all. I was told there was one in a coastal town where the bull was shackled by its horns to a speed boat and dragged off the beach, then towed until it drowned. That sounded hard to beat. However, when I checked this out with a Spanish animal campaigning group they said they had not heard of such a fiesta. Instead they recommended the fiesta at Coria in Extramadura. Here the bulls, two a day all week, were let out into a square where the locals then fired darts at the creature's face through pygmy-style blow-pipes. Once the bull was covered in darts, it was allowed out of the caged square and given the 'freedom of the city!' As it trotted down the ancient side streets, householders brandishing scissors, carving knives and screwdrivers, slashed at its flanks from their windows. The beast was finally despatched with a shotgun blast to its brain. This was explained in some detail and as the fiesta meandered through public streets would give us plenty of opportunity for photographs, so it was Coria we decided upon.

We flew into Madrid and Aylott, used to endless expenses on the National Enquirer, wanted to spend a night at the Palace Hotel, a five star edifice a few minutes walk from the Prado.

It was a fair day's drive to Coria so he talked me into the overnight in Madrid, fortunately I had not told the desk I had fixed up all the background detail on the phone and was able to fob them off with the need to talk to the Spanish animal 'rightists' before setting off.

That night we dined in the Plaza Mayor and planned our modus operandi for getting the story. The Madrid animal campaigners had told me in London that the Spanish were wising up to UK tabloids arriving each summer to stitch them up, and warned me to be careful, the crowd had been known to turn on British speaking photographers. Not speaking any language but English, I decided Aylott and I would pose as Irish tourists.

'They'll never know the difference in the accent and Ireland has never been associated with a sensational press,' I argued, 'and besides, like Spain, it's a good Catholic country!'

Before the night was out, Aylott whose weakness was pretty girls, had got into conversation with a pair of students who had also been dining in Plaza Mayor. One was Julia Rodriques, a girl from Oviedo whose companion Jean Maria from Maine USA, had come to visit Spain after both had studied at the same university. Aylott was not overly convinced by my Irish cover story and wondered whether the girls would like to see the Extramadura part of Spain. Having a Spaniard with us would be perfect. They both jumped at the chance.

The next morning as we breakfasted in the Palace Hotel I rather hoped they would not show up. But soon a rather harrassed-looking hotel flunky led the two young women through the dining hall like a pair of pack-horses. Their voluminous back-packs brushing the tables.

It took the best part of the day to get to Extramadura and we checked into a hotel: the girls had one room and we had another, so as not to compromise our expenses. Aylott whinging over the fact that he could not have his own room.

The scheme worked like a dream, everybody thought we were tourists, although some voiced surprise at Jean having such a youthful father in Aylott.

We put Rodrigues to work translating the local paper which carried the photograph of a beautiful young Spanish girl in the fiesta crowd. It turned out she was the local carnival queen who was a Maid of Honour of the fiesta. We arranged, through Rodrigues, to take pictures of the queen holding up the slaughtered bull's gory ears which she was given as a prize. Day one and we'd struck gold! Fortunately Rodrigues, whose father had fought in the Spanish Civil War on the Republican's side, was an enlightened young woman who thought the bull fiestas 'stupid and sickening' Helping her in her judgement against her countrymen was the promise I had made her of financial reward. And she was paid, too, with all expenses covered.

After that there was no stopping her, she found us a convent where nuns made, by hand, the darts which the citizens of Coria fired at the bulls. We got inside and had an interview with the nuns and took pictures of the sisters hand-rolling the darts.

188

Rodriguez translated the blood-lust of drunken young Spaniards in the local bars to add to my 'colour' : 'Savage senors use bulls as dartboard.'

But eventually the time came for her departure and the pair caught the train, albeit three days later for Oviedo, leaving a phone number and an address.   Fortunately by now, the Daily Star had tired of bull torture anyway, but were so delighted with our gore-fest they asked if we had any more ideas for Dago-bashing.

That night Aylott and I set to plotting our next move to continue our holiday in Spain.

I decided an interview with the political wing of ETA, Herri Batasuna, would make a good story. Great Britain was about to launch itself on the Costas of Spain, if we could get the terror group to warn of bombs buried on the beaches it would stir things up a bit. It meant a long drive north but the Star loved the idea. Aylott and I knew there was only one way of cracking such a tale – with the use of Rodriguez's Spanish, and where did she live? In the north of course.

We arrived at Oviedo at around 10pm tired, thirsty and dust-covered. I spotted an hotel and started to pull over. Aylott waved at me to move on.

'What's wrong with that place?' I asked.

'It's opposite the station,' he sniffed, 'too down market.'

We rounded a street corner and there up in the sky before us was a castle, floodlit.

'That'll do,' said Aylott, again reliving his National Enquirer-no-expense-spared days.

A man dressed in a chocolate brown-tailed coat and a top hat of the same colour, appeared in front of us smiling as we drew up outside the Oviedo Parador. He collected our luggage and our Hertz hire car disappeared from the forecourt as if by magic. My room was the size of an upholstered football pitch.

This story had better work, I thought, as the desk will be watching our expenses like hawks: this was my story idea, not theirs.

Next morning I called up Rodriguez and invited her over to start making the necessary phone calls to Herri Batasuna. With the pace of her countrymen she arrived at about midday and, harrassed that we hadn't even started work, I got her on the phones straight away. All through the afternoon she made calls, each requiring a further call to be made and each time I had to hector her out of her natural manana approach, trying to explain that hacks never wait for people to call back, but must harass, harry and persuade one and all.

Aylott, all this time, was relaxing in his own upholstered football pitch, drinking his favourite 'Cointreau Frappe' and pulling away on Marlboro cigarettes while watching satellite television.

Day two was no better, and late that night after a huge dinner at which we met and dined with the air crew of an Iberian Airways flight, I got a call from the Daily Star night desk. It was Mike Parker the features editor.

'Dick, how you getting on with this terrorist thing?'

'Hello Mike, I'm in the process of setting up an interview with ETA's political wing.'

'OK. Listen, there's a great story in Benidorm.'

Parker went on to mention how chimpanzees, snatched from the jungles of the Congo were shipped to Spain where gipsy hustlers drugged them, removed their teeth and then 'trained' them to pose for seaside snapshots with British and German tourists.

'Dick, we want to rescue one!'

The deluge had covered Mount Ararat and the Daily Star Noah's Ark complex was under way again, and this time it had floated in the nick of time to rescue myself and Aylott.

'Mike that sounds brilliant. Shall we put ETA on hold ?'

'Yes drop that, the editor's mad keen for the monkey. I'll tell him you're on the case.'

This monkey had saved my skin, it would be the least I could do to make sure the Daily Star did not have a hand in its deliverance.

There was only one flight from Oviedo to Madrid the next day. We had to be on it. Early the next morning I tried to raise Aylott. His phone was off the hook. He wouldn't answer his door. I climbed out of the balcony and hammered on his window, still no good. In the end I got the concierge to come up with a key and unlock his room. Immediately the door opened a cloud of cigarette smoke was sucked from his room by the air conditioning and was drawn along the corridor, a thick grey pall. I yelled into the abyss and eventually a semi-detached figure emerged from the smoke dressed in draw-string pyjama bottoms. 'Get your arse into gear, we've got just over an hour to be at the airport,' I yelled.

In the room shut off from daylight by heavy drapes, I could just make out from the flickering TV screen light, a room littered with designer clothing and miniature bottles scattered everywhere. The door of the mini bar was open and the cupboard was bare. 'Get your stuff packed,' I panicked.

'Oh have them send up a porter,' drawled Aylott, as he sprayed himself with Kouros, an after shave which he used as a gentleman's perfume.

I raced round the room cramming his trendy shirts and trousers into suitcases. Then with both his and my cases slung over my back I dashed down to the foyer, sweating in anticipation.

Now the Spaniards at reception, who had spoken English so well on our arrival, were mute with incomprehension as I asked them for our car. On presentation of a large denomination of pesetas they fell in with my request and the car appeared as suddenly, from its mystery grotto, as it had disappeared. Hastily I crammed the boot with our bags and Aylott's photo industry: camera bags, ladders, wire machine and tripod before noticing our back tyre was completely flat.

'Fuck it! We've got a puncture,' I yelled, 'get the spare out quick!'

'Have them call a cab,' said Aylott as cool as you like.

I looked at 'my' photographer, as the more pompous among Fleet Street's hacks would say. This middle-aged man with his thinning hair with its infuriating chestnut highlights, his plastic teeth stained with an obscene amount of orange juice, the mixer for his Smirnoff, and his athletic torso momentarily chilled with Kouros in preparation for another Spanish morning. I seriously thought he was mad.

'We can't leave the fucking hire car here!' I screamed.

'Have them call Hertz,' said Aylott.

And with that he yanked the rent car's ignition keys from the dashboard and dropped them on the receptionist's desk.

191

'The bill, the bill,' I thought with trepidation. This time, surely we had gone over the rubicon. Among other Star hacks our spending had already earned us the unwanted sobriquet of Durham & Aylott Ltd.

Our cab driver, in anticipation of a good pile of pesetas, drove through Oviedo in such a manner that every statistic I'd ever read about how the journey to the airport was a billion times more dangerous than the flight, hovered oppressively over my fevered brow. He made u-turns where u-turns were not supposed to be made, he drove one-way down one-way streets the wrong way and approaching a long traffic queue at a junction, negotiated first the hard shoulder, second the pavement and finally mounted and crossed the roundabout itself to secure swift passage.

We arrived at the airport at bang on take off time and were waved straight through the check-in throwing our bags at them. There on the runway sood an apparition of great beauty, one of the hostesses who had eaten with us and the flight crew the night before.

They had seen the English names on the passenger list and held the flight up by 10 minutes.

'Thought it was you,' said the stewardess as we panted up the gangway.

I had never been so happy to be in the air , and had never drunk a large gin and tonic so early in the day as we flew away from the fear of a failed assignment, arranged by me, to the loathing of one which the desk was responsible for.

Another airport, another hire car. We left Madrid in the lunch hour and headed south east towards Benidorm where we sought out the old part of town away from the readers, and checked in to a lovely art-deco hotel close to the beach.

That evening we found the monkey men. Miserable looking chimps were held by brawny gypsies while a hustler approached the crowds for business. A third man shuffled around close by acting as a sort of monkey minder. Clearly a 'rescue' bid was not going to be easy.

After dinner we went to a bar run by an ex-coal miner from Nottingham. During the course of the evening Aylott had persuaded the fellow and his mates to kidnap a monkey from the gypsies and hand it over to us. I had been making calls from the hotel and so was not party to Aylott's hare-brained scheme. When I returned I discovered to my horror that several thousand pesetas of Daily Star money had been promised as a reward for the snatch! I had to explain that however heart rending the monkey's plight might be, the Daily Star could not be involved in what was likely to be a criminal act. It was as well I did for the true nature of the kidnapper then came to the fore. Robbed of his chance of easy money, he launched into a stream of invective and started waving his fists around.

Once again I hit the phone and discovered a charming retired Battle of Britain Spitfire pilot, Simon Templar, who ran a monkey sanctuary up near Barcelona. In his love zoo was one chimp which had been in the hands of the Benidorm hustlers. For some reason it had proved unwilling to pose with tourists and had been dumped by the monkey men and had eventually turned up at the Barcelona sanctuary.

I explained that the Daily Star was very keen to feature the sanctuary and on doing so, tell the story of the chimp's ordeal and that of his fellow primates. In so doing, I ventured, it could be said could it not, that the Daily Star was at the forefront of helping in the effort of rescuing these beasts, not to say this beast in particular, from an unwanted career as a model?

The chimp benefactor followed the labyrinthine argument very well: 'If you want to say the Daily Star rescued Chico, that's fine by me.'

'Er, well thanks.'

We sped up the Autopiste to Barcelona, and after a vast lunch courtesy of Express Newspapers, during which we debriefed Templar and his wife Peggy on Chico's story, we started on the shoot.

I climbed into the cage of the beast and endeavoured to get it to hug me as a gesture of thanks for its deliverance. Perhaps sensing the fact it was being 'set up' once more for a photographic stunt, the creature refused to be exploited. That was until I stuck a large cherry between my lips and Aylott snapped Chico giving me a 'kiss'.

But before Aylott had a chance to wire the picture we were on the road again.

A gang of British revellers had, in a merry spree, danced on the bonnet of a cab driver in Magaluf. The driver had collapsed and died from a heart attack.

'Drunken Thugs Abroad' was the next story, and on the overnight ferry to Majorca I sat In my cabin to collate nearly a month's worth of expenses. Aylott being dyslexic, was incapable of doing his, and as the signing off of mine were dependant on his being complementary, I was obliged to sort his out as well. As dawn coloured the honeycomb cliffs of the island, I was still at it. Meanwhile if beauty sleep can be obtained via a vodka coma that's what Aylott was getting.

Down in the depths of Magaluf we watched prosperous northern Europeans at play in cheapo Spain. It consisted mainly of young people from Britain, Holland, Germany and Scandinavia discarding huge back-packs in cheap hotels before loading up with cheap rose instead.

The English contingent only ate at breakfast time, to soak up the excess of the night before. Large photographs in garish colours helped them choose their dishes. There was no need to speak any Spanish. Indeed there was no need to speak at all, merely point.

By about 10pm the whole district was legless and Aylott and I weren't too steady either, but we'd done our ground-work in the afternoon and befriended some Spanish police officers, including a female no taller than 5ft., whose long truncheon trailed behind her in the dust
as a result.

Close to midnight we heard the sound of smashing bottles and shouts, and ran down a darkened street. Some gangly youths were brandishing broken beer bottles, there was a sudden slashing movement and an athletic youth dressed only in swimming trunks, was covered in a curtain of gore. Aylott and I got in close and his flash-gun popped. The youth lashed out punching me in the head, but then the police arrived. I and the other youths scattered and the victim was arrested.

Aylott had a great snap, a drunken teenager covered in blood and semi-naked after a bottle fight in a family holiday resort, where a local taxi driver had recently been hounded to death by English yobs. Well pleased I then made enquiries of the police as to our prey's identity. He was Swedish.

Which was a blow.

If we were going to use the picture we had to think of an angle other than 'British Thugs On The Rampage'.

'Just say he's from Manchester, who's going to argue?' said Aylott, slurping his first vodka of the day and keen to get his snap used.

'That would be stupid,' I said, 'the desk will want to know his name, his address, his job. They will want to send another reporter round to show his parents the photograph and get their reaction.'

But 'Swedish Thugs On The Rampage' really took the oomph out of the story. A Swede? Don't they drive Volvos, pay huge taxes for social needs, and behave themselves? A Swede? They don't have street fights, do they? They aren't football hooligans are they? They're all Abba fans aren't they? I tried to read the mind of the desk.

Then Bingo! I had it.

I would write it as a postcard home:-

'Dear Mum, Having a lovely time, got off me face on Rioja, scared a cab-driver to death before having a bottle fight. Went red all over – nothing to do with the sun, mind,' kind of thing. And that's what we did.

The actual piece appeared under the headline: ' So You Wish You Were Here ?', with the strapline: 'Having a bashing time in Majorca'.

The question of the youth's nationality was never questioned. But the desk was now bored with 'Spane' and our holiday was over.

When the Daily Star decided to export its wit and wisdom to Eire, to produce an Irish edition, two 'teams' of 'blunt nibs and smudgers' were sent to Dublin to teach the Irish how to produce news in a tabloid way. Reporter John Mahoney and snapper Tony Fisher were sent from the Manchester office and Aylott and

I were sent from London. We arrived at the Burlington Hotel to be greeted by London picture editor Jimmy Sutherland, who was stressed out with the Sisyphean task of demonstrating the black art of tabloid newspapers to the literal-minded Irish. In the US he'd already experienced trying to inculcate foreigners in the methods of popular newspaper production while working on the National Enquirer. What came naturally to Scots, Welsh, English and Northern Irish was too alien for Americans to absorb. In the end the National Enquirer was virtually run solely by Brits. In Ireland teaching photographers to see the world through tabloid-tinted spectacles was not as easy as it had been in Florida, Sutherland was discovering. The newsroom of the Irish Daily Star reflected the demands of real news-gathering. It was chaotic, disorganised bits of paper and fag packets with phone numbers or addresses on, were scattered all over the place and regularly re-distributed by an over-worked office fan.

Sutherland leant despondently on the bar of The 'Burlo' and told us how he had purchased a seven-day box file for the Irish news editor, John Donlan, so that he could plan his week and manage or create news in a fashion demanded by the pre-conceived scheduling of tabloid newspapers. Sutherland had explained how for Tuesday's newspaper you filled Monday's file, for Wednesday's paper you filled Tuesday's and so on through the red-top week.

'I crept in early one morning after a fortnight to see how the new system was working,' said Sutherland, 'do you know, every file was empty except Friday's, which had a sandwich in it!'

Our brief was to work alongside the new, young staff from the Irish Republic guiding and advising them so that by the time we came to leave they could run a tabloid on their own.

When a photographer was sent to Cork to get a picture of a one-legged hockey referee, and returned with a portrait of his head and shoulders, he was swiftly re-educated by an angry Sutherland. The word spread and all photographers realised they were there to do more than record images, they had to create them. Photographer Noel Gavin's next job was to snap Ireland's youngest football manager. Gavin seemed to be taking an inordinate amount of time over what should have been a straight forward assignment. The reason for this became clear as the image swam towards Sutherland through dark-room fixer: The manager was in the centre of a football pitch dressed as a baby with a dummy in his mouth, peering from a pram.

'There's no such thing as an Irish joke,' said Sutherland, 'they're all true!'

But if the Irish struggled to understand us, the reverse was also true. Leafing through an Irish Independent story one day my eye caught a story about a farm labourer who had run off with his employer's savings. The photograph used to illustrate the story was of a haystack and a ladder, nothing else. The caption read: 'Here is a picture of the absentee farm worker'!

After tabloid news-gathering in the hard-nosed, worldly wise and rat-running Home Counties of England, working in Ireland was a dream. The Irish love to party and were happy to co-operate with our demands as though it was all part of a 'crack', which of course is exactly how we treated it. They seemed to have a highly developed intuition. They sensed immediately where we were coming from. Perhaps it was just that we were so obvious.

After lunch one mid-week day, Sutherland was crying out for something, anything, to fill a large hole on page three of the following day's paper. Recalling that pop singer Michael Jackson was planning a European tour, commencing in Ireland, I rang Dublin Zoo. Jackson, who worked hard at being bonkers, had heavily publicised his love for a pet Chimpanzee, Bubbles. Quarantine restrictions would ensure the beast would remain at the singer's Californian home, so I wondered if the local zoo could supply a surrogate 'friend'.

'Hang on now, I'll put yer through to the monkey house,' came the helpful response from the zoo switchboard. My dialogue with the monkey house warden went something like this:

'Good morning I'm calling from the Daily Star, Ireland's newest newspaper. Do you have any Chimpanzees in your zoo?'

'Sure we do. We have Victoria.'

'Er, I wonder, does Victoria ever listen to music?'

'Sure she does. She loves a good song.'

'So you play music to her then, in her cage?'

'Sure, we can.'

'Does she like pop music?'

'She loves pop music.'

'What about Michael Jackson?'

'Michael Jackson is her favourite.'

And yes there would be no problem in joining her in her cage with a tape-recorder of Jackson's tunes and a photographer, and what time in the morning would we want to come?

'We need it today!'

'Ah, the zoo closes at four o'clock.'

It was now about quarter to, there was a momentary pause, 'Tell you what I'll do now,' our accommodating warden said, 'I'll take Victoria home with me!'

'Fine,' I said stifling any astonishment, 'Fine, we'll see you there!'

Aylott and I stopped at a newsagents to buy a Michael Jackson teeny-bopper poster, we found one with the self-sculpted star shooting one arm into the air, the other cuddling the microphone, and set off. The street of terraced brick houses we entered had a cluster of BMX bicycles around a particular garden wall. Hardly surprising that these kids had gathered at this particular address for there, hanging off the pelmet, was Victoria. Where did Victoria sleep when she came to the warden's house? I wondered aloud. Our good friend stalled.

'Er, do you have a bedroom, a spare bedroom?' I asked.

'Sure we do,' said mine host suddenly regaining the composure of the game.

We were ushered upstairs to the son's bedroom. He was now away at college and his room was used only at weekends. Aylott and I soon had the Formula One race car posters stripped from the walls and replaced instead with the Michael Jackson poster. The next forty minutes were spent with myself coaxing Victoria, as she became sated with bananas, to raise her right paw into the air emulating her 'favourite pop star' for Aylott's camera.

Back at the office the news editor was thrilled with the picture: 'Should we put it on the front page?'

'No,' we said.

But he never forgot the potential of Dublin's zoo, and they were only too happy to coax their creatures into poses worthy of the

Daily Star's suggestions. A week later they called up unsolicited to say a lion cub was being taken for 'a walk' around the zoo grounds on a dog leash.

It was all so different to Regent's Park Zoo's PR machine in London, where similar requests were turned down flat so as not to 'demean' the animals. All very worthy, yet on an earlier Daily Star story I exposed London Zoo for deliberately rearing bear cubs, which were later secretly culled, to pull in the crowds.

Our Irish hosts were beginning to warm to the tabloid way, so we imported some stories which had proved successful in the UK. Sellafield, I soon discovered was understandably - as no Irish jobs were provided by its malignant presence - a highly emotive subject in the Republic. Aylott and I spent days down at Dublin's fish quay in Howth trying to convince trawlermen that giving us fish for scientific testing would help their industry in the long run, even though it might impact on fish-eating in the short term. They all had strange tales of fish with deformities and disease and eventually we found a trawlerman who agreed to help us. Soon Aylott's hotel bath was an improvised wet fish shop full of odd-looking plaice, cod and skate.

A boffin at Trinity College, Dr Ian McAulay, found they had radioactive caesium – 137 and caesium – 134 in them: 'I have no hesitation in attributing them to the discharges from the Sellafield nuclear reprocessing plant' he declared and said he wouldn't eat them. Bingo!

'Monsters of the Deep,' ran the tempered headline.

We also decided to repeat the 'mugger's mile' we'd stigmatised London with on Dublin's main street, O'Connell Street. Aylott and I were due to 'fly on the story' and were taken by taxi to the local football pitch to await a helicopter. We went inside the pavilion for a coffee and half an hour later heard the clatter of chopper blades and spotted the helicopter land on the far side of the playing field. As it was costing big money, Sutherland had ordered Aylott and I to get up and down as quickly as possible so we were a little stunned to find the waiting cab driver in the process of taking the cylinder head off the engine! We abandoned the taxi and ran to the far end of the sports ground, laden like startled donkeys with Aylott's camera gear, to get airborne.

On the weekend we decided to target O'Connell Street, there were just four paltry muggings, Dublin being sleepier than Clapham. So we included all the crimes available: prostitution, pimping, drug dealing, shop-lifting even vandalism. In all there were 33 arrests, hardly a crime wave in the capital city of a western European nation. But we got our spread: 'O'Shameful Street'.

9. FEATURES

The world of features embraces knitting patterns, recipes and health advice: a soft and cuddly place compared with the flinty,rain-driven doorsteps of hard news. It was a fur-lined coffin, as one old cynic described life on Mirror features. 'They want to commune with dolphins' was how Daily Express hack, Alun Rees, in a surreally derisive phrase, once described the feature writer to me.

Rees' jocular put down displays the contempt in which the 'hard news' macho reporter holds the feature writer: a hack engaged in 'women's work' concentrating, as he does on soft news targets. Features are accurately symbolised by an animal: a creature which can't speak and therefore claim it was verballed, demand a retraction or alert the Press Complaints Commission in spite of the fact that a Guardian feature writer once reported 'a dolphin knows 60 words and can understand more than 2,000 sentences'.

So although communing with dolphins might be more fruitful than talking to other animals, it suggests something wishy-washy and other worldly, something spiritual, and mystical: all aspects of human nature which the news reporter, conversely, must nail down with 'facts'. Oddly enough a hell of a lot of features ARE about dolphins and their perceived human-like intelligence!

The feature WRITER and the news REPORTER, there in the job description can be found the language which is at the root of the hack's ire.

Hacks don't want privileged feature writers turning up on the job, overshadowing them. Whether it be a 'writer' sent to do a 'colour piece' about some serious crime, or to write an atmospheric item to go with the funeral coverage of some VIP, or a 'scene-setter' for some major organised forthcoming event. The hack feels he is perfectly capable of doing all this himself. Only when the job goes pear-shaped and few, if any facts, are gleaned will the hack then say 'Well it's a writer's job, they've sent a feature writer down here, let her (the gender used whether male or female) get on with it!'

Many students beavering away at media courses want to be a 'feature writer', what they do not realise is that the best feature writers start out as hard news journalists and that editors prefer feature writers who understand courts, libel laws and how to talk to the public BEFORE they want dolphin communers.

I wanted to be a feature writer after years of being a hack, but for one reason only, to get away from the universally-loathed news editor, Graham Jones.

Coincidentally, Aylott and I, had been down in La Rochelle looking for dolphins, dead ones in this case, when the Jones' regime began. We'd been sent to France after 500 dolphin bodies had been washed up in the Bay of Biscay. We managed to talk the desk into letting us drive down there, ever in mind of the trunk loads of cheap wine we could return with. As a result it stretched the job out. By the time we got to La Rochelle we did not discover any dolphins dead or alive, but we did find some excellent fish restaurants selling illegally -sized portions of their ocean neighbours. While mopping up endless bowls of fish soup with hunks of French bread, a team of schoolboys, employed by us, cycled up and down the coast searching for the dead mammals. As we settled into a gourmet tour of the Vendee, two or three days passed without our boys sighting a dolphin corpse, so I took an 'executive decision', i.e. an autocratic one, and decided to head south.

Bordeaux was tantalisingly close, only a day away, with the promise of a few extra degrees warmth - it was January - and even better wine.

Also there was a dolphin research centre at nearby Arcachon, I could find a good talking head there, I thought, to give us at least, that old reserve, background. Unfortunately our boffin refused to budge from anything but highly complex scientific analysis about the dolphin deaths, and one which pollution played only a small speculative part. Not what Hitchen wanted at all for his headline: 'Dolphins die by the hundred in our dustbin seas'.

So after a splendid dinner in Bordeaux and a good hotel bed, we returned to La Rochelle to the report from one of our schoolboys that, at last, a dolphin, a single dolphin, had been found..

The headless body lay rolling at the water's edge, rapidly decomposing, it was not the snap news editor David Mertens had in mind when we were sent 11 days previously. After those 11 days we did not have much to show for the vast expense bill we had incurred. But, like the dolphins, the old regime was dying and as I checked in with the desk, the late James Wardlaw 'number 14' on the desk, as he was known, told me: 'There's blood in the water: Mertens has gone.' Well that was one good thing, Aylott and I would no longer have to account to the news editor who sent us. The failure of the story could rest with the departed! 'We were on a fool's errand', we would say, much as we liked Mertens.

But his replacement, Graham Jones, was a cold, unsmiling fish, with dead, doll-like eyes, and a 1,000 yard stare which passed right through the beholder.

Not long after his arrival Express Newspapers moved out of Fleet Street.

The dear old 'Black Lubianka,' a magnificent glossy façade - even though it's interior was a shabby warren of cream-painted, tin-walled Wendy houses, was located among a half dozen decent pubs. A place where Ruritanian commissionaires handed out fistfuls of tenners in petty cash for our playtime.

Our new office was the hermetically sealed Ludgate House. Gone were the typewriters and instead computer screens glowed. Gone was the easily accessed newspaper cuttings library, instead a clumsy, complex and time-wasting process, had to be gone through on a computerised library screen. Once the agonising process of 'access' had been achieved the user would discover the cutting had either not yet been scanned in, or more often than not, dispensed with altogether. The new building came with a new policy:

'Express Newspapers PLC.
DRINK OR DRUGS-RELATED PROBLEMS
The Company recognises that persistent excessive drinking and drug dependence are illnesses. Members of staff who believe they have a drink or drugs problem are encouraged to consult the Senior Sister. She is able to give advice and arrange contact with external sources of guidance and treatment. Enquiries will be treated in strict confidence.'

The bit the management hoped the hacks would not get to see was the:

'ADVICE FOR MANAGERS – CONFIDENTIAL'
If an employee who has sought assistance from the Medical Department requires time off work for treatment, the Senior Sister will notify the Personnel Manager. Personnel will make the necessary arrangements with the head of department, who should treat the matter in strict confidence. Other members of staff should not be made aware of the reason for sickness absence.'

Once a hack had officially sought advice from the Senior Sister his problem would be logged with the company. He would be a marked man. I know of no-one who was naïve enough to consult the Senior Sister. One Daily Star editorial head found himself being advised to take some psychological counselling – or else. This was in part office politics, but later when it was discovered that the company insurance would not cover the hefty cost of such head-shrinkery he was deemed fit for work once more…

Lunchtime o'boozing, made infamous by an eponymous Private Eye column, had gone forever.

A new kind of reporter was recruited to sit in the new building. They were a little like automatons, obedient, unthinking, and lacking independence, initiative or imagination. Worse they came cheap too, undermining our hugely inflated wages. They didn't take lunch, they didn't get pissed, they didn't take advances, they put in measly expenses, they didn't leave the office, never mind go on foreigns.

And they didn't come up with any stories. But at least their illiteracy was a comfort to my own scholarly short-comings as this Jones' memo revealed:

'In the interests of all could I just ask you to read the following which is a list of niggles and how to put them right.

'Punctuation:

Too much sub's time is being wasted correcting elementary punctuation errors. Quotation marks " " are obtained by pressing double shift and single quote. Similarly a – (dash) is a double shift and lower case m for mother.

Please make sure you insert a single space after full stops.

One Elevens:

The B.A.C. 1-11 is a passenger jet. The military F111 does not have a hyphen.

Driving cases:

The charge is reckless driving, not wreckless.

Fun:

It is wacko Jacko i.e. he is wacky, off-beat, crazy. He is not whacko Jacko which suggests Jimmy Edwards and spanking.

Pain:

People are racked with pain, not wracked. Wrack (or fucus) is a form of seaweed suggesting again some bizarre Jimmy Edwards flagellation rite.

Deserted Ships:

It is the Mary Celeste not the Marie Celeste. I am pleased to see both Andrew Neil and Brian McArthur got this wrong this week.

I before e except after c if the sound is ee

This rule applies except for one word – seize. Siege, please note,
follows the rule.
Proper Names:
There are two ds in Gaddafi and two hs in Khashoggi and the
Gurkhas are a bit of a laugh (ends with a ha)
Car Crashes:
The lesser injured suffer minor injuries, not miner as if they have
been clobbered with a pit shovel.
Spellings:
Please note the spelling of rhythm, liaison, environment.
Possessives:
Apostrophes should not be used with pronouns: example its, theirs,
ours. It's is a short form for "it is".
Stationery/Stationary:
Please note e for envelope and a for 'alt (stop!).'

Those of us existing hacks who had failed to get out, were a
dinosaur breed, and it wouldn't take much of a volcano to cause
our extinction.

Jones had instituted a monthly champagne award for the
reporter who brought in the best story: in the old days so many
good yarns were produced that champagne was poured for
everybody on a Friday night in the Snooker Club. In the early
days of the Star everybody came up with ideas as the great
socialising that went on in Fleet Street between rivals created an
atmosphere that spurred hacks on to out-do each other.

Jones tried in vain to recreate this spontaneity with hectoring
memos:

'In the last weeks we have had many excellent exclusives
brought in by members of staff. This week the
Trueman/Whittow Hannibal the Cannibal story, Shan
Lancaster's Battling Bimbos and Chris McCashin's BA
pilot/stewards are great examples. It is VITAL we all do our
utmost to make the paper the brightest and the best. Most of
you, I know are fully committed to the Daily Star and would do
anything you could to leave the opposition standing. That's what
we're here for. But I'm concerned – and I know the Editor is too –
that a small minority are not pulling their weight. They spend

too much time chattering to colleagues on other papers. And they say it's not their function to bring in ideas. This despite some hefty claims for entertaining by certain individuals which never seem to bring results. From now on I will require one good TWO-LINE idea from each of you, deadline Wednesday noon. A list will be drawn up and submitted to the Editor at the forward planning meeting Wednesday evening. Ideas such as "I think we should go with Fergie to Mustique" will be struck out and marked as a nil return. Come on, let's come up with the ideas, go for the stories and beat the hell out of the rest of them.'

Fleet Street now was a place rapidly emptying of great newspaper titles. The Daily Mail and Evening Standard had gone to Kensington, The Sun and The Times to Wapping, the Daily Mirror and the Daily Telegraph to Canary Wharf. Reporters of the diaspora still wandered back to Fleet Street to meet up with colleagues from other titles in the pubs they once shared. They were like elephants on the African plains who would plod for weeks driven by the memory of some vast oasis only to arrive and find it a shrivelled watering hole.

I bumped into the immaculately suited Peter Batt, a legendary sports writer as famous for drink as for ink, in Mick's Café - which was no longer open 24 hours, did not serve Vienna steak in the 'restaurant' upstairs anymore – which many said also doubled as a brothel – and was now instead a sandwich bar with wall-hung, too-narrow tables. Batty, as he was known, had two steak & kidney pies in front of him. He turned them upside down, cut open their soft pastry underbellies and filled them up with brown sauce before catching sight of me. Thrilled to meet a friendly face he insisted I join him and started in his deep, rich and very loud Cockney voice to rue the way the industry was headed. Batty, it is fair to say, balanced his eloquently written prose by peppering the spoken word with as many oaths as he could make fit. It was almost as though he was making up for the fact that he had to discipline his writing by omitting the East End vernacular he had grown up with.

'I've got me kids going through university now, but there's no way they're coming into this fucking game. No way. And don't you hide your light under a bushel over there,' he jabbed a fork towards Blackfriars Bridge, 'don't you waste your time over there. I'd give anything to do something else, anything. But what can I do ? Fuck all.

'What makes newspapers different from any other job ? Why do we have the problems we have? There are the normal temptations in any job. Well let me tell you: the fucking temptation in Fleet Street is the fantasy. The fantasy you can be something you're not. I used to believe I was going to be James Cameron, but it's not like that. I've been sacked from every fucking paper in Fleet Street. But I've still got to keep coming back, what else can I do ? Fuck all.

'How old are you ? I'm 50. I'm a fucking old man and I'm telling you get out now while you can. I hate this fucking job I want to commit suicide. It's like the Civil Service in there now, blokes waiting to get their feet under the desk, waiting to get out of harm's way, get their name on a plaque on a desk and heave a sigh of relief. Back in the Sixties, the Fifties, the Forties when there was no television it was different. But now it's just fucking show business shit, some shit about someone in Dallas. Now we've got to stay in watching fucking television all night to be good reporters. It's our version of "the knowledge". Are you listening to to me? I mean I'm just a fucking old Cockney with no education so don't take any notice of me, know what I mean?'

I did and so, too, did Batty himself. Not to be beaten by the evils of TV soaps he joined them and successfully wrote scripts for the BBC series EastEnders.

Graham Jones and I almost immediately fell out. Although he didn't tell me! Instead I would find the most shocking memos CC'd to the editor or higher management waiting in my pigeon hole. Jones had the ability to make the hack feel unthreatened as long as he was morose. As soon as he cracked a thin joke or smiled wanly at you, a devastating report about you had gone to the editor, a copy of which awaited your reception, sometimes even at home. This was a clever psychological trick, to make you feel unloved, unwanted and worthless even in the bosom of your family...

One reporter suffered a nervous breakdown, many went sick regularly as the regime of terror continued in a bid to get people to leave.

Some did, others with good contracts like me endured Mr. Jones, and kept on taking the money.

He could be spiteful too. Once I incurred his wrath for going to a wine bar at lunchtime and thus he sent me to Llandrednod Wells in central Wales, to be there for early morning. I live in Essex, and we were not to run up overnights. Such an assignment , therefore had me on the road at 3 am not getting home until midnight. He would keep you to the end of your shift then send you to knock a door 'on your way home' a door which was usually in the opposite direction.

My saviour was Michael Hellicar, an enigmatic figure and working class lad who had enjoyed considerable success in Fleet Street, culminating in a chief feature writer's position on the Daily Mirror. He had come to the Daily Star as features editor. He was quietly spoken, and, when he spoke at all, his lack of tabloid fuss created an area of intrigue around him and therefore a wealth of rumour. He was a shrewd and well-respected journalist, but then it was also rumoured he had 'damning' evidence of corruption against important executives, which was why, it was said, he survived so long in an executive role.

He was also avuncular, in a sinister way, a bit like Smiley the Le Carre character: one felt compelled to confide in his owlish face, unblinking behind steel-rimmed spectacles even though you had the feeling such a confession would work against you. He was a kind of a priest with a hidden agenda.

But I was fortunate to overhear him one morning saying there was a vacancy in features. I immediately applied for the job, and Hellicar, who 'had the editor's ear' saw that I got it.

It was a huge relief to get away from Jones, but one which caused some envy among the poor bastards still stuck with news, notably Andy Russell, a Northern hack, who was sick as a parrot that I'd managed to bodyswerve the desk.

Delighted that Jones had little power over me anymore, I was determined to make features sing and dance and set to with gusto over Hellicar's first assignment – The Hum.

The Hum is a high frequency noise caused by – no one really knows – but which has thousands of sufferers and equally as many who think they are sufferers.

Aylott and I chased round the countryside talking to people with various forms of sounds ringing in their ears for a three-part series.

We came across one woman who lived in a sort of copper womb rigged up in her London flat, in order to escape the Hum. We got pictures of her in her sound-proof cocoon then drove her out to a copse in Kent which was officially recorded as being the quietest place in England. It all seemed a bit bonkers. But once our humdinger hit the news-stands the letters and telephone calls poured in for days, weeks and months, even years from Hum sufferers.

Shrewdly, Hellicar had guessed the series would create a healthy response, he'd probably done it years before on the Mirror.

To handle all the calls, a special 'Hum Line' was set up by the paper, it rang all day every day. Many of the Hum's victims were upper middle class for some reason. I received many calls from people saying "I don't normally take the Daily Star but I heard you are running a series on the Hum – could you send me the backnumbers?"

The paper soon got bored with the Hum but the Hum sufferers did not get bored with us, they kept on calling long after the series had ended, much to the aforementioned Andy Russell's ire as many came through to the news room reminding him of my escape.

Popularised science, I soon realised, was a subject dear to Hellicar's heart. We were soon into global warming and he wanted an interview with TV science man David Bellamy. Anyone on television helped give gravitas to tabloid features. After interviewing Bellamy at the Royal Geographical Society we had the art desk create pictures of famous landmarks poking up from vast lakes of water, for a two part series on 'Our Dying Planet.'

Day One was 'The Great Flood' in which readers were told that 'Rising seas will drown London and East Anglia'. Scotland would grow vines, after its coasts had been 'menaced' by ice-bergs breaking away from the North Pole, there would be bread queues in London because of flooded wheat fields and the Home Counties landscape would be destroyed by hurricanes. Day Two: 'Death of Venice' had the 'Alps at melting point', ' a malaria plague in Paris', 'camel trains across Italy', Spain would become 'a second Sahara', Holland's windmills 'may still have a use – as beacons for ships', and the bears of Berlin's Grunwald Forest would die of heat exhaustion. Sensational? You bet, sea levels are rising in centimetres a year but never mind, the other papers did not take long to follow the Star's lead.

So if that was science 'fact', imagine what the art desk could do with science fiction. Soon I was on the road once more making calls on those UK citizens who had been visited by aliens. The journey commenced with a visit to a bespectacled solicitor, Harry Harris, in the suburbs of Manchester. In his spare time the fellow had built up a data base of UFO sightings and collected details of those who had seen them.

Propitiously a UFO had been seen over his house the day I arrived, he told me. Whether this particular Star of David had anything to do with the paper's promise of a cheque to help with his expenses, I cannot say.

But the news, from one of his monitors, had us both staring into the sky. After what seemed a respectable period of vigilance, I proposed we got down to looking at his data base. This in in turn led to an interview with housewife Linda Taylor, who had been kidnapped by a UFO snatch squad.

Mrs. Taylor was approaching middle age with a husband 13 years her senior, and lived, like many of those who have vivid accounts of strange encounters with dreamlike creatures, in a dull suburb hemmed in by the infrastructure of a highly populated metropolis. Mrs Taylor was on her way home from a friend's house when on a dark, unlit country road she was stopped by a blinding light. Next thing she knew was that she was in the arms of a 'tall man with blonde shoulder length hair and piercing blue eyes' who took her to a pool where ...... wait for it ...... they stroked dolphins! The spaceship, which had abducted her, was presumably fitted with a dolphinarium.

At the bottom of the page the Daily Star published a 'come on' and invite to readers to send in more stories: 'Have you had a close encounter with a UFO? Send your letters and photos to....' A telephone call to a retired USAF pilot, Milton Torres: 'My Dogfight With A UFO' and a further interview with a former Yorkshire police officer, Alan Godfrey: 'Cop Alan is "Arrested" by Robots', gave Hellicar another three part series. I was surprised to discover the MOD actually have a department dedicated to monitoring UFOs until I realised that unidentified flying objects are just that: only a singular breed is able to identify them.

As a child my father had told me a story about women factory workers in the US who had contracted leukaemia after sucking the brushes with which they were painting the numerals of wristwatches with radioactive night-glow paint. The brushes had required a fine point to get the paint on the right digit and nowhere else. Ever since I had harboured a dread of radiation, radioactivity and armed with such objectivity, and in 1990 I set out on the road to Sellafield and the British Nuclear Fuels Ltd (BNFL) re-processing plant. Features executive Mike Parker had no qualms about sending myself and Aylott on the story, especially once I had told him that BNFL ships, loaded to the gunnels with JAPANESE nuclear waste, docked regularly at Barrow-in-Furness. Parker, knowing the editor's lingering World War II loathing for Krauts and Nips was looking forward to that morning's conference with his scheduled line: 'Japs Turn Britain into Nuclear Dustbin'. The fact that a new re-processing centre THORP was opening soon on the same site gave us a great news peg as well.

Aylott and I drove up into the bleak moorland above Sellafield to find a graveyard. Eventually we found an ancient burial site with moss-covered gravestones, a-tilt, through which, with telephoto lens fore-shortening, could be espied the infamous industrial silhouette of Sellafield on the coast below. Nowadays you could compose such a photograph on a computer, but not then.

A few days in Cumbria gleaned enough copy to write on Sellafield for a week, children with leaukaemia whose fathers had worked at Sellafield, the nuclear waste-carrying ships moored up in the heart of Barrow-in-Furness's two up, two down houses, the cockle fishermen of Morecambe Bay, many of whom had died mysteriously of cancer: 'Poisoned For 100,000 Years', the pipeline which daily disgorged plutonium into the Irish Sea, the smoke stacks which discharged a nuclear gas which had been picked up in Miami: 'They can see the nuclear cloud in Miami. But still the ships of death come in', the predicted swathe of contamination, from Cumbria to Stuttgart, if the wind was NW, after a catastrophic accident. It went on and on.

During our probings we holed up at a hotel in Barrow-in-Furness and on a first night Aylott sent his steak back complaining it was inedible. His card – or rather our cards – were marked.

His complaint did not affect my relationship with the night porter, however, and in the early hours of the morning we yawned on either side of the bar until suddenly he announced he'd had another newspaper up the week before.

Taken aback I blurted: 'Which one?!'

'The News of the World,' he said and explained that his cousin had been the first woman to bring an orphan into the UK from post-revolutionary Romania, and that she was now in the process of trying to adopt the child.

I told him we, too, would be interested in talking to her and bought him yet another drink. I thought no more about it until the following morning when a ringing noise disturbed my search for a cool part of the centrally-heated hotel bedding in which to bury my throbbing head. I bent pillows double, until my cranium – radiating booze rays – warmed the cotton to intolerable levels. I continually scissored my legs across the bed and plunged my arms down the flanks of the mattress seeking cooler pastures. The phone eventually overcame my dehydrated senses and I picked it up.

'Hello, could I speak to Mr. Durman?'

'Speaking'

'Hello it's Shirley Stevens'

'Hello?' I said again, stupidly 'How are you?' battling to make sense of the name.

'Oh I'm fine,' she offered no clue.

'Good.'

'What time did you want to come over?'

'Er, whatever time suits you'

'Could you make it this morning only we've got to go down the social at midday?'

'Yes, fine,' I still had not got a clue, 'see you later then.'

'Yes, would you like the address?'

'Oh yes please.'

'You did want to talk to us about Alexandra didn't you?'

'Oh yes, Mrs. Stevens, very much so,' I said working my brains which Sellafield victim was this?

'Only as I said to my cousin the social workers seem to be trying to stop us adopting her.'

At last the coin broke through the gin-hobbled grey matter.

I leapt from my bed, dressed and hammered on Aylott's door. By lunchtime we had enough words and pictures of Alexandra – the girl dumped by her mother in a Romanian orphanage for a splash 'World Exclusive": 'Girl Saved From Hell' and a double page spread inside: 'Our Little Angel Cost Us A Packet..In Cigs' told how the Stevens bribed their way back to the UK.

The News of the World had already researched the story and taken the pictures, but, incredibly had left the story 'unminded'. By sheer fluke we had stumbled across it.

Mrs. Stevens had asked us if it was 'all right' to talk to us as well as the News of the World. Of course it was, the News of the World is a paper which prefers stories about sex, I explained and it would be as well for the Stevens if there were no sexual skeletons in the cupboard, as the News of the World would be bound to find out, and how would that effect their chances of adopting Alexandra? The Daily Star, in contrast, was a family newspaper. Mr. Stevens suddenly agreed: 'We don't like the News of the World anyway,' he said.

And so we ran the piece across four pages. It was Wednesday, the News of the World would not publish for another four days. The next day we returned to the Steven's house, the Sellafield story was now on hold, for a follow-up.

'We've had the News of the World on,' said Mr. Stevens, 'they were very rude – I knew I didn't like them.'

We had got the story for nothing. The News of the World had told the Stevens they had just ruined their chances of £10,000.

Whether the Stevens' would ever have received such a sum or not we will never know,but they had given the News of the World the full story BEFORE getting any payment.

Meanwhile the local paper, the North-West Evening Mail, took the classic moral stance of an organ which has either missed or which cannot afford the story by becoming high-minded about 'buy ups': 'Rumania orphan in cheque-book journalism row' and based their story on the fact that: 'Many media big guns were chasing hard after the story. The Sunday Times, News of the World, Daily Mail, the Mirror, the Sunday People, TV-AM and Sky TV were all involved before it was netted by the Star.' But all the North-West Evening Mail were left with for THEIR story was a denial from the Stevens that we had paid them! Certainly they WERE paid, around £2,000, but that was weeks later after Express Newspapers' Chairman, Lord Stevens felt morally obliged to help them out. At the time neither Aylott or I paid or promised to pay for the yarn. Celebrating our scoop that night back at the Abbey House Hotel I bought the night porter copious amounts of drink and then confided in him as to our real task, the reason that had brought us to Cumbria. He then told me he knew of a girl, a young girl, who had worked as some sort of assistant at the plant and who had been contaminated.

She had needed to be scrubbed down just like Meryl Streep in the film 'Silkwood'. My mind shot straight back to my father's story of the watch painters. Astonishingly the porter then told me she had left BNFL and was now working at the Abbey House Hotel. Eventually he closed the bar and left me contemplating the icing for our Sellafield cake: an attractive young woman poisoned by the plant, my mind boggled. This was too good to be true, I thought as an ambulance arrived at the hotel entrance and two paramedics went in with a stretcher. No surely not, I stood back amazed.

Back down the hotel stairs they came with a prone body on a stretcher: a young woman's prone body.

'What's happened?,' I asked the hotel manager who was walking beside the patient. He shook his head. "Who is it?" I asked, he ignored me again. I ran up the stairs to Aylott's room, hammered on his door and told him to get his cameras. Before the ambulance men could close their doors Aylott and I were in the back of the ambulance flashing pictures and trying to get a chat with the poor woman.

The following morning as I came into the breakfast room Aylott, who was talking to the hotel manager, caught my eye and gave me a glance of warning. 'Dick, the manager wants to talk to you,' said Aylott.

'Oh what, about the food poisoning from your steak?' I joked. But if ever a joke was perfectly timed this one was. The hotel manager who had been about to report us to the editor, shrank back from the aggressive positon he had taken with Aylott because he thought we may be involved in some consumer survey of his hotel. His fear produced mental headlines which negated any duty he had to bring to order two guests who had hijacked an ambulance taking a member of his staff to hospital. So that was all right then.

Not quite. Though the hotel was squared away the ambulance service was not. A letter from the area co-ordinator was already in the post to the editor. But fortune was on our side again, during our 'investigation' I had told the ambulancemen that the public interest was definitely being infringed by witholding the identity of this patient from us. I explained she could be suffering as the result of contamination from Sellafield, a complaint which is treated as a joke in Cumbria by the many Cumbrian's NOT affected by the plant's malignancy and all Cumbrians whose livelihood depends on the place.

In my efforts to get at the bottom of what, at 1.00 am, after a selection of fine wines, I was convinced was a conspiracy, I had handed over the Daily Star Freephone number and invited anyone in the ambulance service to check out with the editor in person, the very investigation we were involved in. The ambulance co-ordinator had done just that, and had done so immediately. Fortunately the night news editor, Gordon Gregor, had not gone home early and had taken the ambulance co-ordinator's call. Gregor was now alerted to the potential scandal and monitored the editor's mail for the next few days.

I do not know whether Gregor's charm on the night in question, or subsequent censorship of the editor's post, ended the affair, but I heard no more about it. A bouquet of flowers went to the patient and she was soon back at work having suffered 'women's problems' according to a member of the hotel staff. She was not the Karen Silkwood of Sellafield but a waitress at our hotel and seemed highly amused by the whole affair. She was a game lass. We tipped her well.

We continued our probe into Sellafield and did eventually find our Karen Silkwood, a young woman scrawny before she should have been, and bald-headed from the chemo-therapy used to combat her leaukaemia, which she believed was directly attributed to Sellafield.

We wanted to juxtapose her picture and story alongside that of one of the attractive young women used by BNFL as guides for public tours. These automatons used to run bus trips around the plant poo-pooing 'sensational' press reports and depositing day-trippers in the Sellafield shop where gifts, including atom earrings, could be purchased. Unfortunately, try as we might, our real-life Karen Silkwood did not want any publicity. Her silence might have been paid for, we speculated.

The long days and nights spent gathering our material had taken their toll on Aylott, who was as sick of the Abbey House Hotel as the hotel was of us.

His girlfriend at the time was an Aer Lingus air-hostess, a delightful red-head who adored two things – luxury and having a good laugh.

And to impress the undoubtedly lovely Christobel Symons he left Barrow, drove to Manchester and picked her up from the airport. "I've promised to take her to Lake Windermere" Aylott announced.

In classic monkey style, Aylott had done an ad hoc radius around Sellafield on his UK Hotel Guide and found some horribly expensive pile at the edge of the lake.

'But that's miles away from Sellafield,' I complained.

'No one's asking you to come,' came the airy reply.

But I had to keep abreast of my monkey otherwise I could see the whole story going banana-shaped and anyway I'd never been to the Lake District.

Weeks later when confronted with my blank expenses sheet I struggled to fill the columns explaining the nature of the expenditure, why had we been in Lake Windermere when the story was in Sellafield?

I ran the conundrum past the anti-Sellafield campaigner, Simon Boxer of Cumbrians Opposed to a Radioactive Environment (CORE) who I had interviewed earlier. He told me that lake water from Windermere was used to cool the nuclear re-processing centre.

Bingo! 'Enquiries to Lake Windermere – Re: Cooling Water Scandal'

Six months later a lengthy memo was sent to all features staff from the managing editor Peter Beardsley:

'Features Budget
Reimbursed home expenses claims are currently running at £561 per week over budget. This cannot continue and the cutback starts now. Claims for entertaining are at an unacceptable and unnecessarily high level and a drastic reduction is required. The cutback will not be avoided simply by submitting a receipt to support a claim for entertaining. Claims for taxi fares have also risen sharply and must come down. Where fares are claimed they must be accompanied by a receipt no matter how small the fare. A list of hotels throughout the country is now being compiled and you will be required to use them while on assignments. There will be no exceptions unless approved by the departmental head. Please note that agreed meal rates apply on out of town assignments and while the Company pays for subsistance, drinks, hotel room service and in-house movies are on you.'

At least our Sellafield story ran for a whole week and was the splash three days running or reduced to double-page spreads when Coronation Street or East Enders forced the issue back inside.

BNFL filed a record number of complaints – 62 - to the then Press Council claiming our findings were wrong.

By the time every one of those complaints, bar one, were successfully countered, the Press Council had become the Press

Complaints Commission. The only one which was upheld was a strap-line which was written by a sub.

All the other points we were able to counter thanks to the documentation, mostly published by BNFL itself, which had been sourced by Simon Boxer, analysed and explained by him to me. There was one quote which I had to juggle with: 'The most poisonous place on this planet' was a phrase used in quotations as a strapline, trouble was nobody had actually said it, but they would do soon...It was certainly what everyone we had spoken to, thought, and a phone call to one of the residents in Barrow-in-Furness I had interviewed earlier, soon altered that. 'In fact, come to think of it I did say that at the time, didn't I?' And there are those who say the tabloid reading public are stupid.

We returned to Barrow-in-Furness one last time, a year on, to see how Alexandra Stevens was progressing. She had needed surgery for an eye defect, and her parents had faced stiff opposition from the social services department over adopting the child. Aylott was still sweet with Christobel and I met the pair of them at the Steven's home.

Aylott wanted to set up a 'happy' picture of Alexandra tucking into a huge mountain of ice-cream and so we decided to pay our old friends at the Abbey House Hotel a visit for lunch.

When I tried to book rooms for the night as well the reception desk told me they were 'full', a statement which I doubted. The Abbey House was full to the Daily Star, I felt. During lunch in the hotel dining room I got Caroline to call up the hotel reception on Aylott's mobile phone. Remembering The Sunday Post's obsession with little known royals, I said:

'Tell them you are the PA for King Constantine of Greece – It'll mean nothing to them. Say he's coming up on a visit to Vickers (the nuclear submarine builders based in Barrow) and have they a room available.'

She did so and for King Constantine of Greece there was a room available in a special annex.

'Ask them for the room number up front, say you need it for security reasons, that you will have to check out the room before his arrival,' I said. Next I asked one of the waitresses who we'd befriended over the course of our lengthy sojourns at the hotel, if she could get me a crown.

'You know, anything will do, a piece of cardboard perhaps?'

The well-tipped young attendant returned with a piece of cereal box cut into serrations and stapled together probably thinking it was some prop for the Alexandra shoot: Aylott had already ordered a three foot high stack of ice-cream for her to tuck into. Donning my crown I walked round to reception.

'Afternoon, my name's King Constantine of Greece, could I have the keys to room number 58 in the annex please?'

There was nothing to be done but hand them over.

Their revenge was not long in coming. The following day we drove back south down the motorway, Aylott got a call. As he later told me at a motorway cafe, Caroline had left her handbag in their room. In it was her own ID plus one of Aylott's business cards. Someone at the hotel had decided to call the office number rather than Aylott's mobile number to report the missing handbag.

Aylott was grounded, but not for long. No one else could manage quite as well the grotesque and fantastical assignments handed down to the picture desk from the fevered imagination of the editor. Hitchen liked stories about soldiers, lifeboatmen and heroic, handicapped children. His enemies, who did not refer to him as Mussolini, but as Charlie Drake – though never to his face - said that such pursuit and publication of selfless derring-do was made in hope of a knighthood.

I was not surprised therefore to discover the Customs and Excise service joining Hitchen's long list of worthy causes, to be aired through the Daily Star's columns and thus found myself boarding a custom's cutter in Boston, Lincolnshire with photographer Bob Barclay. We were to make a passage with the service around to Great Yarmouth getting pictures and a story en-route about their fight against drug importation. The 'peg' was the fact that the service were commissioning a state-of-the-art cutter. To that end Hitchen had ordered a second photographer, Frank Barrett, up in a helicopter to get aerial shots of the vessel as well. Three staff men, hire cars, hotel bills, a helicopter, it all seemed a bit OTT. For some reason I now forget, there was a cock-up and

219

Barclay and I sailed on, and Barrett flew over, the wrong cutter, we were aboard an existing boat not the state-of-the-art one. Hitchen didn't seem overly agitated by this, nor the fact that the paper ended up publishing the publicity shot of the new launch taken by the Customs & Excise PR department and which we could have had free in the first place: 'HMS Drugbuster. Exclusive: The Star goes on patrol with unarmed heroes'. Hitchen's sanguine approach become clearer when a sub checked my copy.

'Dick what's all this shite about a surveillance camera company helping in the fight against drugs by supplying equipment for customs? It sounds like a plug.'

'I don't know anything about it.'

And there, at the end of the article two new paragraphs had mysteriously appeared: 'The drugbusters call in outside specialist firms, such as Ambex Marine Division of Brighton, to supply and fit super electronic surveillance equipment on the boats.

'It is with such technology that the war on the drug barons is being waged.'

The company was based near Shoreham, West Sussex where Hitchen kept his yacht. Although he later told me the company name had been inserted because they were supplying equipment to the Customs & Excise.

Hitchen's yacht, I had bought for him the same year. It started with that rare thing: a call at home from the editor. It was quite late.

'Dick, are you in tomorrow?'

'Yes Brian.'

'Can you come straight through and see me?'

'Sure Brian.'

Racking my brains as to what I'd cocked up, I strode with some trepidation into the editor's office the following day. He had a copy of Yachting Monthly magazine open on his desk and a ruler placed across the page.

'Have a look at this Dick.'

A box advertisement had been taken by Customs & Excise – them again – announcing an auction in Plymouth, of property as a result of drug seizures. It didn't seem like the sort of story worthy of a national newspaper's attention.

'Could be a good story in this Dick. I want you to check it out ....'

'Sure, Brian, I said.

'And while you're down in Plymouth,' he added, sliding the ruler across the page into the classified ads section, 'could you check this out as well?'

A circled an advert for a 25ft Westerly Pageant sailing yacht confronted me. He then pulled out his cheque book and gave me a signed, blank cheque.

It just so happened that I knew about a design fault with this particular type of boat which involved their bilge keels. As long as a strengthening modification had been made they were a perfectly good boat, if not it was a necessary expense which would need to be taken into account when considering the asking price.

I drove to Plymouth, looked the yacht over, discovered the modification had been made, and then persuaded the owner to throw in a lot of extra kit, including the inflatable dinghy, for the asking price.

Hitchen was delighted and got me to fill in his cheque with a deposit. 'Take your time coming back,' said the yacht-owning editor, 'I'll tell the desk the auction thing didn't work out,' and off I went for dinner in Dartmouth and an overnight at a top hotel. Next day I headed a little further up country, stopping for a swim at Sidmouth, and meandered into the office two-days later. Hitchen berthed his yacht, which he re-named Scoop, in Shoreham Harbour near his home in Hove. Not long after I bought her for him he had her sailed to Portsmouth during a storm. The crew were seasick and left the boat uncleaned and full of leftover take-away cartons much to the horror of Daily Star photographers who were ordered down to the boat to live aboard her while staking-out a tip-off Hitchen had received about a crew of round-the-world drug runners who were about to land a stash of cannabis secretly stowed in their yacht's keel. 'If our lads had put a flashing neon sign shouting PRESS on the deck they could not have attracted more attention,' Hitchen recalled, 'Meantime the villains were removing the dope in duffle bags and yet there were no pictures...while the Customs and Excise half-wits played at being MI5 peeping at the yachts as the crew emptied the dummy keel right under their noses. I'm not sure who had the thickest team. The Daily Star or HM Customs & Excise.'

The 'silly season' brings out the hardy annuals of the Notting Hill Carnival bobby holding a youngster wearing his helmet, topless bathers causing beach outrages, desert-like pictures of dried up reservoirs if there's a drought, or alternatively, puddle-covered cricket or tennis fields if there's a deluge. Cats stuck up trees, nice dolphins playing with children in West Country harbours, or mice sitting on the noses of cats, for as revered journalist James Cameron said, readers love human interest stories and for most of them that means animals.

During one silly season I joined the press pack on the Isle of Wight where we doorstepped the fire brigade for a whole week while they excavated a collapsed well to rescue 22-year-old Romanus Girenus who had climbed down it on an exploration trip: 'Battle To Reach Man In Tomb'

Great Britain was on holiday and the only room I could get was one with twin beds already booked by my old mentor Tom Merrin.

Merrin had also managed to get his company saloon car, unlike many other hacks, onto the island via the Portsmouth car ferry and I, having come with the hovercraft, was glad to ride shotgun with my generous-hearted 'opponent'.

'Don't lock the doors,' he screeched, 'I'm trying to get it nicked. I've told the office I need an estate. I'm forever giving monkies a ride with all their clobber.' Merrin recounted one particular act of generosity one night during a rain storm: 'The monkey said to me: "Are these tyres Michelin? I'm sure they are. I can hear them". When we stopped he was down on his knees in the pissing rain lighting matches to read what tyres they were.' It nicely exemplified the photographer's abiding passion for all things geekily technical.

The days went by and it looked increasingly unlikely that the man in the well had survived. As the firemen got tantalisingly nearer, we were supposed to be keeping a round-the-clock watch on the location. But Merrin convinced me it wasn't worth it: 'The poor bastard died on day one,' he stated confidently, 'Let's go and dine.'

We did and as Merrin turned on the TV news at 6 am the next morning we both watched the reporter from the local television news shivering in the early morning chill with his collar turned up. He HAD kept a round-the-clock watch.

'I am told,' he stammered, 'that the firemen are within 15 inches of breaking through. We should know the answer in the next hour or so!'

'Soppy bastard,' said Merrin, turning off the telly, 'we'll have breakfast and go to the scene of the grave!'

We did and it was.

In order to get on an early ferry Merrin filed his story as a fatality – BEFORE the body was found.

It was accurate as he later found out, on the mainland, while those of us were stuck in holiday traffic trying to get off. Because the poor fellow did not survive it was no longer more than a column of news. Had he been pulled out alive a scrum would have formed at the hospital to get his story.

One of the most unusual 'silly season' stories was that of the African woman who built a giant mud-hut in the back garden of her council flat in Redbridge, Essex in the summer of 1992. The massive earthworks looked more like the preparations for a nuclear bunker. Perhaps she was just digging in the hope of finding something worth keeping. But by the time photographer Ian Showell had finished snapping her, complete with a flowered umbrella he'd dug out of his boot, and I had written about the culture she'd left behind in Cameroon, the piece became Homesick African builds herself Mudhut.

Redbridge Council did not like the publicity she was getting and her neighbours weren't keen on a cross between an archaelogical dig and World War 1 communications trench being excavated over the fence. So the council threatened to re-posses the flat unless she removed the hut.

Or there was the one about the Chinese illegal immigrant who reached Britain undetected and took up residence in a Sittingbourne wheely-bin: 'Wife finds illegal migrant in the rubbish', and housewife Janet Moore added: 'Of all the wheelie bins in the world he had to pick mine' as she posed for a picture looking shocked as she lifted the bin's lid.

The silly season was also the time when all the top executives, from the editor down through deputy-editor, woman's editor, showbusiness editor, sports editor, features editor, picture editor, and political editor took themselves off to a five star hotel in the countryside for a two day 'think tank!' or 'drink tank' as it was known by those not invited. When they were organised under the Turner regime they would be in the Cheshire area, while Hitchen preferred Surrey. It was a time to let off steam and nobody cared how much it cost: Express Newspapers were paying. Blundell said: 'You went out to get totally rat-arsed every night, jump in the fish pond and chase the swans and rip up the billiard tables. I can recall Andy Carson, the Manchester deputy editor, doing his tin whistle party trick as he danced the length of the restaurant table singing: "Hail, hail the Pope's in jail what the fuck do we care".'

At one such bash the new TV editor Stafford Hildred was so drunk – his water carafe, alongside his name lable on the conference table had been half filled with vodka by his colleagues as an initiation ceremony – that when his time came to outline his ideas he couldn't speak. The mission statements written out in bold felt tip pen on giant sheets of paper pinned to a blackboard were turned over until: 'The escape route is under hut 15 in the latrines' and similar came round and everyone broke for a three-hour lunch. The evening session at one such conference broke up because there was a 'grab –a-granny night disco in full swing and executives kept disappearing,' Blundell said.

Between the shedfulls of wine and cordon bleau food, not to mention liasons dangereuse, these brain storming bacchanalias determined the direction the paper was going in and how to improve it.

All lowly hacks and snappers were memo'd beforehand by their heads of department to submit at least three ideas. Those who were worried about their careers submitted literally layers of 'ideas' others effecting a macho stance would submit less than the required number. Aylott and I would say 'they've had all ours' but would nevertheless come up with an assortment of contrived stunts we hoped would carry us to far away and exotic places.

These ideas, if they were any good, would immediately be re-submitted by the head of department under his own name. If the idea was approved the hack who put it up would be assigned to the 'story'.

To the best of my knowledge Aylott achieved the greatest coup in this category when, in 1988, while shunting in through West London traffic one morning, he was sat jammed in auto fumes staring at a giant billboard poster of a tropical island.

Golden Wonder crisps had glued the banner up around the country with the offer to those unconcerned about saturated fat and salt ingestion to 'win your own paradise island'.

Aylott ran the idea past me, 'We've got to find out where it is and go there first. It's bound to have snakes, mosquitoes, sharks, scorpions, well anyway at least cockroaches.'

It was a classic piece of tabloid inspiration. I hit the phone and the Golden Wonder air-head told me it was somewhere in the Seychelles archipelago. That was good enough to stand up the threat of some tropical beasties.

The desk went potty, they loved it, but not enough to send me as well. I'd had another memo exchange with the managing editor Peter Beardsley who this time had gone to my immediate boss Michael Hellicar with this:

'I do not believe the Features home expenses budget, already overspent by £8,700, can afford to keep Dick Durham in the style to which he clearly aspires. Entertainment to the tune of £171.15 is unreasonable.'

Aylott flew out instead with a Starbird, who was probably more expensive. But she proved reluctant to leave the luxury of an hotel on a neighbouring island and Aylott's piece was more travel-logue than corporate stitch-up. But still he got to see the Seychelles.

As for the executives' own drink tank ideas, I can only recall one from Jimmy Sutherland: 'You know the Sun have got a box on 20 things you never knew about such and such?'.
'Yes?' I said.
'We're going to do 21.'

10. BRAND AWARENESS

All journals need to attract advertisers and endeavour to produce stories which will fit certain consumer profiles. Some magazines even tailor stories to lure in advertisers and run the 'story' adjacent to the advert. On newspapers it's a bit different. British Airways are not going to buy space to announce cut-price fares on the day Concorde crashes, Webley are unlikely to advertise shotgun cartridges in the week that a trio of drug takers are blasted to death in a country lane. The vagaries of news cannot be fitted to match consumer goods. However, softer sections of the paper can and do.

For instance, the holiday pages. All holiday companies use press relations companies to 'interface' with Fleet Street and the bigger regional newspapers. Every year well ahead of school half-terms or summer holidays, Fleet Street 'travel editors' are bombarded with offers of buckshee holidays all over the world. They can go skiing, scuba-diving, rock-climbing or simply toast on a beach anywhere from Sydney to Seattle and all points inbetween. With such a global empire at their feet and the ability to hand out the 'freebies' – after all they can't go on them ALL – it is not surprising that the travel editor's job is one of the most secure in the volatile world of Fleet Street.

Certainly the Daily Star's travel editor Brian O'Hanlon was a well travelled man as was his editor, deputy editor and on down the chain.

As a family man, one of my favourite holidays was taking the ferry from Plymouth to Santander for the drive straight into sunny Spain. The ferry crossings were like that of a cruise liner, a fact I did not hesitate to mention in the glowing travel pieces I wrote. And so readers learnt that Collioure in French Catalonia was a place where 'Wine Is Good For The Art!'. For in a local bar, paintings of Picasso hang.

'Picasso was an artist in more ways than one sense – and he often paid for his booze by doing a quick sketch for the landlord.' Collioure was thus a 'painter's paradise that will appeal to every palette'.

Writing about the family holiday also paid for *my* bar bill in Collioure.

Later, during another vacance to the Dordogne we visited the replica of the Lascaux cave which holds the paintings of cave-men. The real version had been closed to the public for years in order to preserve the art. But even in the mock-up cavern, photography is forbidden.

I was puzzled, how could flash bulbs spoil the acrylic daubings of mammoth, ibex and bison? I was told the owners of the cave held the copyright! But the sub-editors were not interested in any of that and so Daily Star readers learned that: 'There were none of the Flintstones' luxuries for the cavemen who lived in south-west France 32,000 years ago. But those Cro-Magnon chaps were dab hands at the yabba-dabba-doodle.............of elephant, horse and goat....in the belief that cave paintings would make the real thing turn up so they could eat. Nothing much has changed as the stomach still figues large in the thoughts of Dordogne man.'

Other freebie holidays were less exotic, like the time we went to a West Country holiday camp, although on that occasion it was as a favour to the newspaper on my behalf and not the other way round. Early in 1996 the sing-song voice of the then news editor Hugh Whittow 'The Welsh Wizard' trilled down the phone: 'Dick? How old are your kids?' They were then seven and five. 'Listen can you do me a favour? Can you go and spend a weekend at Pontins, it won't come off your time, you can take days in lieu.'

He was very apologetic at having to request one of his reporters should undergo what he clearly perceived was an onerous task. In the light of his own regular tours of the USA with his family courtesy of the travel editor, it was perhaps not surprising. But why on earth did he want to take me out of 'the area' -I was by now covering East Anglia, Kent and Sussex from home - to give me a buckshee weekend? The answer was soon forthcoming.

A former Pontin's holiday camp had been sold and turned into a prison. This had inspired the Daily Star cartoonist, Bill Caldwell, to draw the daily laugh at the expense of Pontins, suggesting that all their camps already shared a lot in common with HM prisons! Ha Ha.

Pontins did not see the funny side of it however and told the advertising department that if that is what Express Newspapers thought of them then they would withdraw their advertising, worth a rumoured £1 million a year.

'Have a word with the PR,' Whittow continued singing, 'and sort if for us can you mate?' I was to go and enjoy the delights Pontins had to offer and write it up as a travel piece for the holiday page. I did indeed contact the PR woman and suggested I go to their camp in Norfolk, not too far from my patch.

'Oh that one won't be open,' came the reply 'You'd be better off going to Brean Sands near Weston-super-Mare, and you cannot possibly experience all that Pontins has to offer in a weekend, you must take a week!' On the latter point she was adamant and I did not think Whittow would thank me for refusing and provoking the wrath of Pontins further.

'And remember, Hugh,' I said to Whittow, once it was all fixed up 'this is not coming out of my time OK?'

My wife Cathy and I, plus daughters Kate and Emily, arrived at Brean Sands on a warm spring day. The girls stripped off and made a beeline for the swimming pool, followed soon after by myself. My bald pate parted the waters as I dived in but by the time I'd surfaced I looked like the lead singer with Status Quo, with several rogue strands of children's hair draped over my dripping cranium. At reception Cathy had collected £180 worth of meal vouchers which we soon discovered could be exchanged for wine. We therefore dined outside the camp most nights and returned to drink the Chateau Pontins.

We spent the days touring the beauty of Somerset: Glastonbury Tor, Wells Cathedral, Cheddar Gorge and Wookey Hole. There was a great 'greasy spoon' across the road where we had breakfast, all in all it was a very pleasant week and my copy reflected this.

Pontins got their glowing critique – the Sales and Marketing director Simon Sheard wrote to the editor: 'I particularly liked the quote of Dick's five-year old daughter Emily,"I want to stay here for two thousand, hundred, million years!" Thanks for the support!'. Express Newspapers' advertising revenue was no longer in jeopardy and we had an extra week's holiday. Everyone was happy.

Each year the Daily Star raised its own profile with the Daily Star Gold Awards. This was a lavish ceremony to which the great and the not so good were invited to receive a star-shaped alloy pendant on a piece of red ribbon for being heroic. The awards were a southern phenomena – that is to say the ceremony is held in London. To promote The Daily Star in the north it was felt more appropriate to hold the 'Blackpool Bash'. This was a roadshow in which unlucky staffers had to stand and shout:

'What do you read?' and when the answer came back 'The Sun' or 'The Mirror", were obliged to offer Daily Star T-shirts.

As far as The Daily Star Gold Awards were concerned the heroic deeds to be celebrated could be performed by little children who had overcome great physical obstacles, soldiers in war zones, policemen, firemen etc. It was always a tricky piece of organisation because nobody on the paper could guarantee that the big names, which pull in the publicity, would turn up. Consequently the executives were loath to promise the ordinary 'heroes' that they would be dining with certain soccer stars or showbiz guests. As the years went by, however, the awards took on a little more gravitas, thanks to Hitchen's 'pull', as at first Margaret Thatcher turned up to hand out the tin 'gold' awards and then star of stars, Princess Diana. While covering a Russian trade show in London's Islington I was ordered by the newsdesk to see if I could find someone with links to Boris Yeltsin so that we could invite him along to present the 'awards.'

So the desk were understandably nervous when in 1993 they got a phone call alleging one of their 'heroes' was a fraud. Lined up to be decorated with the pendant was Pat Daley, a housewife, who had rescued her 'war-hero' husband Gerry from muggers. Gerry, who had been in the Army serving in Northern Ireland, or so he claimed, had survived a bomb attack which had left him partly physically handicapped. The pair ran a charity shop in East Sussex. But a phone call had alerted the desk to the fact that all Daley's neighbours found him hard to recognise from the glowing account of his life which had appeared in the Daily Star. The great fear of the incumbent news editor Graham Jones was that somehow The Sun would get to hear of the cock-up and turn up at the Savoy to put the mockers on the Gold Awards ceremony. Brian Hitchen, by now a CBE and with potentially much bigger gongs in the offing than those he was conferring on our in-house heroes, would not be amused.

I was sent down to East Sussex to try and retrieve the invite which would secure the Daley family's presence at the Savoy. There was no-one at home when I called, so more out of habit than anything else, I started banging up neighbours. Soon I was chatting to a loose-tongued old gent who laughed at claims that his neighbour was a crippled war hero. Apparently Daley dug a local allotment seemingly unimpeded by war wounds. 'He's known as Billy Bullshit round 'ere,' came the discomforting remark.

Later in the day Mrs. Daley answered my knock. She was delighted to have a representative of the Daily Star call and Soon I was ushered in and chatting over tea in her comfortable lounge. The problem the Daily Star was confronted with, I lied, was that IRA activity was building up on the mainland and our police sources had told us it was feared that a high profile target was being sought, possibly in London.

I let her mull on this for a while then added: 'And what with your husband's service in Northern Ireland ....' I left the sentence hanging, but she readily understood. I explained that as a security measure all the invites were being recalled so that they could be stamped with a special code, did she still have hers? Of course she did, and immediately handed it over and making my excuses I left. Jones, of course, wasn't satisfied: could I go back and get the rail warrant which had been issued to the family for their travel to London?

I suggested that the only way to prevent the Daleys coming to the Savoy was for me to take them to lunch on the day in question, as a consolation prize.

'Brill' said Jones, concerned only that his arse was no longer on the line. I returned to their home, this time husband was in residence. I explained to him that we would need his old army number for 'security reasons!' Strangely enough he couldn't remember it, and rather took a stab at what it might be. Unfortunately it did not check out when I later rang the MOD. Now I returned once more to break the bad news. Mr and Mrs Daley could not be placed on the list of guests for the all important 'security reasons' but by way of an apology we, that is to say I, would take them out for lunch at a restaurant of their choice. They chose a local hotel and on the big day I turned up and drove them there.

They seemed quite relieved and Mrs. Daley ordered Liebfraumilch with her meal, at which I insisted she have champagne, which she tried but did not like. So I drank Moet & Chandon while they sipped their hock.

All methods of promoting newspapers have their pitfalls. The Daily Star can claim a first for initiating Bingo throughout its pages. The Sun then followed with Zingo, but when an administrational error in The promotions department produced 150,000 winning numbers it was left to the editor, Kelvin MacKenzie to get the paper off the hook.

Extra type-setters were brought in to print the names and addresses of the multitude of 'winners'. They ran through the back pages of the newspaper, each taking a few pence each from the win. The strap-line at the top read 'Every One A Winner!' The front page MacKenzie reserved for the poor sap in the promotions department, who was taking the can. There he was in dunce hat under the headline 'The Sun shows you the sinners' His name and home town were published as though he were a common criminal, and that night as he got off his commuter train, the local paper team were waiting outside his house, to interview him.

When the Daily Star in conjunction with the Daily Express, started the Millionaire of the Month Bingo game, they discovered they would have to spend a small fortune on TV commercials trying to convince readers it was for real. 'This was one of the problems with big prizes : you can get more interest if you are giving away ten grand because people know you can pay ten grand. They don't know how you are going to pay a million. At least that was the case until the Lottery started, people have since been educated to big money,' said Hitchen.

Don Mackay had to babysit one of the first successful candidates, who I will call Tom, at the Savoy, along with photographer Stanley Meagher. Meagher & Mackay got along famously with the newly enriched Tom who had promised to pay off Meagher's mortgage and supplied Mackay with a continuous supply of lager. When a reunion was fixed up for Tom and his long lost family, in Herefordshire ,Mackay escorted him down there while Colin Bell from the Daily Express had been sent on ahead to await the newly monied fellow's arrival. Such tactics were to ensure no other newspapers, local, national or news agencies got to talk to him. The problem for Bell was that he had to wait the best part of a week before the party arrived. He got bored and when eventually Tom turned up Bell had already been celebrating rather too successfully. As a jolly jape – and as a matey dig at the Star - he stepped forward and said: 'Good to meet you Tom I knew you'd win, the whole thing was rigged.' Travelling with the party were adjudicators from Touche Ross, who were making sure the millionaire game was credibly run. They did not see the funny side of Bell's very public remark and he was immediately recalled to London.

But even more disturbing phone calls started to come in to the London newsdesk this time concerning Tom and none of them were complimentary. He had, it would seem, an uncertain place in the affections of his neighbourhood. A worried Brian Hitchen sent Alastair Buchan down to Hereford to work as a fixer inbetween writing the odd feature on the newly wealthy fellow. 'I was dispensing £500 in used notes to people making claims about him,' he said.

'We just wanted them to go away. I had one father who was alleging Tom had broken his daughter's back, and a garage owner, alleging he had screw-drivered scratches along his cars.' The angry father refused 'on principle' to take the hush money until Buchan, taking a pee upstairs, stuck his head round the door of the master bedroom,'It was covered in crucifixes.'

And so after appealing to the father's Christian nature Buchan was successful. But while his problems could be bought off, the hacks were more unpredictable.

By now Hitchen had decided to get Tom out of Hereford, out of England, and Buchan was told to get the winner to Heathrow along with Mackay and Meagher.

But MacKay, who had fallen in love with a local barmaid, refused to go.Worse, Tom, who had become Mackay's best friend, would not go without him. Mackay had to talk Tom into leaving his town with Buchan, a fellow Scot and trusted friend. Next Buchan discovered the winner's promise of paying off Meagher's mortgage. 'I had to talk Stanley out of it – I told him that if it got out he would be finished professionally.' Eventually Tom was flown to Sri Lanka. Hitchen had told him that now he was a millionaire he would not have to pay for anything – people would queue up trying to ingratiate themselves with him – and they would pay instead. 'It's only when you've got nothing they won't give you any,' he had said.

So when the foreign trip came up Tom's first words were 'Who's paying?'

'The Sri Lankan Tourist Board,' Hitchen was able to reassure him.

In the best hotel on the island Tom 'fell in love' with his chambermaid and announced his intention to marry her.

'We can't have that we'll look bloody ridiculous,' stormed Hitchen.

Buchan was ordered to prevent the match. And Meagher talked Tom out of buying her a £30,000 gold necklace. Then Tom discovered she lived in a shack with no running water. She had to fetch water from a nearby stream, so he bought her a pump. Then Tom met the very large boyfriend of the girl and backed off. Later a 'photo opportunity' was arranged between Tom and 'Miss Sri Lanka.' When Tom later found Buchan talking to 'his girlfriend', who was being paid to pose with snorkelling gear with the Croesus of Hereford, he went into a sulk and demanded Buchan be flown back to the UK for chatting up 'his bird'.

The Daily Star's executives need not have worried in the end for there were so many skeletons in the cupboards of the rival newspaper's millionaire winners - the Daily Mirror's candidate from East Anglia had a shop-lifting conviction and was allegedly a 'soldiers friend" - that dog, for once, did not eat dog.

Arguably the Daily Star's greatest asset was the Beau Peep cartoon strip carried on the back page. By Roger Kettle and Andrew Christine it was the story of Dennis Pratt a dozy member of the French Foreign Legion. The strip was once so popular that the paper's executives tried to cash in on it further by announcing another kind of award altogether: the Dennis Pratt Award For Outstanding Stupidity. Readers were asked to nominate those they thought suitable for a Pratt sticker. And there were scores of nominees, some like, John French who wanted to start an Orange Order in Portsmouth and also ban Wimpey Homes, Maria Giles who campaigned for the Radical

Party whose manifesto was to promote pornography and Rickie Powell the Beastie Boys roadie who tried to outgross the group, all got their awards: for the story 'A Pride of Pratts.' But Mrs Ivy Wilson of Carshalton, Surrey was left off the list and wrote in to complain:

'Dear Sir,
It has been weeks now that I have been waiting for my Pratt badges.....I bet you say you're out of them.......I've waited so long......could you send them please.......it's been so very, very long. You must have caught up with everyone's letters by now, So please be kind send mine on now would you? I've been waiting patiently and not seen anything in the paper saying sorry.'

Another important ingredient of any newspaper is the astrology column. There is a knack to convincing even the credulously suggestible that Gipsy Rose Lee is accurate on a daily basis and such soothsayers can earn a lot of money. Consequently several would-be Zodiac forecasters try selling their predictions to newspapers. Nigel Blundell's reply to one such unsuccessful candidate – a Ms Caroline Gerald of Stafford – ran:

'Dear Ms Gerald,
Thank you for your letter offering your services as a clairvoyant promising "accurate personal predictions". I feel, however, that your services may have been of more use to the addressee of your letter "Mr Lloyd Turner, Editor, The Star, 121 Fleet Street" if you had presented them to him two years ago. Because it was shortly after then that he unexpectedly left the employ of Express Newspapers. Subsequently there have been two further editors, the newspaper is no longer titled "The Star", and the address is no longer "Fleet Street".
'I imagine that by now you can at least predict my reply.'

When the headmaster of Stowe School, Christopher Turner, banned another cartoon strip which appeared in the Star – Judge Dredd – because of it's use of incorrect grammar and slang, I was despatched to the public school armed with a pile of papers to hand out to the pupils: 'The Star Is Tops With Toffs'.

'The boys of a Brideshead-style school have given your Star a big thumbs up.'

Jolly hockey-stick pupils of Stowe School gathered round as we handed out free copies.

Their verdict: "The Star is tops for fun".............'

For a time the Daily Star employed The Sun's TV critic Garry Bushell but he did not stay long and following his return to The Sun started publicly describing his former Star colleagues as 'winos and pissheads'. Lawyers from the Daily Star went to the High Court seeking an injunction restraining Bushell from repeating the accusations. Private Eye's Street of Shame column also reported how night editor Peter Hill, who they said had been dubbed 'Thrush' by a secretary for being an 'irritating little cunt', had entered Bushell's office armed with a crossbow and later used it to fire off a sharpened pencil while being 'unsteady on his feet'. Hill then asked Bushell if he could get him an 'unlicensed pistol' because he lived in Brixton and feared being burgled. This was all contained in an affidavit produced by Bushell at the High Court. Bushell had now set himself up as a target for a missile far more deadly than a sharpened pencil. Some years down the road, the chance came for the Daily Star's executives to get their own back and I was sent off to doorstep Bushell outside a girlfriend's house in Tunbridge Wells, Kent. After we photographed him leaving her home early in the morning his wife, Carol, told us: 'You can't throw 22 years of marriage away on shagging.'

Bushell was hardly a major celebrity but he was the Daily Star's public enemy number one and the 'story' was splashed across the front page: 'Telly Garry Broke My Heart' and the wretched Carol was described as the 'wife of a TV star'!. Just to make sure the bemused readers knew who he was, two pages inside on 'the love rat with stars in his eyes', carried a short biography on the beefy-faced hack: 'Garry Bushell has become one of Britain's best-known entertainment personalities after shooting to fame as an outspoken TV pundit............He was once Gotcha'd by practical joker Noel Edmonds, who had him caged on his House Party.' So now we knew.

There was no hint that the Daily Star's new editor, Phil Walker, who succeeded Hitchen, had also 'Gotcha'd' Bushell by using his newspaper in a personal vendetta.

11. WAR

The ego leads you into one hell of a mess. There I was comfortably ensconced on the second floor of Ludgate House, double-glazed against the cruel world and with no more troubling matter that to find five 'case histories' of people unfortunate enough to have been abducted by aliens. That there was a war going on I could not ignore, almost every page of the newspaper was covered with it. It had begun for the Daily Star with the front page headline: 'Bangdad' after the first bombing of the Iraqi capital in January 1991. The man whose idea that headline was, night editor Peter Hill, had thought it up days before it was needed. He couldn't wait to use it.

Now I, too, was to join this war. Foolishly, perhaps, I had requested the job. I had asked Brian Hitchen for the chance to cover a war, even though I had moved into features from news. I had asked to be sent to the Falklands War a decade earlier, but another reporter Mick Seamark, had already been earmarked for that one: thanks to Hitchen having sent Magaret Thatcher a big bunch of red roses. For until then the Daily Star had not been included in the MOD's guest list for war.

This time round the Daily Star already had reporters in the field. They had staffers in Saudi Arabia where the bangs for Baghdad were coming from. We had staff in the Gulf itself on a Navy ship where other Baghdad-bound bangs were originated. We had a photographer and yet another reporter in Jordan where victims of the Baghdad banging were expected to flee. We even had somebody in Israel peppered with bangs FROM Baghdad. He was Iain Mayhew, a features executive there on holiday. That's where I came in. It was Friday night when the news editor telephoned me and told me I was going to Israel: "It's where we all want to be isn't it?" by way of bolstering up my sheepishness now that my chance of glory had arrived.

I hired a driver to take me to Heathrow. We had hurtled round the M25 chicaning in and out of the lorries through the night. As we drove BBC Radio 4 , dedicated to cover the war on FM, told us how Bruce Cheeseman a reporter, had gone missing somewhere out in the war zone.

I wondered what the office would say if I went off a-hunting UFO abductees after all? I set aside the thought: I wanted to see my name corralled in a little box on the newspaper's front page. In a war zone.

'Don't suppose this is one you're going to enjoy?' said John, my driver, cheerfully.

'No,' I said, affecting nonchalance. I did not add that I had put my name forward, that I could have been safely using my investigative powers to track down alien kidnappers.

'Mind you, those shonkers don't mess about,' John broke in again.

'Sorry?'

'The Jews, they don't mess about, once they get going.'

238

'No, true.'

'And they've got the bloody weapons to zap 'em.'

It was the perfect word to describe this war. So far the newspapers were full of 'pin-point' bombing attacks that had 'clinical accuracy'. Our imaginations were criss-crossed with precision bomb sights every time we read of another military target being 'taken out'.

Just a couple of days ago I had stood with my wife Cathy and one-year-old daughter Katie at Battle Abbey in East Sussex. Down into a peaceful valley we looked and tried to imagine the Hastings beach-head where Normans charged the Saxons. A zap was an abstract assault and less troubling than a crunched bone, a cracked skull, the twang of a bow string or the clatter of battered armour. Reading later how King Harold took a sword blow to the thigh, which went 'through the bone' produced a wince. A zap was cleaner, just a line ending in a symmetrical star of detonation. But of course a zap was a lie. At the end of a zap would be flesh torn to the bone as well. A zap was something which belonged to the vocabulary of alien-hunters and hunted.

The El Al check-in desk officer at Heathrow put my hungover and banging head through an interrogation that would have unearthed a Palestinian, had there been one, from my genetic make-up stretching back to my great, great grandfather's maiden aunt. Exhausted from anticipation and dehydration from my send off dinner, I went to collapse in the departure lounge and then my scrutineer discovered I'd got a first class ticket, not economy. Unbelievably I had to go through the questioning all over again at the correct check-in desk!

On the flight to Tel Aviv there was only one other passenger, clearly Saddam Hussein's missile attacks on Israel were having the desired effect.

Ben Gurion airport was strangely quiet too, for an airport. I'd never been there but I assumed it was normally a busy place. The hire car I drove into Tel Aviv took me through equally empty highways. I soon discovered that every evening Tel Aviv was evacuated by its citizens and workers, most of them anyway, in a long traffic jam which the Daily Star headlined 'Exodus' which I'd read before somewhere.

I felt like a brave pioneer venturing into danger, my duty to inform the world about the suffering being inflicted by an evil dictator, this was better than skate-boarding ducks and, so far so good, no dressing up. Then I arrived at the Hilton Hotel and found it packed to the seams with Fleet Street's finest and all manner of world newsmen and women. It was a bit of a let down to my idea of being a lone truth hunter, but welcomingly reassuring.

Talk at the hotel was of Alun Rees' exclusive for the Sunday Express, in which he revealed how he witnessed an Iraqi Scud attack when two missiles sailed over the roof of the Hilton, which is on the beach, and crashed harmlessly into the sea. Other reporters who had not seen the attack suggested Rees had filed the story in order to get Saddam to close down his range and leave the Hilton a safe haven. It seemed ingenious to me, but Rees was outraged at the suggestion and adamant he had seen the missiles go over. He told me how he saw the sea 'bubbling' with the impact of something large which had dropped out of the sky. Rees, being from a military family, had a better idea than most of us of just what would happen if a Scud should land carrying a chemical war-head, an idea reinforced by the Israeli Defence Force who had spelt out the modus operandi to Rees in the event of such an attack. If there were a gas attack we would be locked in sealed rooms for 24-40 hours while the agent cleared, we would thus be incapable of covering the story, 'and I don't fancy being stuck in a sealed room with a lot of sweaty Israelis for three days,' Rees said after being told the rooms had been stacked with enough rations to sustain life for the best part of a week.

Rees had been in Tel Aviv seven days ahead of me and had been 'on location' for every missile attack on the city. He had lived through all the Scud strikes and was now considering the merits of operating from Jerusalem, a safer location because of its large Palestinian population. Many journalists had covered the war from there throughout. Rees argued that, because the censor would not let us name streets for fear of improving the Iraqis' range, and that we also could not use victims' names, as it was thought Saddam's regime would use a Tel Aviv telephone book to find out where his missiles had landed and as the Daily Express was getting bored with stories of missiles dropping on Tel Aviv, he might as well cover the story from Jerusalem and get some sleep.

Later when Rees, then a staff reporter on the Daily Express, discovered he was getting no extra pay for filing to the Sunday Express, he became very angry. He demanded a neutron bomb be dropped on Baghdad. 'Then save one for Damascus, another for Teheran and take us all back to 1948 with oil suppliers in friendly hands and fuck the ragheads,' he said and set off for Jerusalem.

The parties were good at the Hilton, and the wine flowed freely, which is why I stayed on and the place was packed with incredibly glamorous East European prostitutes, which was why others stayed.

In the Jerusalem Post I learned how to prevent a gas-mask fogging up by leaving a piece of potato in it, and how to get reluctant children into their protective cots, by luring them in with a favourite toy. Readers were advised to 'rearrange family albums' or focus on somebody worse off to alleviate stress. There was also an emotional hotline I could dial if I wanted someone to talk me through it.

The first time the air raid sirens went off I was in the restaurant of the hotel having dinner. To see men in green army fatigues, many Israeli Defence Force officers were also billetted at the hotel, get up and run from their tables was not a little worrying. But I was with Frank Barrett, a notoriously tight photographer. While there was white wine on the table he refused to leave until we'd drunk it all. Then Barrett, Neil Syson of The Sun and I made our way to my room on the 11th. floor. An angry IDF man in his gas-mask approached us menacingly down the corridor and demanded we go to the sixth floor where the sealed room was located. We took the fire escape stairs and hid until he passed by, knocking on doors to make sure the hotel rooms were empty. Then we went back to my room. From the balcony we saw four large flashes away to the north-east somewhere over Haifa. One far away, low, thud sounded. Syson speculated that the IDF were not keen for us to see how many Scud missiles were coming over and therefore wanted us out of the way in the sealed room. Half an hour later the all-clear sounded. An IDF briefing informed us two Patriot anti-missile rockets had successfully downed one Scud. Debris had scattered over residential and wooded areas of Haifa. But another Scud missile had demolished a two-storey residential building about 1/2 a mile from the Hilton. The 500lb, 'conventional' warhead exploded injuring scores of Tel Aviv residents too poor to join the nightly exodus. About 60 suffered cuts, others were seriously injured. One woman was carried from the mashed concrete with no legs, a baby was undergoing surgery for serious head injuries. Three people died from heart attacks in the vicinity of the bomb.

The following night I was taking wine with Mayhew, the Daily Star executive who had been on holiday in Israel when the war had broken out. We were in his hotel, the Hotel Dan down the coast a little way from the Hilton. The sirens went off again and people started running, pulling on gas masks. It was unsettling, seeing everyone take a 'zap' seriously. Mayhew and I sat in a room sealed off from potential clouds of nerve gas or cholera spores, a damp towel laid across the door crack. After a few minutes we decided our sanctuary was faintly ridiculous for hacks sent to 'cover' the attacks and so we left and ascended the two floors to Mayhew's room to see if there was anything we could actually witness from his balcony. The missiles travelled at 3,000 miles an hour and arrived in Israeli air space within 6 minutes of being fired from western Iraq so such a languid approach to reporting was to prove fruitless.

From Mayhew's hotel balcony we peered myopically into the night sky in a farcical bid to obtain first hand eye-witness material for our employers. Meanwhile the irritating Cable News Network , on Mayhew's television, were already reporting a Patriot anti-missile missile having been fired at at least two Scuds. Their 'live' reporter stood on the roof of his hotel. Presumably he had boldly spurned the sealed room drill. Mayhew and I slumped on his hotel bed and succumbed to CNN's ubiquity. Their Jerusalem office reporter was on but at least he was wearing his gas-mask. Later others jeered at this: Jerusalem was not thought to be under threat, holding as it does, holy Islamic as well as Christian relics.

After 1/2 an hour the all-clear sounded: one long continuous howl of the air-raid siren, as opposed to the wee-oh, wee-oh when it's not all clear, and we went back to the bar where another CNN-tuned TV held us in thrall. Like rabbits in the car headlights we froze in front of the live TV. There was a feeling that if we moved we might miss something...

The bar staff were relieved to see us, and not just because we hadn't paid. From them we learnt where the missile had fallen. Shortly after an ambulance whistled by throwing up water from huge rain puddles. Mayhew, being my superior, decided he would go to the scene and I would return to the Hilton for the Israeli Defence Force briefing. I joined the reporters from the other British national dailies.

If any of them were rattled none showed it. But I was relieved the rather forced jokes about Scuds and Saddam Hussein, the songs they were going to make up, the T-shirts we would have printed with gas-mask logo, had stopped. An impassioned Colonel Raanan Gissin, the deputy chief spokesman of the Israeli Defence Force, was imploring reporters not to give the location of the hit in their reports and therefore help Saddam's missile launch crews improve their range. Gissin affected a macho image through continuous gum-chewing as he briefed reporters. Slim -hipped, short and dark with rolling brown eyes, his handsome Levatine face sat atop a taught sinuous neck. That's what you noticed about all the Israeli military, their necks. They were not necessarily powerful or broad, but they were all without a trace of fatness whatever their age. From that alone you knew these men were fit.

Colonel Gissin was annoyed by several things, first and foremost the French TV or radio crew he believed gave away the location of the missile impact, secondly inaccurate reports that the warhead contained the feared chemicals, thirdly the fact that reporters were already filing stories about the dead when no fatalities had yet been confirmed.

With white chest hair among the black sprouting from his unbuttoned green fatigue shirt he said: 'I don't want to give you this in bits and pieces, there is a statement being prepared so please if you have some patience.' After the briefing he explained to one elderly lady, a very painted, very coiffured, very chic Jewish lady, why the state was still recommending to its citizens that they put on their gas masks and shut themselves in sealed rooms rather than seek the shelter of bunkers, despite the latest Scud attack on Israel being conventional and not chemical. It was because a direct hit on a bunker would blow it up killing most of the occupants and therefore clock up a higher casualty rate than if people were 'spread out' in their sealed rooms. Not only that, but IF there were a gas attack the chemicals, being heavier than air, would tend to drop to earth and bunkers are harder to seal.

This only partly reassured the old woman. She wanted someone to safeguard her totally from fate, not just give her a calculated measure. It was truly a home-owner's nightmare.

Deputy Foreign Minister Benjamin Netanyahu's description 'live on CNN' of Saddam Hussein as a 'Master Terrorist' was a good one. As I watched the injured stretchered away from the scene, courtesy of CNN, I reflected that still the war was a zap war for me in the comfort of the Hilton. It was no longer a zap war for Mayhew. His night at the scene of the impact had made its mark on him. His Nordic looks which long ago had earned him the nickname 'The Vision', had taken on a sickly, ghoulish pallor beneath the Mediterranean roast turkey tan his holiday had turned him.

The following morning it was my turn to visit the scene of the Scud's grounding to get the full picture. I took a mini bus with Gordon Hay of the Daily Mirror and Paul Harris of the Daily Mail, along with an L.A. Times photographer to the bombed suburb of Tel Aviv. The area was taped off and civil defence crews were dealing with a surreal landscape of severed gas mains, torn and exposed electric cables, tangles of telephone wires. Uprooted olive trees and splintered telegraph poles were festooned with bedding, and clothing. Domestic objects looked puzzlingly sordid, torn from their proper place in private dwellings and revealed to the public gaze. It was not unlike what we dreaded seeing: human parts torn from their proper place. The typical

Tel Aviv dwelling is a functional, unfinished structure. The squat blocks of lightweight concrete are punctured by square, unimaginative windows and balconies moulded in situ in the block work. The roofs support gas tanks, water tanks and all the other paraphernalia of utility exposed to the sky. Air-conditioning units bulge in crude, bolt-on appendage from the upper storey walls. When a Scud hits such a complex and exposed habitat, the resulting ruin is a dangerous cocktail of live cables, leaking gas and sudden fountains of water main.

One old woman was trying to find some order in the ruins of her home. She was still surrounded by her four walls it was just that they were now horizontal. She was dusting off the powdered concrete of her home's collapse from a picture frame in her kitchen which now had only fresh Mediterrranean air for walls. She proclaimed it a miracle that the photograph the frame contained, of her two-year-old grandaughter, had survived undamaged. The streets of the surrounding area were littered with Venetian blind slats, scattered like sycamore pods on the ground. Later we were taken to a hotel where one nine-year-old girl, with her bus-driving father, three brothers and mother now homeless, were being sheltered. The girl had drawn a crude picture of Scuds flying across the sky knocking over orange trees and her daddy crying beneath. It had not been copied from CNN. The zap was losing it's definition.

Every night more and more of these ramshackle Israeli breeze block homes would lie in ruins. There were classic stories such as the air raid shelter next to a school which took a direct hit leaving the school untouched, interviews with Holocaust survivors who had managed to dodge the gas of the chambers at Auschwitz only to face the threat of the same chemical, Zyklon B, on the warheads aimed at Israel.

Saddam Hussain woke me up one evening as I lay dozing on my hotel bed. The air-raid warnings sounded. I got up quickly, dressed and as I did so somebody on reception spoke through my telephone set like big brother telling me to 'go to the sealed room on the 6th. Floor.' Suddenly I heard a large bang over the city to the north. Then a starburst over the sky not a mile away. In the clear night sky I could see some smoke trails. I telephoned the office, and as I did so I watched a silver bullet streak across the sky from the north. It did not seem higher than my balcony on the 11th. Floor. It was one of the anti-missile rockets, the Patriot. I ran down the fire escape stairs, more bangs were going off, you could feel the vibration.

This turned out to be a seven-strong Scud attack. All Scuds had been hit by Patriots but there were 40 injured from the resulting flying debris, one dead. In the morning Barrett and I went to Tel Aviv's main hospital Ichilov, to photograph one of the casualties: a four-year-old girl. Glass splinters had been removed from her brain and one leg. She lay in her cot her face cut and bruised, her eyes blacked and a bandage around her head. I was disturbed by Barrett's attempts to get a more moving picture. He was trying to move the teddy bear closer to the girl's sedated head. But my discomfort soon vanished when the surgeon who had operated on her, moved the teddy himself and then unwrapped a Barbie doll and placed that beside the girl's head as well. Encouraged by his co-operation Barrett moved a chair close to the bedside and stood up on it for some moody elevation. Every Israeli understands the value of international propaganda against their foes.

By now 20 Scud missiles had been fired by Iraq at Israel without Israeli retaliation. It was rumoured that if a Scud hit a school and certainly if a chemical weapon was fired, then Israel would retaliate and retaliate with a nuclear weapon.

Wearing a gas mask added to the claustrophobia already created by the low night sky full of threat, although once I had discovered the mask had a rubber straw attachment, enabling the continuous consumption of champagne, I had no objection to donning the thing. But the rubber smell insinuated Itself into the pores of the skin: after a few minutes wear my face stank like a car tyre store.

As soon as the sirens went off we were supposed to head for the sealed rooms within the hotel, having donned our personal gas masks. However, we hacks were loath to go into the rooms for the aforementioned reasons outlined by Rees. We hung back awaiting others to go first. After a few days we got used to the air raid sirens: Scuds did not come anywhere near the Hilton so

246

perhaps Rees' exclusive had an effect, and eventually we stopped even *heading* towards the sealed rooms.

Barrett and I managed to inject some tabloid 'light' by interviewing Miss Israel in both her glamour gear and her Israel Defence Fatiques, every person in Israel has to do a stint in the army. After a while inevitably London got tired with Scud attacks: they just weren't killing anyone. Their disinterest rubbed off: we held Scud parties on the balconies of the Hilton. Our fireworks, the Patriot Anti-missiles bursting against the Scuds as they came in.

ITN's Colin Baker held mock TV interviews with us assembled hacks for our 'eye-witness accounts'. One night we were banned from a local bar for staging a 'raid' on it. We all burst in throwing 'air' hand grenades and holding 'air' rifles, which understandably didn't go down too well. Eventually we braved driving out in the centre of Tel Aviv away from the safety of the coast. On the first such sortie Gordon Hay, of the Daily Mirror, the Daily Mail's Paul Harris, John Passmore of the London Evening Standard, The Sun's Neil Syson and myself were at a Jewish café about a mile from the hotel. Suddenly the air raid sirens went off and we were led into a deep basement. We noticed that huge unsealed openings led up into the street level. We fiddled with our food as we tried to ignore the fact that we would be totally unprotected in a gas attack. When the sirens went off again we dashed en masse out of the restaurant and started running down the unlit and empty streets making a bee-line for the safety of the untargeted beach.

As we galloped along John Passmore, puffing along with the rest of us, said: 'Just a minute, that's the all clear!'

Sure enough we listened and the crescendo of the sirens was going in reverse: the threat was over. Amazingly we had actually paid for the meal, if ever there had been an excuse to 'do a runner' we'd missed it.

My own fears were based on what had ACTUALLY been fired at Israel, namely TNT. I liked to get plenty of reinforced concrete over my bald pate when the alarms sounded. The Hilton was 17 storeys high. One hoped a Scud could not penetrate so many floors and yet one still wanted to be up a few storeys to avoid the ground-hugging gas. The Scuds were not very effective at killing people, not directly anyway. There were road accidents when cars hit rubble in unseen streets. Some new born babies suffocated in their gas-protected incubators. All very horrible, but not cataclysmic in a land as troubled as Israel.

One day I checked in with the newsdesk informing them of a story I had filed on an American academic who had given a talk on terrorism. They weren't interested. The paper used nothing of the stories I had filed the day before, which included a civil engineer who had lost his parents, brother, four aunts, four uncles and a cousin at Auschwitz and who was now facing a potential gas attack from Iraq with German made weapons.Another was a story about a baby born during a Scud attack, her first impressions of human kind were that they looked like black frogs until midwives took their gas-masks off. So a little peeved, because the Daily Mirror used something on each of these, I asked if they were losing interest in Israel. 'No mate, don't worry,' said Stuart Winter, 'you're here, you're number 13 on the schedule, yeah here it is, "Durham: Scud Watch."'

As our newsdesks reduced the Scud, or Skoda missile, as we by now had dubbed them, attacks to a few paragraphs inside the paper, we went sight-seeing, courtesy of Israeli Defence Force who took us up to the Lebanese border where a lantern-jawed young major went on the record to say he would have no hesitation in going into another sovereign territory, in theory anyway, and killing people he believed were a threat to Israel. In fact, he said he had already carried out raids into the Lebanon, on the other side of the then buffer zone. It was most incredible listening to such candid views coming from an army officer faced with a press corps, especially after the weasel-worded sophistry of our own Ministry of Defence spokesman, Ian McDonald, which we had experienced during the Falklands War.

The IDF took us on another sight-seeing tour, into the Gaza Strip, re-named the Gazza Strip by assorted hacks after the star England soccer player, Paul Gascoigne. We joined a platoon of heavily armed Israeli soldiers in the chase after a gang of stone-throwing Palestinian children. Again I was shocked at the IDF's disregard for discretion. From the cast iron gateway to some hovel, a skinny Palestinian waved a dead mouse at us and an interpreter explained that was what some were reduced to eating as a result of the Israeli imposed curfew on Gaza. Palestinian workers who held jobs inside Israel were under strict curtailment for fear their number might harbour terrorist sympathisers to Iraq.

One night at the Hilton I dined with an ex-Mossad agent who worked as a newspaper tipster and whose name I had been given by Hitchen. I apologised for my lack of in-depth knowledge concerning the ancient hatred between the Israelis and Palestinians, but wondered if he had any sympathy for the Palestinians' plight. 'You must understand two things,' he said, 'the first is that no other Arab nation wants to harbour Palestinians because they are too militant and the second is that no other Arab nation wants to harbour the Palestinians because, having lived so long side by side with us, it is said of them that they have the smell of the Jew about them.'

Clearly this was an issue not best suited to the simple reductionism of culpability sought by a tabloid man.

On the days the IDF did not supply tours for us we used our hire cars to make our own. I read the obligatory newspapers while floating in the Dead Sea, and climbed the heights of Masada. In Jerusalem we were amused by the Sun's Neil Syson and his fast forward history lesson. He posed with a pretend knife and fork at the scene of the Last Supper, and on asking what had happened at the Mount of Olives actually looked skyward when Paul Harris of the Daily Mail pointed up saying: 'Jesus ascended to Heaven.'

I had no desire to treat a Scud attack as a spectator's sport anymore, especially as my despatches barely credited a mention after 10 days or so.

At one stage during a Scud attack I rang home and stuck the telephone receiver out of my bedroom window so that my wife, Cathy, could hear the all-clear. She had been watching CNN on the TV. So rather than leave my hotel room I got her to give me the run down on what had happened. I then filed it to the office as a standing piece and went out to investigate, satellite TV had its advantages. As long as I was the only one watching it.

The real battle started when I returned to the office and tried to get my expenses through. Managing editor Peter Beardsley fired first:

'The level of your claims for entertaining is unacceptably high at £1,651.40 as is the "gratuities" claim of £131. Simply submitting receipts does not necessarily justify a claim or make it acceptable. I have expressed my concern about your claims to Nigel Blundell (deputy editor) who is aware that they are being returned to you for an adjustment to a more reasonable and acceptable level.'

I returned fire, with a breakdown of the price of glory:

'When I drove into Tel Aviv from Ben Gurion airport I had the impression it was a city built for motorists. I thought it was one of those souless metropoli designed and conceived around the car. The reason I thought this was because there was not a human being in sight. The place was empty.

'I was soon told that in normal times Tel Aviv is like a Middle Eastern Calcutta, an ant heap of pedestrian activity. But because bus-sized lumps of TNT were falling on the streets of the Israel's financial capital every night people felt safer if they put more than their scalp between them and Iraqi Scuds. Because of this, journalists working there were seen as a "captive audience". We faced extraordinary mark-ups from the taxis, the restaurants, the guides, the interpreters, in fact anyone who remained in Tel Aviv during the war felt their services worth the increase.'

For once I won the memo war: my expenses were paid in full. However the days of lunching contacts big time was coming rapidly to a close. Beardsley took my expenses to task again just a week later with his final memo to me before he retired:

'The attached claim of £520.42 for five days (£307.07 of it entertaining) represents 64 per cent of the Features weekly expenses buget for 12 people. You do not appear to be getting the

message: the Managing Director has cut staff expenses and
ordered that budgets must be adhered to.
'The level of your claims for entertaining is not acceptable and, for
the record, is substantially in excess of that of any other member of
the Features staff. I cannot think of a logical explanation for that.
'We can tackle the matter in either of two ways:

  1. You can bring your expenses down to a reasonable level; or
  2. I do it.'

Don Mackay, the scrapyard alsation mentioned earlier, felt he
was made for conflict. He, by the time of the Gulf War, was on
the staff of the Daily Mirror and he was duly sent to Riyadh to
follow events from there. Eleven years later he was still hacking
away on the Daily Mirror but was overlooked for enlistment as
younger men were sent to cover the US attack on Afghanistan: 'I
do war,' he complained to the newsdesk when he realised he was
not part of the 'draft'. But later in the bar he explained: 'I know
what the desk are doing, they want to blood their young lions!'

12. SHOWBUSINESS

The late George Best personified the rise and fall of the
celebrated person in Britain like no other. All people in the
public eye must rise, be adored, be made so famous that they
interest a vast number of newspaper readers and then start a
well-documented decline: the longer and more scandalous the
better. Best's career as a footballer was relatively short

compared to his life as a celebrity. The trouble was he did most of the celebrating himself and because of that had crossed the line, as far as the press were concerned, from sport to 'showbiz' and the show was himself. He had written – or had ghost-written – five books about himself. A further eight have been written by others. Most detail his life among 'the stars', hob-knobbing with actors, film stars, pop idols and bedding a variety of Miss Worlds, actresses and models. In 1990, twenty years after Best's finest days on the field, the Daily Star serialised the latest of the Best 'autobiographies': The Good, The Bad and The Bubbly.

Snapper Aylott and I were sent to 'mind' the story – to make sure no rival newspapers tried to muscle in on Best's latest reconstruction of his life. This turned out to be a farce: the paper were paying him £20,000 and should have had full access to their investment. Instead Aylott and I ended up 'doorstepping our own buy-up' while Best acted like some capricious potentate, changing his mind by the hour, cancelling arrangements, and then failing to show at re-arranged times. His latest girlfriend – Mary Shatila – was deployed as the organiser of his futile existence. She pretended he had a busy schedule to slot us into. The reality was that his life was so hugely empty the echoes were deafening. Rather than face up to middle age with its spread distending his once athletic torso, its time greying the raven locks and beard, he drank and talked incessantly about the 1960s when he was a secular god. Shatila was simply the PR of this chaos, making a life, which needed no routine, try to fit the demands of people living in the real world like Aylott and I. Well, sort-of real world.

The Daily Star wanted fresh pictures to go with the serialisation. And they wanted them in the places forever associated with the Best footballing legend. We spent the first day on assignment never actually meeting Best or Shatila, but waiting on the end of a phone either outside his flat in Chelsea or at Euston station where, through Shatila, he had agreed to meet us to take a train to Manchester for a visit to his old club: Manchester United.

'He was all ready and packed, then fifteen minutes before we were due to leave he just said he couldn't handle it,' Shatila said at the end of the day.

As the arrangements on day two began to crumble we discovered that his 'local' pub, the Duke of Wellington was up near the Edgeware Road and so we met him in the bar, where he was drinking champagne, and eventually talked him and Shatila into taxi-ing across to Euston, via his flat to pick up an overnight bag.

"You've done well, you've only had to wait a day to get George. Most people have to wait a week,' said Shatila, as though Best was the chief executive of Manchester United rather than a former player. We had half an hour to kill for our train at Euston, time enough for Best to seek refreshment so we went to a bar in the station concourse.

It was a scruffy, crowded and smoke-filled station establishment peopled with dull-eyed customers who appeared to have missed several days' worth of train connections. I was amazed to see every head lift up and a kind of rapture spread across - what had moments before been - brutish, mean and ignorant faces. Suddenly they had a sort of pathetic beauty.

'Vodka tonic,' Best said characteristically omitting the 'and' , as though the alcohol was a health cure, as many pages from my note book went to paperless autograph seekers. Best did not turn away any pleaders for his name.

On the train up he started talking at length about what sudden fame on the football field can do to a young man. I got the impression it was a kind of psychologically received cop-out he had adapted from interviews over the years to explain his profligacy. He trotted it out in 'and let this be a warning' style for the latest soccer star, Paul Gascoigne, who, Best told me, was not as good a footballer as he, Best, had been.

Shatila started breathing nervously at all the notes I was taking. The Daily Star had paid for the serialisation rights to Best's latest ghost-written book, nothing more.Occasionally she would start up, but never quite broke through Best's mantra of his life, to complain that we had not paid for this bit.

When we met Best at the pub he had been finishing off a bottle of champagne. On the train, after the vodka, he ordered a bottle of the driest white wine. He ate nothing. At Manchester our cab was flagged down by an Asian passer-by who insisted Best alight to pose with his family for a photograph.

Once we had checked in to the Crowne Plaza Hotel we all took a taxi to a nearby restaurant. Owned by one Felix Izquirdo-Moreno, 47, a fellow befriended by Best during his fly-aways to the Spanish Costas for sun, sangria and sex, back in the early seventies. Eventually Best had employed him and brought him back to Manchester with him.

It struck me as a rather ordinary place serving run of the mill food, but you could tell it was important for Best to hear how good the joint was and I obliged.

Next morning Best had changed his jeans, trainers and black jogging top for smartly-pressed trousers, polished leather loafers and a blue and white striped business shirt, ready for his meeting with Sir Matt Busby. The ageing Scot turned up at the Old Trafford ground in a new Mercedes saloon. We were introduced and led through to the office they still kept there for him. On the wall hung a lop-sided portrait of Sir Winston Churchill. 'He always told me that was his favourite man,' Best later explained.

Later out on the empty pitch a groundsman was towing a lawn-mower. No one is allowed on the hallowed turf normally, but the groundsman simply switched off his engine as Best was encouraged to become a lone footballer by Aylott. As Busby watched Best's ball control for Aylott's camera he muttered to me: 'I feel partly responsible for what happened to George. I should have taken better care of him.' Quite how the old Scot could have reigned in the working class Belfast lad who was being offered the world as an oyster and was more than willing to supply the Tabasco, he did not explain. Both Best and Busby then sat in the stalls and Aylott captured a classic shot with the old man wiping away a tear as Best looked adoringly on. It was the only time in the six days we spent with Best that he showed any respect for himself, did not have a drink in his hand, and turned up on time. Perhaps the old manager had been a better influence on Best than he was prepared to admit to himself.

After that it was back to the restaurant. Champagne for Best, white wine for Shatila. Two acolytes lured Best away and Aylott and I were left to entertain Shatila. The two acolytes and a heavily made up blonde who looked like Thomas the Tank Engine, with her brightly painted round face, became the impromptu audience for Best who ignored Shatila for several hours while he told ill-timed, poor jokes, at which his new friends laughed uproariously. The scene was pathetic and I attempted to show Best this by emitting an exaggerated guffaw at his next joke. It was a mistake. 'I'll fucking kill you, you cunt,' he said curling his hands into fists and thrusting his face forward. I was suddenly the summation of all the bad press he'd courted over the years. For a minute I was what he hated about himself. The acolytes dutifully looked threatening as well and I rejoined Shatila saying I thought I'd now blown my chances of continuing to work with her George. The newsdesk had wanted me to get him to Belfast to kick a ball around in the streets of his youth.

'Oh take no notice, he'll be fine tomorrow,' she said reassuringly and then was promptly sick over my trousers – twice. Keeping up with George was like partying with Caligula.

Worried that the subject of our serialisation would depart in the early hours, I was up at 4.00 am and hovering in the foyer. The night porter was helpful. 'They're still in their room,' he said and waved me round to the staff side of his reception desk the back of which comprised a computerised screen. 'There you are, room 217. 05:30, mini bar accessed, one bottle of champagne.' I was lucky, for Best had tired of Manchester and apparently his girlfriend too. In the early hours he had left the hotel, Shatila, baggage and all in an attempt to get back to London but fortunately had missed the last train. All that was left for him was the continued distraction of champagne. Aylott and I collared Best at 6.45am, and as he had champagne breakfast, the fast being broken in this case was of champagne, tried to talk him into Belfast that day. But he was missing his mates in the Duke of Wellington. He promised he would fly the following day and left for London. Next day Aylott and I made our separate ways to Heathrow. Once again Best did not show.

His human answer phone, Shatila, did not return any calls again until in desperation Aylott decided the only way to get them onside again was more money. With the promise of £1,000 in cash for that one trip to Belfast, all expenses paid of course, Aylott's mobile phone bleeped into life once more. It was now Friday, we'd been all week with Best. I was outside the Duke of Wellington before morning opening time and Aylott was outside the Chelsea flat. One way or another we ought to manage a 'hands-on' contact. Sure enough I was buying him Moet & Chandon by 11:00. By midday Best was full of enough champagne to feel in the mood for co-operation once more. From there we at last got him to the airport. Although there was time to get the 2:30 shuttle, Best did not want to rush, so we sat in the departure lounge while he drank 'vodka tonic' for the next two hours until the following flight. Once on the plane Shatila asked me why the engine kept changing noise, was it 'normal?', I told her it was like the changing of gears in a car. Then she sought reassurance from her boyfriend. 'I like fear,' he said and as the plane climbed into the clouds, added 'It's going to get worse now Mary,' with the little chuckle he often used. 'Oh don't,' she gasped as she grabbed my hand. I was now worried in case the attention being lavished on me by his woman, because I was being sympathetic, would send Best off into another unco-operative mood. But once on Northern Irish turf we drove off towards the Belfast backstreets where Best had kicked a ball around as a lad and Aylott captured him on the street where his boot first touched pig's bladder. His father Dicky, 70, still lived in the council house on the Cregagh estate where Best was born, and where Loyalism was displayed with Union Jacks, and St. George's flags, a permanent fluttering fixture to the little terraced houses.

'If you wanted to find George he'd be up there in the top field kicking that ball back and forth in the pouring rain,' his father recalled. 'He used to spend his pocket money on OXO cubes for him and his team. His mum used to take kettles of hot water up for them to drink.'

Best would also play for so long in the cold he could not untie his boot laces and would have to cut them off. Dicky's own interest in football was, by now, reduced to posting a spot-the-ball competition every week to the local paper.

Meanwhile, Best, for the first time seemed genuinely animated, pointing at the flags with amazement, talking about how after a huge explosion on his estate, his uncle went to help out some residents trapped in a blazing room and came away with a set of female arms.

On our last day in Belfast, Best quaffed another two bottle champagne breakfast at the Europa Hotel, courtesy of the Daily Star, and 'vodka tonic' at Belfast International before flying back to London and heading straight to the Duke of Wellington for more champagne. On route Best concentrated briefly on a newspaper cross-word, but soon he was back to the retrospection that is his life – a Gothic burden of 1960s memories. 'I met Jimi Hendrix. He never drank, but he was on all sorts of other stuff. He was a crazy man and a very nice guy. I met him two months before he topped himself,' Best said, reaching his own verdict on the rock singer's death.

On our way back to the Duke of Wellington from Heathrow in a taxi, Best pointed to a large hoarding of posters: 'Look there's one of my fans' and gave his little cackle. I laughed as I saw a huge picture of Clint Eastwood's face.I thought at first he was making some semi-serious comment on his fame. He wasn't, he was referring to a poster next to the film star which showed a young boy wrapped in dozens of different football scarves advertising the comprehensive soccer coverage boasted by B/Sky/B.

Back in the Duke of Wellington on an upholstered bench, Shatila sat the opposite end to Best. He started holding court with a large ice-bucket in front of him. Between the couple were two friends. One a Cockney trying to sell boxed shoes, the other his girlfriend. Shatila turned to me and said: 'The real story of George has not been told. There is a reason why his women have left him. I know what it is....' she trailed off teasingly. I would leave some other poor beggar to cheque-book chase that one. Earlier Best had told me that while his other football colleagues read comics and went to the movies, he read the classics and went to the theatre. Cross-words were a test for this intellect. I had, indeed, read that Best was an intelligent, charming, talented man turned into a mental cripple by fame. This was the take celebrity journalists like Michael Parkinson had on Best. But in my view Best loved fame and was addicted to it as much as the bottle. If he could not be famous for balls why not booze? Two livers Best, the celebrity celebrated for celebrating.

The last thing Best said to me was that he was due to appear on the Terry Wogan TV show in a few weeks' time. 'Watch it,' he said with his hirsute grin, and his shy cackle, 'it's going to make news.' He would not be drawn on why. I did watch it. It did make news. Best had gone on the show drunk. The pundits blaming the BBC for entertaining Best before he went on air could not know he had planned it all along.

The Daily Star's serialisation of Best's latest life story produced a healthy mail bag of reader's letters. I have kept one from a Mr H. E. Harris from Plymouth:

'Why, oh why, do you write about a has-been? There are men who have given their lives for their country and made it safe for others to enjoy a good life. They have had their guts spilled out and lost limbs. They were news for a week. Now we have a story that makes me puke, about a man who could have made it in this world of ours...... Those men who gave their lives have been forgotten. For a few pounds they died and yet this man gets paid large sums of money to pay for his drink and women..........it is reporters like you who want to make him some kind of superman and to make money for him to waste on his drinking bouts and for him to tell yarns about the women he has had........you reporters are as bad as he is. I have met people like you in my days, you add words to a story to make it look good but it is a load of bunk. So Mr Dick Durham keep on writing your stories about has-beens you may make a good liar yet............I am a disabled person who looked after his beloved wife for 12 months until she died. I was let down by the hospital who said when she became a cabbage they would look after her.......but this story would look tame to you it would look small to you, it would not interest you because this is real life.'

Well Mr Harris, if ever you read this, I hope it makes you feel a little less bitter to know that Mr Best only received £19,000 for

258

his serialisation. The £1,000 in cash paid to him to fly to Belfast was deducted from the final sum.

The late actor Richard Harris was also a legendary drinker, but unlike George Best it was his boozing and brawling life-style that helped make him a household name and not the other way round. For his character helped land him the role as Frank Machin, the hard drinking Yorkshire miner, who dreams of becoming a top rugby player. When 'This Sporting Life" came out in 1963 he became famous and two years later was as well known in the US as in the UK. But he had enemies too. One of them was Brian Hitchen, who detested the Irishman for his support – as Hitchen saw it – of the IRA. I was summoned to Hitchen's office and told: 'Dick, I want you to go and stitch up that bastard Harris. He's a fucking apologist for terrorism and should not be lionised by a gullible public.'

It was 1981 and Harris had been appearing on the London stage in Camelot, to rave reviews with royalty fawning in the audience, an irony Hitchen found hard to bear. 'I've also heard he has a penchant for black prostitutes,' added Hitchen 'so much for being a spiritual king.'

Harris was staying at the Savoy and photographer Tony Sapiano and I were invited up to his suite, where he was ensconced with his latest girlfriend Anne Turkel.

Both tall and lanky they filled the room like a couple of outsize Barbie dolls.

Harris pushed a mini tape-recorder in front of me to record the interview, threatening to sue if I misquoted him. Fortunately I had a load of questions ready to ask him about his life as a thespian, and so the tape wound on and on while Harris regurgitated his stage life. While he might have been a powerful, if limited, actor he was in real life much larger than it, eloquent, witty, profound. He needed no script. He soon tired of talking about his professional life and started to talk instead about the 'pricks' he'd met. One was a neighbour of his on his islet in the Bahamas. 'For Christ's sake, I'd gone there for peace and quiet and this fucking idiot, who also had a pad on the island, was insisting on meeting me. I kept putting him off until one day I saw him coming along the beach with his family paraded behind him. I quickly set up my home movie showing a blue film, opened the curtains and sat there masturbating with a brother of mine in front of a plate glass window! I never heard from him again!'

Now Harris was fired up and wanting to talk all day. He was on the wagon then and probably bored. It was a great time to strike.

'What about your links with Noraid?' I said casually. That was it, he was off, the tape-recorder had run out and had switched itself off, but the actor did not even notice. And we got a spread out of 'Superstar hits out at the men of violence. Richard Harris brands the terrorists who duped him into supporting them.'

'If one of my sons was killed by an IRA bomb then I would walk down the Falls Road with a machine gun,' he said.

Another of Hitchen's pet hates was drugs and anyone who had anything to do with them. So it was that when Geoff Baker, the most prolific showbiz reporter ever employed by the Daily Star, came up with a story about TV soap star, Gary Holton, being a heroin addict, he was immediately despatched to Spain where Holton, star of Auf Weidesein Pet was filming, to 'front him up'. At first Holton denied the claim, then he relented and said he HAD been an addict but was now clean. The actor knew the game was up and decided to capitalise on his ignominy. He told Baker he would give him a frank – though not free – full interview for £15,000. When Baker called The Daily Star, Hitchen refused to pay up. They had the story anyway. It was front page news, four days running with the rest of the tabloids racing to catch up and former girlfriends burrowing out of the woodwork to sell their story, too. By the end of the week Britain's hottest and sexiest TV star was dead – from an overdose of alcohol and morphine.

'Congratulations, your first kill,' said Hitchen to Baker upon the hack's return to London.

' I felt awful, I still do' Baker said.

'He'd of killed himself anyway, what you worried about?,' Hitchen comforted, 'don't worry about him – he knocked himself off. I don't like dope dealers.'

Shortly afterwards Baker left Fleet Street: 'I was quite naïve then,' he said, 'and when the full impact hit me, I found it hard to take, it was hideous and unethical.' He didn't give up newspapers for a life of poverty, however. He went on to work as the PR man for Sir Paul McCartney, before falling out with the crooner. Baker was last reported as working as a roadsweeper in Weymouth, rather than sell the 'inside story' of life with McCartney. No doubt the old hack still felt the scars of his 'first kill'.

The rise and fall, the ebb and flow of personal reputations – especially those on television - is the bread and butter of Fleet Street. It is the showbusiness reporters who are expected to wheel these stories in. The ordinary hack just gets the occasional celebrity doorstep to watch as 'leg men' for their 'showbiz' colleagues. Not many stars reach the satus of uninpeachability, and what's more they know it. When their time comes round to be hung out to dry then those with good advisers make cash out of it. They who refuse to play ball will get trounced in print anyway as the following contract taken out on Coronation Street star Chris Quinten shows:

'This is an agreement between Mr Chris Quentin, his wife Leeza, and the Daily Star.
In consideration of the sum of £10,000 I agree to supply to The Daily Star exclusively the full pictures and stories as follows:
Chris Quentin's marriage to Leeza. Life in Los Angeles. The baby Leeza is expecting. Future home and career plans for both. Life and times in Coronation Street. Views and feelings pertaining to previous.
Also first picture and story refusal on new baby.
I will make myself available to the Daily Star exclusively from now until a period of seven days after publication.
As a goodwill gesture, a cash deposit of £2,000 will be made into a special Escro account held by my lawyers on signing this contract.
I agree that the full United Kingdom exclusive rights to the stories and pictures belong to The Daily Star.
I will not talk to any other newspaper, radio, TV or media representative without full permission from The Daily Star during the term of this contract.

*I undertake to provide or pose for pictures with my wife Leeza.
And I will not pose or provide pictures for any other news media
without the permission of The Daily Star during the seven-day
period.
I will assist The Daily Star in any other manner they request.
Full payment will be made on the pictures and story meeting The
Editor's satisfaction.
Signed.....'*

The contract, sent from Los Angeles, to assistant editor Jimmy
Sutherland at the Daily Star's office at 121 Fleet Street, had a
memo attached to it from the reporter involved in the Quentin
story. I have omitted his name as he is still working for the
paper.
The memo reads:

*'Enclosed is the revised contract which Chris Quentin has
approved. He didn't notice that there's no mention about copy
approval in it.
He has faxed a copy to his lawyers and I hope the deal will be
sealed when I speak to him again at 10am my time today.
In the meantime, while we sleep here, his lawyers will be studying
the contract before speaking to Quentin.
His brief may contact you to check on deposit details etc.
Quentin seems quite happy with the deal now. But if he spots the
absence of copy approval, which we can't give, there could be
snags again.
That's when I'm happy to turn him over with all the stuff I already
know from our chats together.
We'll know one way or the other shortly.'*

Many ordinary hacks get fed up with their paper being swamped
with showbusiness stories – often tales of the telly push out real
stories which reporters have worked hard to break. So when
readers come on complaining in the same vein, we take heart.
Once on a night-desk shift I took a call from what I at first
thought was one such reader in Manchester. She was irritated
that The Daily Star had a long-running soap story on the front

page for the best part of the week. I tried to defend the paper's coverage pointing out that the civil war in Lebanon (then a major story in the broadsheets) was on page nine, admittedly only in three paragraphs but it was at least there. I took down her name and contact details intending to leave a note on the night-log hoping to lobby harder news into the paper. After I did so I asked her what SHE would like to see on the front page.

'Maybe the Bingo?,' she said. I tore up the night log note.

Those in showbusiness who do get through their professional careers without ever becoming a tabloid target are those who live happy lives, making no enemies and who keep up excellent relations with the press. In my experience such people included comedian Eric Morecombe. I always had his home telephone number, and as far as I know he never used the services of a press agent. He would always return calls with a witty one liner for the accursed symposiums of 'what the stars think' that are the bane of every hack's existence. Other media friendly stars included the popstars Noddy Holder, David Essex and Sir Cliff Richard. The actor Edward Fox also gave out his phone number and was always breathtakingly honest. Another helpful star was comedian Frankie Howard. Of those who were very un-media friendly my favourite story is of the diminutive clown Ronnie Corbett. While playing at a charity golf tournament he was asked by photographer Ken Lennox to pose in some long grass growing adjacent to the course. The idea was that the grass would envelope Corbett and only his raised golf club would be seen in the picture. For a man who used his child sized body to earn a good living he amazed the world-weary Lennox when he went ballistic and refused to co-operate.

One of the easiest jobs for the regular hack was to re-write an embargoed magazine interview with a star. The deal was that the paper got a transcript of the interview the day before the magazine hit the newsagents. We could then run the story in the following day's paper to coincide with the magazine's first day of sale, on the understanding that we mentioned the magazine. One piece I did on actress Shirley Maclaine's 'loneliness' at the top invited letters from many readers.

One from a Mr T J Etheridge of Peterborough asked for a forwarding address:

'.....as I believe I maybe the answer to her worries in life. 'Given this opportunity to correspond to her I could enhance my claim to make the lady a happy woman once more. For the record if she would like first hand information before corresponding, I am a single man aged 52 years owning my own house. I have been in full employment from leaving school as an engineer over these latter years after training. My salary is a fairly stable one but most probably not to the extent of Miss Maclaine's salary as a top actress in her own rights. But if both parties are prepared to love one another for the rest of their days in this world why worry too much on salaries.......'

Another came in from a Mr Gerald Reginald Leddington of Broadwas on Teme, Worcestershire.

'Dear Miss Maclaine,
I feel we have something in common I am a bachelor aged 48 years old having spent much of my life looking after my Mother who passed away some two years ago. Over the past two years I have been seeking Miss Right but have failed in getting anyone. So therefore this puts me in the same position as yourself.
'Should you know of anyone who would like to share my life with me perhaps you could put them in touch with me, there is a Miss Right somewhere but I have been unable to find her.'

Like Best, Paul Gascoigne became a celebrated person because of his prowess on the football field and therefore his life off the field was put under the microscope warts and all – especially the warts. The drinking, wife-beating, clubbing all came spewing out: sometimes the result of dogged newspaper work, other times large injections of cash induced the celebrated to agonise over where his or her life had gone wrong. Gascoigne then, like Best, became more famous for his failings than his skill and with such 'star quality' became owned by every member of the public who saw him. Many of them reached for the nearest telephone to tell a newspaper what he was up to. At the height of his celebratedness, The Daily Star received a tip-off that 'Gazza' had checked into a health farm. So reporter Madeleine Pallas, of blonde mane and long legs checked in, too. Like the readers mentioned above, Gascoigne was in need of companionship but appearing at Pallas' door naked was an unusually direct way of starting a relationship.

'He asked me to go fishing with him at midnight, but I'd already seen his tiddler,' was the headline which had deputy editor Nigel Blundell heading straight for Chairman Lord Stevens's office once again.

'What is this girl doing at this place?,' demanded Stevens.

'Because Gascoigne was staying there and I sent a reporter along to see what he was up to.'

'It's entrapment.'

'It's not it's simply following a story'

'I will NOT have this sort of thing in my newspaper.'

Hitchen thought it wise to get Blundell out of the office and harm's way for a while and so he and his reporter girlfriend – Sue Blackhall who later became his wife – jetted off to Palm Beach, Florida for a holiday. Unfortunately for them the fevered imagination of picture desk executive Bert Reavely, another old Enquirer hand, but a man so nervous of missing a scoop he was inclined to overreact upon receipt of minimal intelligence, had been given a tip-off and passed it onto Hitchen. The sister of Country & Western singer Dolly Parton wanted to reveal the married crooner's secret sexual life with another man. Just as Blundell and Blackhall were slapping on the sun oil they were ordered to fly to Knoxville, Tennessee where she would meet them at the Hilton Hotel. There would be 10,000 US dollars waiting for them to hand over for the full story. By way of authenticating her relationship with the singer their informant started off by telling the duo that Dolly, who had suffered a gum disease as a child could not afford a proper set of false teeth, so she had a set made of wood. And what's more she still wore them. Blundell and Blackhall said they would just go to their hotel room to get the cash and crept out of the hotel, back to the airport and continued their holiday.

They had flown a thousand mile round trip to talk to a nutter. The wisest stars knew that to keep their twinkle the best policy was to remain mute when confronted with the press. Liz Taylor came out of her home in Kensington one morning to find me with the milk bottles, but did not even tell me to get off her property, but simply walked to her waiting car.

At St Martin-in-the-Fields Church in the West End I followed Lauren Bacall to her taxi outside hoping to secure an interview. She got in the back and I knelt down on the pavement to ask feebly: 'Er, where you off to now?" She looked me straight in the eye, smiled, and cut me off with the electric window.

In death of course, there is escape for the celebrity, but not for their nearest and dearest. Famous death is always a big story for newspapers large and small and on a night shift in April 1984 I was watching comedian Tommy Cooper live on TV when he collapsed on stage. The night news editor, Peter O'Kill, ordered me to call Cooper's wife Gwen. I did so and to my horror discovered that she never watched him on telly. 'Oh, well, er, it's just that he, er, fell over...and, well I'd better put the phone down as probably someone will be trying to get through.' He was already dead from a heart attack.

Cooper was a favourite of the press and rarely, if ever, got 'turned over'. Once during an interview at his home with the Daily Star's Michael Hellicar, Cooper, a heavy drinker, vomited over his living room floor. He called his wife: 'Can you come here, dear? Michael's been sick.' A joke that was not aired in the subsequent story.

During pop star Freddie Mercury's last months in 1991 journalists were continually probing to cofirm whether or not his drawn appearance was as a result of HIV/AIDS. Graham Jones sent me to his father's home in West London to see what he had to say on the subject. I banged on the door, his father answered, I asked the question and the door banged on me.

13 Royals

My greatest royal scoop was to reveal to the world that Prince
Charles and Princess Diana received 22 toasters among their
wedding gifts. Time was when anything a royal said or did was
news and the Daily Star's royal correspondent, James Whitaker,
flew around the world covering similar inane and innocuous
'stories' at huge expense on 'Windsor tours' as the royal beat was
cynically known among the royal hacks.

The ordinary hack got the doorsteps, the Bank holiday jobs and
the night shifts of the royal court coverage. I have driven to
various polo fields in the Home Counties to witness Prince
Charles blaming his horse, the ball or photographers for his play.
I have stood outside various of the London palaces to record
Sarah Ferguson's choice of clothes, current weight and even
demeanour.

Official royal stories, the ones 'The Firm', as the press call the
Windsors, want the public to read, are not given the same
prominence. Once traffic held me up on the way to witness the
inauguration of Prince Andrew's new job aboard the warship
HMS Brazen in Plymouth. By the time I arrived the ship was out
in Plymouth Sound being followed by the press boat. I
commandeered a speedboat driven by two Londoners in
swimming trunks who were swilling cider from glass flagons. By
the time we got within half a mile of HMS Brazen my summer

suit was drenched and a high-powered navy inflatable with armed SBS men aboard sped out to meet us before we could get near enough to act as a floating suicide bomb. I had to 'pick up' the story from Daily Mirror hack Geoff Lakeman when he got ashore later in the day. It made three paragraphs the following day in the Daily Star and the Mirror used nothing.

It was 'Lady Di' , and later 'Princess Di' who upped the anti of royal coverage, if that were possible in a royal-obsessed media. As soon as she was in the frame as a Prince's boyfriend, camera men followed her every day of her life. She was tall, blonde, sexy, looked like a film star and was a royal-to-be to boot. Even as plain old 'Lady Di' everytime she appeared on the front page sales soared.

Because of this every member of the Daily Star staff received a 29-page memorandum before the royal wedding of Charles and Diana on 28 July 1981. It comprised the 'fixed positions' of each employee along the royal wedding route. It included a phalanx of staff watching TVs in the office. There was feature writer Rob Gibson who would do the 'wrap' -the overview of the whole proceedings-, fashion editor Sandy Williams who would comment on the wedding dress and its design, and TV editor Ken Eastaugh who would monitor the output on rival television stations. But most important of all in the office line up was showbusiness editor Pat Codd. He was also a major in the Territorial Army and had a skill which was in great demand that day: lip reading. His job was to jot down the royal asides, diplomatic or otherwise, from the lips of all and sundry who appeared on the TV screen, especially of course the happy couple themselves.

Chief crime reporter James Nicholson was to be based at police headquarters in Paternoster Square. Sat in radio cars were reporters Tom Roche in South London and Joe Clancy in North London, on 'river watch' was reporter Shekar Bahtia, endearingly dubbed the 'Sepoy runner' by news editor Phil Mellor.

For the procession itself feature writer Peter Batt was fixed at the Victoria Memorial; reporters Mick Seamark, and David Evans were based along The Mall, feature writer John Beattie was standing under Admiralty Arch, reporters Frank Curran, Barry Gardner, Ramsay Smith, George Dearsley, Lynne Greenwood, Hugh Whittow, Chris Boffey, Pat Moore, David Newman, Robert Wilson, Ian Monk, Winn Walsh and feature writer Cathy Couzens were placed at strategic points between Trafalgar Square and St Paul's Cathedral, including well known 'venues' along Fleet Street itself! Inside the cathedral was royal correspondent James Whitaker.

After the procession, from St Paul's to Buckingham Palace, all staff were moved to new positions along the Mall to cover the beginning of the 'honeymoon route' from Buckingham Palace to Waterloo Station and reporters Shyama Perera, Brian Wells and myself were to cover respectively, Horseguards Parade, Whitehall and Parliament Square. Photographers Frank Barrett, Ken Lennox, Dave Ashdown, Doug Doig, Alasdair Loos, Tom Stoddart, Tim Cornall, Joe Bangay, Simon Phythian, Tony Fisher, Tony Sapiano, Lawrence Lustig, Stan Meagher, Bob Barclay, John Dawes, Stuart Goodman, James Milne, Colin Gower, Alan Steele, Peter Wilcock, Robin Jones, Richard Blake, and Mark Bourdillon were deployed along the route, in helicopters, on balconies and on a cherry picker. A helicopter and a fixed wing plane were on standby to fly their unprocessed film to Manchester - where the paper was then printed - to a landing facility specially prepared by Express Newspapers which was near the Great Ancoats Street office. Less urgent pictures e.g. those of the cheering subjects were wired up from London.

In case anything else happened in the world that day, the office was manned for 'general stories' by industrial editor Tom McGhie and freelance hack Syd Brennan.

One hundred and thirty two London streets were closed off to traffic at 4am with 8,000 barriers on the day. According to the press briefing given by the Met and City Police, 'the criteria upon which manpower levels are determined are as follows: 1. Scope and importance of the event (the first Royal Wedding since Princess Anne's in 1973 and the wedding of a very popular Heir to the Throne) 2. The time of year (it is the height of the tourist season).' Officers from both the Metropolitan and City Police as well as extra policemen drafted in from Bedfordshire, Essex,

Hampshire, Hertfordshire, Kent, Surrey, Sussex and Thames Valley were to secure the wedding of a 'very popular Heir to the Throne'. Military Police and police from both the Metropolitan and City Mounted Branch provided horseback escorts for the Queen as well as Charles and Diana. Metropolitan Police Commissioner Sir David McNee wore a silver waist sash, medals and white gloves, his Assistant Commissioner Wilford Gibson wore boots, spurs and sword. The Commissioner of the City of London Police, Peter Marshall and his Assistant Commissioner Ernest Bright were also draped with swords. They were the lucky ones: there as spectators. The ordinary bobbies lining the route missed the whole procession as they had their backs to the newlyweds having been ordered to stand facing the one million strong crowd along the streets where every office block, shop and apartment had been checked for snipers among the workers, customers and residents.

The operations room at New Scotland Yard monitored the entire route of the procession on screens linked to 12 closed-circuit TV cameras.

Department of the Environment 'stewards' were on hand to guide people to temporary lavatories and first aid posts. St John's Ambulance were 'in charge' of lost children.

Next day a grainy black and white picture of Charles and Diana pressing closed lips together on the balcony at Buckingham Palace appeared on the front page.

'THE KISS' was the headline under the red-top Daily Star masthead which was shaped like a crown for the day. It was, readers were told 'A moment to treasure'. The army of staff had been upstaged in the paper with a commissioned colour picture taken by Lord Snowdon of 'The wedding couple in vivid glowing colour in a unique souvenir edition.'

It was the last day Charles and Diana would be held in high esteem by the press. It would now be downhill all the way with 'the pack', as we call even ourselves, in hot pursuit. By November that year Diana fell pregnant. In December print and TV editors were invited to Buckingham Palace where they were asked not to intrude on the royal couple's privacy. The only editor not to attend was Kelvin MacKenzie of The Sun. That unnerved the executives at The Daily Star who were in direct competition with the 'current bun.' In January Brian Hitchen was hunting for ideas on how to cover the story with which to assuage his boss – Lloyd Turner was then editor – and was not happy with the input from his staff:

'With the exception of a handful of people the response to my memo on ideas for the Royal Baby presentation has been abysmal. Come on, let's shake out some of that stardust from your typewriters. The prize for the reporter who does not submit any ideas at all will be eight dog-watches outside Buckingham Palace during Royal baby Watch.
Trust me!'

The handful included, of course, royal correspondent James Whitaker and photographer Ken Lennox who were getting the cream jobs following the newlyweds to exotic locations. They were going to be FULL of ideas...

And just a month after Hitchen's memo the duo found themselves jetting off to the Bahamas where Charles and Diana had gone for a holiday.

To get at the couple sunning themselves on the beach, Lennox had to crawl on his belly for half a mile through thick undergrowth armed with his telephoto lens. It was a very long shot but nobody picking up The Daily Star doubted for a minute that the bikini-clad, statuesque figure, five-months pregnant - with Prince William-, was the Princess of Wales.

The Press Council said it would investigate to see whether both The Daily Star and The Sun, whose photographer captured the same images, had 'breached' the council's Declaration on Privacy.

Next day Lloyd Turner apologised in an editorial explaining that it had acted out of 'deep affection' for the royal couple.

MacKenzie also apologised and explained that the coverage 'brought a breath of summer into the lives of millions of our readers back in chilly Britain'. He also re-published the photographs disingenuously explaining to his 'millions of readers' that this was what all the fuss was about...

'The surreptitious taking and the publication of these long range pictures of the Princess of Wales on a beach when she was five months pregnant and wearing a bikini was a gross intrusion into her personal privacy. Whether the beach was public or private is immaterial to this offence. There was no legitimate public interest to excuse that intrusion,' the Press Council ruled. They even defined what the public interest was not: ' "In the public interest" is not synonymous with "of interest to the public",' they ruled.

They were not impressed with either paper's apology: 'The Sun's offence (is) seriously aggravated by two matters: firstly The Sun republished the offending pictures alongside its "apology" – particularly in editions circulating in areas where their first appearance would not have been seen; and secondly, it sold the pictures to the foreign press.'

Lloyd Turner plucked at that particular straw and on the day after his paper was 'condemned for bringing discredit on the British Press' added at the end of his editorial:

'We did not sell any of the pictures to overseas newspapers or magazines. We said the day after publication of the pictures that if we had upset the Princess, we were deeply sorry. That apology was very genuine.'

Pass the sick bag, Alice, as another of Express Newspapers' employees – Sir John Junor, editor of the Sunday Express – might have said.

And while Palace press officers rubbed their hands with glee at their triumph they overlooked one thing: there is no humiliating a tabloid newspaper, a beast which knows no shame. From that day on Princess Diana's name rarely missed a single edition of The Daily Star.

At first the stories were harmless: 'Princess Diana is to stand in for Princess Margaret at a charity gala.', 'Princess Diana celebrated her first Mother's Day yesterday.....as a godmother.', 'Princess Diana revealed yesterday that she doesn't like Mondays.....at least when it comes to kissing.' But everywhere she went, everything she did, anything she said was recorded. Anyone vaguely connected was dragged into the limelight, too:

'Princess Diana's former uncle, Tory MP Sir Anthony Berry, was yesterday banned for drunken driving.'

All the above are just a few of the stories I covered as an ordinary hack. So you can imagine how many stories were actually fielded on Diana with the attention of every newspaper's royal correspondent working full time and other reporters finding more and more of their 'diary' duties pegged on the royal cover girl.

But Diana's astonishing revelations about her life among the Windsors was a decade away and the biggest royal story of the 1980s was the story of Michael Fagan, the man who sat on the Queen's bed.

Unfortunately it was a story which the Daily Star did not get a sniff of and Hitchen was livid as this memo to all staff reveals:

'A staggering saga of incompetence......

'That was the intro on the splash in this morning's Daily Mail. It could have been tailor-made to describe the Daily Star's coverage of the biggest and most important Royal story this decade.

It has highlighted gaps in the Daily Star's expertise which angers and disturbs me.

'The story of the intruder in the Queen's bedroom began, not in the Daily Express, but on the editorial floor of the Sunday Mirror on Friday morning where an executive decision was taken not to print it.

They had all the details. From there it was taken up by the Daily Express who, quite rightly, had a field day with it.

'To have had not the faintest whisper from supposed Palace sources on a story that was by now three days old, suggests that our much vaunted Royal contacts were not worth a tarnished tiara. To have not detected even the slightest tremor of the story along the police grapevine from much entertained "contacts" was really nothing short of amazing.

'There are some who feel it was time that the Daily Express had a story. I do not see it that way. I'm a bad loser and I do not expect that sort of attitude from anyone. This isn't a game where we take turns in having exclusives. It's a daily fight for survival. I know we do not have a big staff. I know that we were out-gunned on the

doorsteps. But in this sort of story it isn't the numbers that matter. It's real contacts who can provide real facts. That's all it takes – plus a burning desire to win.

'Time after time over the last few days we have missed the good lines. Even the Press Association has sometimes had to tell us what was going on........'

On the day of the Express's exclusive, news editor Phil Mellor caught an earlier train from his home in Meopham, Kent to London Bridge station where he hailed a cab to Fleet Street. He was first inside the Black Lubianka. As each reporter turned up so Mellor sent them out to the Fleet Street pub of their choice and told them to wait there for instruction: 'For Christ's sake don't get pissed,' he warned.

When Hitchen walked in he demanded to know where everyone was.

'I've got them all out on various doorsteps, Brian,' said Mellor.

Hitchen stormed into his office and turned the photograph of his 'chief crime reporter' James Nicholson, dressed up in his Bat cape, to the wall.

Mellor, sensing the heat Nicholson was in for, waited in the corridor for his arrival to head him off.

'Jimmy, Brian's not best pleased,' he started as the black suited Nicholson strode along the bacon-smelling corridor.

'I've had 36 news editors in my time,' drawled the Black Prince, 'and you're the biggest bozo of them all. I've got an appointment with the DPP at eleven.'

And so he had. Nicholson spent a lengthy lunch – as Mellor fretted away telling Hitchen he had a good follow up and hoping against hope his crime man would pull something out of the bag – with Sir Thomas Hetherington the Director of Public Prosecutions. Nicholson got the whole story in the form of evidence, and statements and returned to the office.

'He had few lines to jog his memory written on a fag packet,' said Mellor, 'and I sat down and wrote it as Nicholson dictated it. It made pages one, two and three next day. "I hope it's accurate," I said to Nicholson.'

'You wrote it,' came the Prince's reply.

When James Whitaker left the Daily Star to wear ermine for the Daily Mirror instead, a tall, slim, bespectacled, and earnest young man arrived in the Fleet Street office of the Daily Star from Manchester. There he had worked as a sub and in his spare time edited various trade union newspapers as well as becoming chapel clerk of the NUJ. His extra curricula work gave some indication of Andrew Morton's dedication to his ambition. For in those days he was working towards what he hoped would be a job as a political correspondent. Morton always had an eye on the bigger picture – at least where his career was concerned – and did not waste time in the drinking dens of Fleet Street.

At first he was given general news stories to cover. And in true Daily Star style the Clark Kent lookalike was not able to avoid at least one 'dressing up' story. When the film Superman opened, Morton was obliged to dress up in the figure hugging flying reporter's garb and was photographed emerging from the chrysalis of a telephone box, minus his spectacles and with an S on his chest. But he soon showed, what Editor Lloyd Turner thought was, an ability to get in close on 'top people' stories. This was especially true after he managed to dance with divorcee Lynne Frederick, first wife of TV show presenter Sir David Frost while trying to get close to the story of their marital breakdown. In a newsroom full of be-suited, short-arsed, misfits: brawling Scots, hard-drinking Northeners, and thieving Cockneys, here at last, Turner, an Australian, believed was some glamour. Turner had lost Whitaker, who while not being glamorous, at least spoke posh. Now he had Morton. Diana, already becoming well known for her flirtatious nature, might even fancy him, Turner cunningly reckoned.

'When they told me I was going to be royal correspondent I felt physically ill,' Morton said, ' sure I was personable but whether they thought Di would fancy me or not I hadn't a clue. Though it is quite flattering.'

Once Morton was appointed royal correspondent his was the only phone in the tin office to be white: all the others were grey. After appearing on the Terry Wogan show, to discuss the harrassment of the royals by the press, Morton could not quite handle his new found fame.

'I've been stopped twice from the tube station to the office by people wanting my autograph,' he told me the following morning. But Morton was not one to lose focus for long. Soon he set to work becoming the expert on his subject. He would spend hours after his daily shift poring over the Express Newspapers' cuttings library, making notes and taking photostats on the royal newspaper history. He began to write coffee table books on the royals, but when Brian Hitchen 'inherited' Morton, as he put it, after taking over as London Editor he was unhappy. When he discovered that The Daily Star had agreed to pay Morton £40,000 to serialise his book 'Inside Kensington Palace', Hitchen's famous dander was up. As far as he was concerned his royal correspondent was simply re-flogging the fruit of his privileged job, much of it, Hitchen believed, from Express Newspapers' library.

'It was a cuttings job – admittedly with good pictures – but when I saw what we were paying Morton and the TV ads we'd gotta do to promote the series – and remember we'd got no money – I said we can't do this. We've got to re-schedule the thing because we can't afford it. But Turner told me that was the agreement, that's it. And I thought well I don't need this guy anymore,' said Hitchen.

So Morton had to go.

Hitchen's legendary instinct about reporters had for once, failed. For Morton would go on to break the most astonishing story ever told about the royal family.

Hitchen remained unsentimental about the issue: 'People afterwards, when he became famous, said would you have fired him if you had known? And I said "yeah" . I said I had a greyhound once that never won and Morton was like that. The potential was there but I couldn't afford to wait around, like I couldn't afford a greyhound that wouldn't run.'

Hitchen knew that Morton would go on turning out books and making a bundle and he could not countenance that.

'He wasn't going to profit by it again, on the Daily Star's account, you know somewhere warm for him out of the rain. I don't like lazy buggers, and he was bloody idle.'

But then had Morton, who went on to live in London's Hampstead on the fruits of his world–famous book published in 1992, Diana – Her True Story, remained on the Daily Star he believes he would never have cracked the story.

'I would have left the Star anyway,' he said, 'I had always made myself different. I didn't hunt with the pack. Harry Arnold of The Sun and James Whitaker of the Daily Mirror were the old lags of the game. By the time I came to write the Diana book I wasn't a royal reporter anyway and because of the way I went on my own when I was one, Diana saw me as an outsider, which was how she saw herself.'

So it was one misunderstood soul meeting another. Except that Morton understood exactly what he was doing: as always he'd done his homework.

Phil Mellor, the news editor at the time, had taken Morton under his wing and helped him switch from sub-editor to reporter. He said: 'We used to help write his intros and everything and then he made five million on a book,' he said with exasperation.

Before Morton's revelations I met Diana at a hospital scanner, tape-cutting 'photo opportunity'. She was much thinner in the flesh and quite gawky, I thought. She didn't seem to wear the royal status easily and was most definitely rather shy.

Hitchen, who met her many times said: 'I thought she was fantastic, she was wonderful. I can never understand why Charles turned his back on her for that fucking old goat Camilla Parker-Bowles.'

The fact that he did confirmed in the eye of the public that the royals couldn't be taken seriously any longer. Charles' choice of woman left the Windsors open to more ridicule than even their infamous TV appearance on It's A Knockout.

One person Diana would not have fancied was Sun royal photographer Arthur Edwards, who surprised many when the luxury he chose when interviewed on Desert Island Discs was not a machine for jellying eels. Even today every time the royal family is in the news a very long tongue comes poking out of The Sun's pages. It belongs to professional Cockney Edwards and it is always snaking towards royal rear-ends. I don't blame the old snapper, he knows where his bread is buttered, and he clearly had reasonable contacts among royal flunkies. And of course he is now part of the establishment and no longer required to stake-out and snatch pictures of royals, like he did for years when pursuing the Princess of Wales. Long before anyone knew about the demons Diana was plagued by, Edwards was holding court, as was his want, on some royal doorstep and said: 'On my baby's life, Charles does not know what to do with Diana she's a fucking nutter.' Clearly the royal magic, even then, was wearing thin. When Ollie Wilson, a former Daily Star showbusiness reporter, started freelancing for CNN text in their West End TV and internet studio, he was upbraided for filing royal stories under Entertainment instead of News.

It was a small but significant symptom of royal demise.

Epilogue

Whatever is wrong with the press it reflects British society better than any other institution. It is in the hands of a complete cross-section of citizens from ill-educated drifters like me to privileged Oxbridge men like Alastair Campbell, who became Prime Minister Tony Blair's spokesman, but who started his mercurial career with shifts in Fleet Street including many on the Daily Star. For all its faults the press, has, at times, more integrity than the Palace of Westminster. It's a sobering thought that behaviour similar to Campbell's alleged distortion of intelligence over weapons of mass destruction, which caused a furore, but which did not prevent the invasion of Iraq in 2003, would have got a reporter fired on the Daily Star. 'Standing the story up,' is a recognised procedure in Fleet Street, however if the story is found to be false in the first place its creator will be shown the door.

The news gathering practices revealed in this book have not changed greatly, but the behaviour has. The Street of Shame column in Private Eye magazine is still running, but is tame these days and even back in my time it only scratched the surface of 'baffled pissed old hackery'. Eye stories of the tired and emotional Daily Star executive Ray Mills who urinated on his litter bin to put out a cigarette fire, or the piece of Daily Star reporter Mark Christy's ear found between the teeth of Sunday Sport editor Drew Robertson after a fight were funny and secretly regarded as a badge of honour by the subjects. But during my time in Fleet Street at least 12 journalists, who I knew personally, died from drink-related illnesses. There was the editor who, a self-confessed alcoholic, was persuaded that champagne was not a real drink and sipped the odd glass, bottle, then crate and was eventually rescued one night running out in front of London buses on The Strand. He died shortly afterwards. Then there was the reporter who told all his colleagues he had beaten the booze, but who had not included his wife in the deception. She found him dead, choked on his own vomit. Another reporter, fired for continually wrecking stories after heavy drinking was inconsolable: having got to the top then having blown it. He returned home to Glasgow and drank himself to death. Yet another who was made redundant and never came to terms with it, could not shake off the vice he'd handled well enough while in Fleet Street. His liver imploded from excessive wine drinking and he was found dying with blood running from his mouth. Then there was a feature writer whose habit of triple vodka for breakfast did for his pancreas.

Even the afore-mentioned Campbell is a recovering alcoholic and commendably makes no secret of it.

In December 2013 I returned to St Bride's Church, the place I used to visit 40 years earlier as a fledgling reporter to look at the famous Fleet Street names recorded on the pews. This time it was to light a candle for one I had known: Brian Hitchen and his wife Nelli had been killed in a road accident while on holiday in Spain. All those in Fleet Street who had known Hitchen, which were many, were stunned. That a legend should end in such a random fashion perplexed the legions whose job it was to confer culpability because there was no one to blame, it was an accident, pure and simple.

Others survived: one in true hack spirit actually flogged the story of his reformation! Daily Star back bench sub-editor the skeletal Dave Nicholls known as 'the drink on the stick' around the office, beat the booze and sold his story to... The Sun!

Despite all this the bar-room camaraderie among the hacks, while all the newspapers were based in Fleet Street, was unique. To this day there is a strong nostalgia for the 'Street'. When Roy 'Slippery' Chaplin, a sports photographer on the Daily Star died his wife dutifully carried out his last wish and sprinkled his ashes in small deposits throughout all his favourite Street drinking dens. But the happy endings are in the minority. Before its mass redundancies, when Express Newspapers employed thousands of people across four titles I was told the number of hacks who had lived long enough to draw a pension was 11. The first lord of the Daily Star, Lord Matthews accepted the drinking habits of his hacks as they used the pubs around Fleet Street. The second lord of the Daily Star Lord Stevens had a bar built in the new building Ludgate House, hoping to keep them near their desks. It was not a good idea: it meant they spent longer actually drinking. The third lord of the Daily Star Lord Hollick, a teetotaller, closed the bar down and now there are no more lords anymore and the hacks are more likely to be found sipping bottled water at their work stations. There is no longer any place for booze and a slurring diction: for newspapermen are at all times on call at the end of a mobile phone.
When they are not busy hacking them, that is.

HOLD THE BACK PAGE

After my last day on a national newspaper I went to the local career centre. I was offered a job as a shop assistant in a bakery; a security guard 'with good communication skills' ; or a care assistant in an old folks' home: 'Though you would need training for that,' the manager said.
It seemed there was still time to do something useful.

end

Printed in Great Britain
by Amazon

45920388R00159